# WOMEN'S HOUSEHOLD DRAMA

*The Other Voice in Early Modern Europe:*
*The Toronto Series, 66*

MEDIEVAL AND RENAISSANCE
TEXTS AND STUDIES

VOLUME 544

# The Other Voice in Early Modern Europe: The Toronto Series

**SERIES EDITORS** Margaret L. King *and* Albert Rabil, Jr.
**SERIES EDITOR, ENGLISH TEXTS** Elizabeth H. Hageman

## Previous Publications in the Series

The Other Voice in
Early Modern Europe:
The Toronto Series

**SERIES EDITORS** Margaret L. King *and* Albert Rabil, Jr.
**SERIES EDITOR, ENGLISH TEXTS** Elizabeth H. Hageman

### Previous Publications in the Series

# The Other Voice in Early Modern Europe: The Toronto Series

**SERIES EDITORS** Margaret L. King *and* Albert Rabil, Jr.
**SERIES EDITOR, ENGLISH TEXTS** Elizabeth H. Hageman

## *Previous Publications in the Series*

The Other Voice in
Early Modern Europe:
The Toronto Series

**SERIES EDITORS** Margaret L. King *and* Albert Rabil, Jr.
**SERIES EDITOR, ENGLISH TEXTS** Elizabeth H. Hageman

### *Previous Publications in the Series*

The Other Voice in
Early Modern Europe:
The Toronto Series

**SERIES EDITORS** Margaret L. King *and* Albert Rabil, Jr.
**SERIES EDITOR, ENGLISH TEXTS** Elizabeth H. Hageman

*Previous Publications in the Series*

The Other Voice in
Early Modern Europe:
The Toronto Series

**SERIES EDITORS** Margaret L. King *and* Albert Rabil, Jr.
**SERIES EDITOR, ENGLISH TEXTS** Elizabeth H. Hageman

*Previous Publications in the Series*

CLAUDINE-ALEXANDRINE GUÉRIN DE
TENCIN
Memoirs of the Count of Comminge *and*
The Misfortunes of Love
Edited and translated by Jonathan Walsh
Volume 48, 2016

FELICIANA ENRÍQUEZ DE GUZMÁN,
ANA CARO MALLÉN, AND SOR
MARCELA DE SAN FÉLIX
*Women Playwrights of Early Modern Spain*
Edited by Nieves Romero-Díaz and Lisa
Vollendorf
Translated and annotated by Harley
Erdman
Volume 49, 2016

ANNA TRAPNEL
*Anna Trapnel's Report and Plea; or, A
Narrative of Her Journey from London into
Cornwall*
Edited by Hilary Hinds
Volume 50, 2016

MARÍA VELA Y CUETO
*Autobiography and Letters of a Spanish Nun*
Edited by Susan Laningham
Translated by Jane Tar
Volume 51, 2016

CHRISTINE DE PIZAN
*The Book of the Mutability of Fortune*
Edited and translated by Geri L. Smith
Volume 52, 2017

MARGUERITE D'AUGE, RENÉE
BURLAMACCHI, AND JEANNE DU
LAURENS
*Sin and Salvation in Early Modern France:
Three Women's Stories*
Edited, and with an introduction by
Colette H. Winn. Translated by Nicholas
Van Handel and Colette H. Winn
Volume 53, 2017

ISABELLA D'ESTE
*Selected Letters*
Edited and translated by Deanna Shemek
Volume 54, 2017

IPPOLITA MARIA SFORZA
*Duchess and Hostage in Renaissance
Naples: Letters and Orations*
Edited and translated by Diana Robin and
Lynn Lara Westwater
Volume 55, 2017

LOUISE BOURGEOIS
*Midwife to the Queen of France: Diverse
Observations*
Translated by Stephanie O'Hara
Edited by Alison Klairmont Lingo
Volume 56, 2017

The Other Voice in
Early Modern Europe:
The Toronto Series

**SERIES EDITORS** Margaret L. King *and* Albert Rabil, Jr.
**SERIES EDITOR, ENGLISH TEXTS** Elizabeth H. Hageman

### *Previous Publications in the Series*

MARY WROTH, JANE CAVENDISH,
*and* ELIZABETH BRACKLEY

# Women's Household Drama:
## *Loves Victorie, A Pastorall,* and
## *The concealed Fansyes*

~

*Edited by*

MARTA STRAZNICKY *and* SARA MUELLER

Iter Press
Toronto, Ontario

Arizona Center for Medieval and Renaissance Studies
Tempe, Arizona

2018

Iter Press
Tel: 416/978–7074        Email: iter@utoronto.ca
Fax: 416/978–1668       Web: www.itergateway.org

Arizona Center for Medieval and Renaissance Studies
Tel: 480/965–5900       Email: mrts@acmrs.org
Fax: 480/965–1681       Web: acmrs.org

**Library of Congress Cataloging-in-Publication Data**
**Library of Congress Cataloging-in-Publication Data**
Names: Straznicky, Marta, editor. | Mueller, Sara, editor. | Container of (work): Wroth, Mary, Lady,
  approximately 1586–approximately 1640. Love's victory. | Container of (work): Cheyne, Jane,
  1621–1669. Pastorall. | Container of (work): Cheyne, Jane, 1621–1669. Concealed fansyes.
Title: Mary Wroth, Jane Cavendish, and Elizabeth Brackley : women's household drama : Loves
  victorie, A pastorall, and The concealed fansyes / edited by Marta Straznicky and Sara Mueller.
Description: Toronto, Ontario : Iter Press ; Tempe, Arizona : Arizona Center for Medieval and
  Renaissance Studies, 2018. | Series: The other voice in early modern Europe. The Toronto series ;
  66 | Series: Medieval and Renaissance texts and studies ; volume 544 | Includes bibliographical
  references and index. | Loves Victorie / Mary Wroth -- A Pastorall ; The concealed Fansyes / Jane
  Cavendish and Elizabeth Brackley.
Identifiers: LCCN 2018023621 (print) | LCCN 2018041593 (ebook) | ISBN 9780866987493 (ebook) |
  ISBN 9780866986021 (pbk. : alk. paper)
Subjects: LCSH: Women--Drama. | Marriage--Drama. | English drama--Women authors--History
  and criticism. | LCGFT: Drama. | Comedy plays.
Classification: LCC PR1263 (ebook) | LCC PR1263 .M23 2018 (print) | DDC 822/.40809287--dc23
LC record available at https://lccn.loc.gov/2018023621

Cover illustration:
*An Allegory with Venus and Cupid* (ca. 1545; oil on canvas), Bronzino, Agnolo (1503–1572) / The
National Gallery, London, England / The Bridgeman Art Library BAL5361.

Cover design:
Maureen Morin, Information Technology Services, University of Toronto Libraries.

Typesetting and production:
Iter Press.

# Contents

# Illustrations

# Acknowledgments

I wish foremost to thank Betty Hageman for inviting me to edit women's household plays for the Other Voice series, for her expert and patient editorial guidance through the many phases of this complex project, and more generally for her ongoing commitment to recovering and transmitting the voices of early modern women to future generations. As many readers of this volume will know, Betty is a pillar of our scholarly community and every one of us is in some sense indebted to the tremendous contributions she has made to the field. I want to thank Sara Mueller for readily joining the project at a time when it was proving impossible for me to complete it alone. I also wish to thank Alison Findlay and Mary Ellen Lamb for taking an interest in this edition and for being so generous with their expertise. Sara S. Hodson, Curator of Literary Manuscripts at the Huntington Library, helped to confirm important facets of the paper and binding of HM600. Thanks to the staffs of the Huntington Library, the Newberry Library, the British Library, and the Folger Shakespeare Library for their generous assistance. Jelena Marelj was an astute research assistant at a crucial stage of our work. Queen's University provided research and administrative leaves that enabled me to give this work undivided attention. I thank Iter Press and the Arizona Center for Medieval and Renaissance Studies for permitting portions of the introduction to *Loves Victorie* to be published in *Sidney Journal*. Lastly, deep thanks to my close friend and colleague Louise Noble for her intellectual fellowship and unending support.

*Marta Straznicky*

This edition of Jane Cavendish and Elizabeth Brackley's plays has benefited tremendously from the wisdom and insight of many people. First and foremost, I must thank Marta Straznicky for her generosity, knowledge, patience, and leadership in keeping this project moving forward. I must thank her too for inviting me to be a part of this edition. Betty Hageman's unfailing eye for detail, knowledge of the period, and vast editorial experience has made this a far better work. I would also like to thank James Fitzmaurice for his generosity in providing thoughtful and helpful comments on an early version of the Cavendish introduction, and Tiffany Stern for meeting with me and helping to clarify some tricky parts of the Bodleian manuscript. Brent Nelson and Georgiana Ziegler both provided assistance at the early stages of this project. The staff of the Bodleian Library, University of Oxford were extremely helpful, most particularly Michael Webb, Curator of Early Modern Archives and Manuscripts. I also wish to thank Elizabeth Frengel, Research Librarian, the Beinecke Rare Book and Manuscript Library. Finally, Lindsey Banco's keen editorial eye and constant support are as appreciated as ever.

Thank you, too, to Philip Mueller and Teena Mueller, as well as to Sadie Banco, who was born in the early stages of this project and is now writing household drama of her very own.

*Sara Mueller*

# General Introduction

## The Other Voice

The three plays collected in this edition belong to a rich and vibrant tradition of household theatrical activity that involved early modern English women as patrons, spectators, performers, and readers, while also affording opportunities for playwriting and dramatic design that were not available in commercial theater until the late 1660s.[1] The country homes of England's nobility were the scene of many kinds of theatrical activities, from full-scale dramas produced by troupes of traveling professional players to performances of a wide range of more modest entertainments by family, friends, or members of the household staff. Household drama differed in many respects from professional drama: it was usually written for, and performed in connection with specific times of the year or local festivities; it was more topical, referring to people, places, and events that may not be discernible to an audience in a different place or at a different time; and it was frequently more experimental because it was not produced in a regulated public setting for paying spectators. The involvement of women as authors of household drama is an important aspect of its experimental nature; it is just as much a hallmark of this theatrical tradition as is the absence of women from professional playwriting before the closing of the theaters in 1642. If we are to hear the voices of early modern English women dramatists, we must turn to household theater.[2]

In a different sense, the voices of early modern English women dramatists resonate in the material texts in which their plays have survived, whether as manuscripts or as printed books.[3] Editions such as the present volume necessarily intervene between the earliest extant texts and the contemporary reader, and it is therefore vital that we become aware not only of the interventions that editors and technologies make in the transmission of these women's plays, but also of the

---

1. On the extensive involvement of women in early modern English theater, see, for example, Pamela Allen Brown and Peter Parolin, eds., *Women Players in England, 1500–1660: Beyond the All-Male Stage* (Aldershot, UK: Ashgate, 2005).

2. Two plays by women did, however, appear in print during this period and therefore necessarily circulated outside the domestic context: Mary Sidney's *Antonius* (1592; reprinted as *The tragedie of Antonie* in 1595), and Elizabeth Cary's *The tragedie of Mariam* (1613).

3. For a survey of early modern women's manuscript and printed plays, see Marta Straznicky, "Private Drama," in *The Cambridge Companion to Early Modern Women's Writing*, ed. Laura Lunger Knoppers (Cambridge: Cambridge University Press, 2009), 247–59. On women as play readers, including readers of other women's plays, see Straznicky, "Reading through the Body: Women and Printed Drama," in *The Book of the Play: Playwrights, Stationers, and Readers in Early Modern England*, ed. Marta Straznicky (Amherst: University of Massachusetts Press, 2006), 59–79.

meanings that are embedded in the very materiality of their texts.[4] Accordingly, this edition of Mary Wroth's *Loves Victorie* and the Cavendish sisters' *A Pastorall* and *The concealed Fansyes*, all of which survive in handwritten copies dating from their authors' lifetimes, draws on specific manuscripts as copy texts and attempts, insofar as possible, to represent or at least describe their idiosyncrasies and inherent ambiguities. *Loves Victorie* is here edited from the autograph manuscript now at the Huntington Library in San Marino, California; *A Pastorall* and *The concealed Fansyes* are both edited from the scribal copy of the plays now in the Bodleian Library, University of Oxford.

## Household Drama in Early Modern England

Household drama had a long history in England prior to the seventeenth century and is often defined by its occasional nature.[5] Household plays were written or performed in a specific context, were often performed by members of the household themselves, and were conceived with particular audiences in mind. According to Suzanne Westfall, household theater was also "deliberately ephemeral, multimedial, and frequently nontextual or metatextual."[6] For this reason, much of the information we have about household theater comes from administrative records or audience accounts; it follows too that most of this evidence documents the household theater of elites, in part because their literacy rates far exceeded those of the lower classes. Yet because of the characteristics described above, we must also acknowledge that there is much about household theater of this period that is unrecoverable.

The texts and records of household theater that have survived show a wide variety of plays and entertainments performed in households, ranging from elaborate spectacles to intimate family theatricals. Early records of household theater

4. For a history of editing plays by early modern Englishwomen, see Marion Wynne-Davies, "Editing Early Modern Women's Dramatic Writing for Performance," in *Editing Early Modern Women*, ed. Sarah C. E. Ross and Paul Salzman (Cambridge: Cambridge University Press, 2016), 156–75.

5. The household was one of the most common venues for performance before commercial theaters were built in London in the latter half of the sixteenth century; it continued to be prominent throughout the seventeenth century. For an overview of the earlier period of household drama, see Suzanne Westfall, *Patrons and Performances: Early Tudor Household Revels* (Oxford: Clarendon Press, 1990), 1–49, and Greg Walker, *The Politics of Performance in Early Renaissance Drama* (Cambridge: Cambridge University Press, 1998), 51–75.

6. Suzanne Westfall, "'A Commonty a Christmas Gambold or a Tumbling Trick': Household Theater," in *A New History of Early English Drama*, ed. John D. Cox and David Scott Kastan (New York: Columbia University Press, 1997), 39–58 (39). The twenty-four printed volumes of the *Records of Early English Drama* (*REED*) record many examples of household theatricals and touring troupes sponsored by the nobility. For a list of the published collections, see http://reed.utoronto.ca/print-collections-2/print-collections/, accessed May 6, 2018.

show that some household plays were performed by troupes of professional tour-ing players such as the Earl of Pembroke's Men, the Queen's Men, or the King's Men; this tradition of touring was a common practice for the London acting companies, especially when the theaters were closed for public health or politi-cal reasons.[7] Some elite households had their own troupes of players, and some households, especially those of courtiers, staged lavish masques and entertain-ments for royalty and inner court circles.[8] Elizabeth Russell, for instance, wrote a pastoral entertainment to celebrate the arrival of Queen Elizabeth at her estate at Bisham on August 11, 1592 that featured Russell's daughters in speaking roles.[9] Similarly, Mary Sidney Herbert, aunt of Mary Wroth, wrote a pastoral dialogue to entertain the queen on a planned visit to Wilton House in 1599. Although the visit did not occur, Sidney's dialogue was nevertheless printed and took its place within a rich tradition of Elizabethan household entertainment.[10] On a less exalted scale,

7. Peter H. Greenfield, "Touring," in Cox and Kastan, *A New History of Early English Drama*, 251–68 (258–59). For a geographic analysis of touring performances in early modern England, see Mark Brayshay, "Waits, Musicians, Bearwards and Players: The Inter-Urban Road Travel and Performances of Itinerant Entertainers in Sixteenth- and Seventeenth-Century England," *Journal of Historical Geography* 31, no. 3 (2005): 430–58.

8. Westfall, "A Commonty," 13–49, discusses households that had their own players. See especially her discussion of the chapel gentlemen and children.

9. Elizabeth Cooke Hoby Russell, "The Bisham Entertainment for Queen Elizabeth I, August 11, 1592," in *The Writings of an English Sappho*, ed. Patricia Phillippy with translations from Greek and Latin by Jaime Goodrich (Toronto: Iter and the Centre for Reformation and Renaissance Studies, 2011), 147–57. Although the entertainment was printed anonymously in Oxford by Joseph Barnes in 1592, critics have argued persuasively that Russell was its author. See Alexandra F. Johnston, "'The Lady of the farme': The Context of Lady Russell's Entertainment of Elizabeth at Bisham, 1592," *Early Theatre* 5 (2002): 71–85; Peter Davidson and Jane Stevenson, "Elizabeth I's Reception at Bisham (1592): Elite Women as Writers and Devisers," in *The Progresses, Pageants, and Entertainments of Queen Elizabeth I*, ed. Jayne Elisabeth Archer, Elizabeth Goldring, and Sarah Knight (Oxford: Oxford University Press, 2007), 207–26; Elizabeth Zeman Kolkovich, "Lady Russell, Elizabeth I, and Female Political Alliances through Performance," *English Literary Renaissance* 39 (2009): 290–314. Russell also staged a wed-ding masque at her home in London on June 16, 1600, in honor of her daughter's marriage. On the context of the masque, the text of which does not survive, see Phillippy, *Writings of an English Sappho*, 270–73, and Davidson and Stevenson, "Elizabeth I's Reception at Bisham," 221–22. Phillippy dis-cusses Russell's interrelated creative engagements with painting, masques, and embroidery in "Chaste Painting: Elizabeth Russell's Theatres of Memory," *Early Modern Women: An Interdisciplinary Journal* 7 (2012): 33–68.

10. Mary Sidney Herbert, "A Dialogue betweene two shepheards, *Thenot* and *Piers*, in praise of *Astrea*," in *The Collected Works of Mary Sidney Herbert, Countess of Pembroke*, vol. 1, *Poems, Translations, and Correspondence*, ed. Margaret P. Hannay, Noel J. Kinnamon, and Michael G. Brennan (Oxford: Clarendon Press, 1998), 89–91. On Sidney's dialogue in the context of entertainments at Wilton House, see Marta Straznicky, "Wilton House, Theatre, and Power," in *The Intellectual Culture of the English Country House, 1500–1700*, ed. Matthew Dimmock, Andrew Hadfield, and Margaret Healy (Manchester: Manchester University Press, 2015), 223. On the country house as a safe space for

plays were also written and performed by family members for one another, and women participated in this tradition as well. Lady Rachel Fane, for instance, wrote short entertainments that reimagine life at her family home, Apethorpe.[11]

While the term "household theater" may suggest homey, amateur plays put on with more enthusiasm than skill, this was not necessarily the case. Household entertainments could, at their most elaborate, be stunning examples of environmental theater. A famous example is the Earl of Hertford's *The Honorable Entertainement given to the Queenes Majestie in Progresse, at Elvetham in Hampshire*, staged for Queen Elizabeth in 1591. This entertainment, which took place over four days at Hertford's estate, involved lavish banquets, woodland spectacles, and various other extravagant shows, including a mock sea battle staged in a crescent-shaped pond that was specially dug for the occasion.[12] Spectacles of this magnitude reflect not only the wealth, but also the size and complexity of an elite household, which could number as many as 250 persons and in a very real sense function as public space.[13] Furthermore, as Julie Sanders has shown, households were not discrete entities: they intersected with other spaces, both local and national, and should therefore be considered as sites of cultural exchange, in some respects even as avant-garde, rather than simply imitative of London theatrical trends.[14] For many households of this scale, theatrical displays were anything but private and amateur: they were a vehicle for promoting dynastic interests and advertising the family's wealth and power.[15]

A relevant example of the sophistication and cultural complexity of household theater are two masques commissioned in the 1630s by William Cavendish, the father of Jane Cavendish and Elizabeth Brackley, to be staged at the family

women dramatists, see Marion Wynne-Davies, "'My Seeled Chamber and Dark Parlour Room': The English Country House and Renaissance Women Dramatists," in *Readings in Renaissance Women's Drama: Criticism, History, and Performance, 1594–1998*, ed. S. P. Cerasano and Marion Wynne-Davies (London: Routledge, 1998), 60–68.

11. Centre for Kentish Studies U269 F38/1–4. For an edited text of one of Fane's entertainments, see Marion O'Connor, ed., "Rachel Fane's May Masque at Apethorpe, 1627," *English Literary Renaissance* 36 (2005): 90–113 (105–13). See Alison Findlay, *Playing Spaces in Early Women's Drama* (Cambridge: Cambridge University Press, 2006), 96–101, for a detailed discussion of Fane's works in a household context.

12. See *Elvetham: 1591*, in *Entertainments for Elizabeth I*, ed. Jean Wilson (Woodbridge, NJ: D. S. Brewer, 1980), 96–118.

13. Westfall, "A Commonty," 41.

14. See Julie Sanders, "Geographies of Performance in the Early Modern Midlands," in *Performing Environments: Site-Specificity in Medieval and Early Modern English Drama*, ed. Susan Bennett and Mary Polito (Houndmills, UK: Palgrave Macmillan, 2014), 119–37.

15. Walker, *Politics of Performance*, 51–53.

homes of Bolsover Castle and Welbeck Abbey.[16] The masques were written by Ben Jonson, a successful commercial playwright in London and prolific writer of masques for the royal court.[17] They were commissioned specifically for the visit of King Charles I to Cavendish's estates while the court was on progress through the kingdom.[18] Both masques survive in acting texts with Jonson's annotations for performance at the Cavendish estates; that he later revised and prepared the texts for print shows that they were also meant to have an audience and cultural reach beyond the occasional and site-specific performance for which they were initially written.[19]

Julie Sanders has argued that these and other household theatricals had a significant impact on the public theater in London, particularly on the representation of women because the household setting enabled women performers to depict a different range of female perspectives and experiences than was possible for male actors.[20] This is indeed a key distinction between household theater and the London stage and also holds for women's involvement as patrons, writers, and designers. Women did not perform regularly in public until the 1660s, and it was during this period, too, when the plays of professional women writers such as Aphra Behn were first produced. Long before this time, however, household

16. The masques were *The King's Entertainment at Welbeck in Nottinghamshire* (May 21, 1633) and *Love's Welcome at Bolsover* (June 30, 1634).

17. Jonson was out of favor as a writer of court masques by the 1630s, though Newcastle continued to patronize him. Lynn Hulse writes that "Newcastle patronized several literary figures including Jonson, Brome, Shirley, Flecknoe, Dryden, and Shadwell. He particularly admired Jonson, whose masques and plays were a major influence on the Duke's own writings." "The King's Entertainment by the Duke of Newcastle," *Viator* 26 (1995): 355–405 (311). Jonson celebrated Newcastle in two epigrams and is a prominent figure in a manuscript compilation prepared by John Rolleston for the earl (British Library Harley MS 4955). See note 19, below.

18. Lynn Hulse, "Cavendish, William, first duke of Newcastle upon Tyne (*bap.* 1593, *d.* 1676)," *ODNB*. Cavendish himself wrote several plays, including plays for household performance and for commercial performance in London. Hulse notes that his *Witts Triumverate, or The Philosopher* "was written for performance before the king and queen in the winter of 1635–6," although there is no record of it having been staged. Cavendish also wrote a Christmas masque for performance at Welbeck and had two plays performed by the King's Men at Blackfriars Theater (*The Varietie* [ca. 1639–41] and *The Country Captaine* [1641]).

19. The acting texts are in British Library MS. Harley 4955, a composite manuscript of verses, poems, and entertainments prepared for William Cavendish, Duke of Newcastle. The manuscript is in the hand of John Rolleston, Cavendish's secretary, who also prepared the two manuscripts of the Cavendish sisters' plays. For an analysis of British Library MS. Harley 4955, see Hilton Kelliher, "Donne, Jonson, Richard Andrews and The Newcastle Manuscript," *English Manuscript Studies, 1100–1700* 4 (1993): 134–73. The two masques were first printed in 1640 in the collected edition of Jonson's works. For a modern edition, see *Ben Jonson: The Complete Masques*, ed. Stephen Orgel (New Haven, CT: Yale University Press, 1969).

20. Sanders, "Geographies of Performance," 133.

theater provided women with opportunities to commission, sponsor, write, and perform theatrical works. The women likeliest to create household theater were the wives and daughters of noblemen who were themselves patrons of writers and other intellectuals. Women like Wroth, Cavendish, and Brackley, who were well educated and raised in cultured households, had the learning and opportunity to write drama that spoke to issues central to their lives and those of their families.[21] It is no accident that the plays collected in this volume are written by elite women whose education, familial circumstances, and personal inclination converged to enable them to write, circulate, and probably stage their plays within their households. Their plays were not printed and available for sale by booksellers; instead, they were copied by hand, sometimes in multiple versions, and shared within select networks of readers (see the section Manuscript Culture, below). This does not mean that their plays did not have a social function; rather, it suggests that their social function was meant to be controlled.[22]

One of the most fascinating aspects of household theater for the contemporary reader is how the plays were able to use the whole household—the public and private spaces of the house, the gardens and grounds, everyday household objects, the people who performed in the plays, and the audiences who would watch the performance—for their theatrical impact. The opportunities to use household space and objects, and the potential to complicate the usual roles individuals had in day-to-day life through the identity they would assume in a household performance, means these plays are full of theatrical potential. This ability to use and exploit domestic space for dramatic purposes differs from plays performed in London's playhouses, which Shakespeare describes in the prologue to *Henry V* as the empty "wooden O":

> Can this cockpit hold
> The vasty fields of France? Or may we cram
> Within this wooden O the very casques
> That did affright the air at Agincourt?[23]

The space of household theater, far from being a nondescript "wooden O" that could one day be the fields of France in the battle of Agincourt and the next the

21. On the household as a secure space in which Wroth and the Cavendish sisters could negotiate and perform identity, see Lindsay Janelle Yakimyshyn, "Security and Instability: Mary Wroth, the Cavendish Sisters, and Early Stuart Household Plays," Ph.D. diss., University of Alberta, 2014. For details on their upbringings, see the sections on Life and Works in their respective introductions, below.

22. This important point is made in a seminal article by Margaret J. M. Ezell, "To Be Your Daughter in Your Pen: The Social Functions of Literature in the Writings of Lady Elizabeth Brackley and Lady Jane Cavendish," *Huntington Library Quarterly* 51, no. 4 (1988): 281–96.

23. William Shakespeare, *Henry V*, in *The Norton Shakespeare: Third Edition*, ed. Stephen Greenblatt et al. (New York: W. W. Norton, 2016), Prologue 11–14.

woodland setting of *A Midsummer Night's Dream*, was full of signification and resonance since it was the space in which day-to-day life was lived. Everyday space used for performance can exploit the meanings and significations that it already has for the audience. As Alison Findlay puts it, household theater creates "an imagined locale that is superimposed on a physical household through the processes of composition, reading and possibly production."[24]

This facet of household drama offers tremendous potential to represent and explore locally relevant issues in a range of rhetorical stances: they can be humorous, affirming, ironic, playful, subversive, unsettling, or even uncanny. Because the domestic is never "merely" the domestic, and because the personal is also political, household theater was effectively a political theater. As Westfall notes, authors and designers of household theater

> made topical use of local history, current events, or persons in attendance as systems of reference devised to entertain, to deliver subtle and not-so-subtle suggestions, and to include household members in a hermeneutic circle. This circle could be so closed that at times the line between spectators and performers becomes blurred.[25]

The first lines spoken in Cavendish and Brackley's *A Pastorall* explicitly acknowledge this possibility: "This is a brave world for us now for wee / meatomorphise every body."[26] Here the authors call attention to how, through their play, they have temporarily transformed, or metamorphosed, household space. Similarly, both Wroth's *Loves Victorie* and Cavendish and Brackley's *The concealed Fansyes* reimagine the circumstances of their authors' day-to-day lives. In *A Pastorall*, Cavendish and Brackley go even further by creating identities completely outside of their experience—those of witches—and then staging that imagined reality in the place where they actually lived.

The household, then, is a dramatic context that offers a fascinating window into a particular time and place in a way that is arguably more local and more specific than most other theatrical forms of the early modern period. As a political theater acted in personal, domestic space, household theater offers its authors, performers, and producers opportunities to incorporate and thus influence the lived reality of the audience in ways that are unique to the venue. The women whose plays are presented in this volume, and other women who were variously involved in household theater, seized this opportunity for creative agency: their work both demands and repays scholarly attention in this context.

---

24. Findlay, *Playing Spaces*, 45.

25. Westfall, "A Commonty," 53.

26. Cavendish and Brackley, *A Pastorall*, Antemasque, 5–6.

## Manuscript Culture

In addition to being a venue for theatrical performance, the early modern household was also an important site of literary production. A multitude of handwritten documents survive from this period and reveal that manuscripts performed many different functions in the household, both private and public: account keeping, preservation of estate records and administrative papers, personal and business correspondence, contractual agreements, taking of inventories, training and education, recording of culinary or medicinal recipes, to name just a few.[27] Although England saw the advent of print during the early modern period, manuscripts continued to be the dominant mode of textual production, accounting for some 80 percent of the paper imported into the country in the sixteenth and seventeenth centuries.[28] Handwritten lyric, dramatic, and prose texts make up a small proportion of the large and varied field of household manuscript activity, but they represent a vital, complex literary culture that differed significantly from print in terms of authorship, readership, and the material nature of the text.[29] The significance of these differences between print and manuscript cultures is perhaps nowhere more evident than in the agency afforded to women, specifically in household settings, as authors, readers, compilers, editors, and collectors.[30]

27. Margaret J. M. Ezell, "The Laughing Tortoise: Speculations on Manuscript Sources and Women's Book History," *English Literary Renaissance* 38, no. 2 (2008): 331–55 (337).

28. Mark Bland, *A Guide to Early Printed Books and Manuscripts* (Chichester, UK: Wiley-Blackwell, 2010), 83. England did not have a large-scale domestic paper manufacturing industry until the late seventeenth century; most writing paper was imported from Western Europe. See Bland, 29–32.

29. For an overview of early modern manuscript culture, see Harold Love and Arthur F. Marotti, "Manuscript Transmission and Circulation," in *The Cambridge History of Early Modern English Literature*, ed. David Loewenstein and Janel Mueller (Cambridge: Cambridge University Press, 2002), 55–80. Love and Marotti have each also published seminal full-length studies of early modern manuscript culture: see Harold Love, *Scribal Publication in Seventeenth-Century England* (Oxford: Clarendon Press, 1993), and Arthur F. Marotti, *Manuscript, Print, and the English Renaissance Lyric* (Ithaca, NY: Cornell University Press, 1995). On the circulation of household entertainments in manuscript, see Gabriel Heaton, "Elizabethan Entertainments in Manuscript: The Harefield Festivities (1602) and the Dynamics of Exchange," in Archer, Goldring, and Knight, *Progresses, Pageants, and Entertainments*, 227–44.

30. A number of recent essay collections and editions address women's involvement in manuscript culture: George L. Justice and Nathan Tinker, eds., *Women's Writing and the Circulation of Ideas: Manuscript Publication in England, 1550–1800* (Cambridge: Cambridge University Press, 2002); Victoria E. Burke and Jonathan Gibson, eds., *Early Modern Women's Manuscript Writing: Selected Papers from the Trinity/Trent Colloquium* (Aldershot, UK: Ashgate, 2004); and Jill Seal Millman and Gillian Wright, eds., *Early Modern Women's Manuscript Poetry* (Manchester: Manchester University Press, 2005). Important titles in this field have recently appeared in The Other Voice in Early Modern Europe series: Lady Margaret Douglas and Others, *The Devonshire Manuscript: A Women's Book of Courtly Poetry*, ed. Elizabeth Heale (Toronto: Iter and the Centre for Reformation and Renaissance

The composition of literary works in manuscript was a choice for male and female writers alike, offering more control over circulation, more speed and efficiency in reaching readers, the evasion of regulating authorities, the possibility of creating beautiful and unique copies of one's work, and the opportunity to participate in literary communities centered on family, personal acquaintance, or common interests.[31] Although some manuscripts were made for strictly private use, many were written for a particular readership or occasion and as such were inherently social texts, bonding individuals and groups of readers within the larger fabric of communal life. Writers were also readers, and readers frequently became writers, annotating, supplementing, copying, or otherwise contributing to the re-creation of the manuscript. Handwritten texts were thus changeable documents and were intended for continued use. They were frequently also traveling objects, not unlike printed books in this respect, moving outward from their domestic place of origin to other desks, rooms, and houses—virtually any sites where reading and writing were done. The survival of so many literary manuscripts from the sixteenth and seventeenth centuries indicates that they were valued and carefully preserved.[32]

Hundreds of manuscripts by early modern women have survived, a vastly greater quantity of writings than were printed, and they reveal a much wider range of cultural and authorial agency than does the print record.[33] In addition to creating imaginative works in handwritten form for their own use, women copied their own and others' writings, prepared attractive presentation manuscripts of their work for select readers, showed and circulated their handwritten texts to guests, compiled collections of works from both printed and manuscript

Studies, 2012); Katherine Austen, *Book M: A London Widow's Life Writings*, ed. Pamela S. Hammons (Toronto: Iter and the Centre for Reformation and Renaissance Studies, 2013); Lady Hester Pulter, *Poems, Emblems,* and *The Unfortunate Florinda*, ed. Alice Eardley (Toronto: Iter and the Centre for Reformation and Renaissance Studies, 2014); and Mary Wroth, *"Pamphilia to Amphilanthus" in Manuscript and Print*, ed. Ilona Bell and Steven W. May (Toronto: Iter; Tempe: Arizona Center for Medieval and Renaissance Studies, 2017). On the politics of editing women's manuscript writing, see Victoria Burke and Elizabeth Clarke, "Julia Palmer's 'Centuries': The Politics of Editing and Anthologizing Early Modern Women's Manuscript Compilations," in *New Ways of Looking at Old Texts*, vol. 3, ed. W. Speed Hill (Tempe: Arizona Center for Medieval and Renaissance Studies in conjunction with Renaissance English Text Society, 2004), 47–64.

31. Love and Marotti, "Manuscript Transmission and Circulation," 56.

32. For a database of manuscripts of early modern women's writing from the sixteenth and seventeenth centuries, see *The Perdita Project: Early Modern Women's Manuscript Catalogue*, http://web.warwick.ac.uk/english/perdita/html, accessed May 6, 2018; and *Perdita Manuscripts, 1500–1700*, http://www.amdigital.co.uk/m-products/product/perdita-manuscripts-1500–1700, a complementary database linking detailed catalogue descriptions with complete digital facsimiles of the original manuscripts.

33. Ezell, "The Laughing Tortoise," 334; and Michelle O'Callaghan, "Publication: Print and Manuscript," in *A New Companion to English Renaissance Literature and Culture*, ed. Michael Hattaway (Oxford: Wiley-Blackwell, 2010), 1:162.

sources, corrected and annotated texts, read aloud from manuscripts, kept and collected volumes of others' works, and acted as patrons and editors. Many of these functions are evident in the literary activities of Mary Sidney Herbert, Mary Wroth's aunt and mentor.[34] Although Sidney had access to a number of stationers and worked with them to bring some of her own and her brother Philip's works into print, she also chose to preserve other writings in manuscript, preferring to circulate them more closely among members of her family, literary circles, and even the court. Her translation of the *Psalmes*, for instance, continues work begun by Philip before his untimely death in 1586. Mary transcribed and edited the poems he had translated, as well as completing the work with her own translations of the remaining psalms. The *Psalmes* survive in eighteen manuscripts, in various hands and differing from one another in many ways. One copy in Mary Sidney Herbert's handwriting has a unique dedication to Queen Elizabeth, showing that it was prepared for a very restricted readership. As Margaret Hannay has documented, several of the individual psalms circulated independently and were enclosed in people's correspondence, two were set to music, and others survive in variant forms in multiple kinds of manuscript.[35] Mary Sidney Herbert's literary agency with respect to the *Psalmes* thus includes transcribing, editing, translating, composing, and disseminating the work, functions that are documented in the material texts themselves and that reach well beyond the activity of writing per se.

The physical nature of women's manuscripts obviously differs in important respects from print, but individual manuscripts also differ from one another, not only in the uniqueness of their texts but also the uniqueness of their material makeup.[36] The kind of paper used, the way individual sheets are gathered, the handwriting and the number of hands present in it, signs of wear or use, and the nature of the binding, if any, can, among many other facets, tell us a great deal about the date and authorship of a manuscript, its relationship to other documents, its conceivable purposes and readerships, and its perceived value.[37] Accustomed as we are to reading early literature in the medium of print (and increasingly in electronic form), it is important to remind ourselves that texts

---

34. For an excellent study of the range of Mary Sidney Herbert's authorial activities, see Margaret P. Hannay, "'Bearing the Livery of Your Name': The Countess of Pembroke's Agency in Print and Scribal Culture," in Justice and Tinker, *Women's Writing and the Circulation of Ideas*, 17–49. The account here is indebted to Hannay in many of its details. On manuscript practice in the Sidney family more broadly, see H. R. Woudhuysen, *Sir Philip Sidney and the Circulation of Manuscripts, 1558–1640* (Oxford: Clarendon Press, 1996).

35. Hannay, "Bearing the Livery of Your Name," 37.

36. For bibliographic descriptions of a range of early modern women's manuscripts, see the introductions to the individual texts in Millman and Wright, *Early Modern Women's Manuscript Poetry*.

37. On writing practices in the early modern period, see Helen Smith, "Women and the Materials of Writing," in *Material Cultures of Early Modern Women's Writing*, ed. Patricia Pender and Rosalind Smith (Basingstoke: Palgrave Macmillan, 2014), 14–35.

preserved in manuscript belong to a particular culture of reading and writing and can therefore convey information about the literary texts and activities they record that are not present in their printed or other forms.

In the case of manuscript plays, these activities may include performance. A presentation manuscript such as the Penshurst version of Wroth's *Loves Victorie* may not have any of the features found in playhouse scripts, but this does not mean that the play was not performed, just that this particular copy of the play was probably not used in performance.[38] A manuscript translation of a play by Euripides written by Lady Jane Lumley around 1550 poses similar questions: the play survives in a notebook that includes Lumley's academic translations and thus seems to be anchored in a schoolroom setting, yet the peculiar nature of her translation indicates that her main interest was in preparing an actable text.[39] Conversely, verbal features of play manuscripts that strongly suggest physical enactment, such as the prologue in the Cavendish sisters' *A Pastorall*, do not, in themselves, constitute definitive evidence of performance, only that a performance was envisioned. Even the presence of detailed stage directions can be indeterminate, for such directions can just as easily be intended to help readers visualize the action as be instructions for, or records of, enactments. In fact, playhouse manuscripts from this period are notoriously lacking in detailed stage directions because staging was worked out by the actors in the course of rehearsal and performance. Printed plays, on the other hand, can be and were read in ways that simulate the experience of acting and playgoing. In praising the genius of Shakespeare's "Tragick Vein," Margaret Cavendish writes that "he Presents Passions so Naturally, and Misfortunes so Probably, as he Pierces the souls of his Readers with such a true sense of Feeling thereof, that it Forces Tears through their Eyes, and almost Perswades them, they are Really Actors, or at least Present at those Tragedies."[40] Although she is describing the experience of reading plays in print, Cavendish blurs the boundary between reading, spectatorship, and performance in terms that can also enrich our understanding of manuscript plays as performance texts.

There are too few extant manuscript plays by women from this period to make generalizations, but the ones we do have resemble the manuscripts of academic, civic, and male-authored household drama more than they do those

---

38. On early modern theatrical manuscripts and their physical characteristics, see William B. Long, "'Precious Few': English Manuscript Playbooks," in *A Companion to Shakespeare*, ed. David Scott Kastan (Oxford: Blackwell, 1999), 413–33, and Paul Werstine, *Early Modern Playhouse Manuscripts and the Editing of Shakespeare* (Cambridge: Cambridge University Press, 2013).

39. See Straznicky, "Private Drama," 248–50. For a description of a successful performance of Lumley's *Iphigenia* in 2013, see Wynne-Davies, "Editing Early Modern Women's Dramatic Writing," 172–75.

40. Margaret Cavendish, *CCXI Sociable Letters* (London: William Wilson, 1664), 246. On early modern women play readers, see Straznicky, "Reading through the Body."

originating in the professional theater.[41] The absence in women's play manuscripts either of external evidence of performance or internal verbal or formal features specific to playhouse texts does not so much argue against a stage history as point to a theatrical and literary context situated elsewhere and configured differently than the professional theater of London. That context is the early modern household which was, as the section above makes clear, the site of a rich dramatic culture in the sixteenth and seventeenth centuries. The manuscripts of women's household plays materialize this culture in unique ways.

## *Note on the Text*

The overall aim of this edition is to foster and facilitate an understanding of women's household drama with respect to the materiality of their texts. Accordingly, we present texts of *Loves Victorie*, *A Pastorall*, and *The concealed Fansyes* in their original spelling (including capitalization, contractions and abbreviations, with the exception of i/j, u/v, and long s in the Wroth manuscript, and *ff* in the Cavendish and Brackley manuscripts, which have been normalized), punctuation, lineation, and, insofar as possible, features of the manuscripts' layout (indentation, placement of songs, speech prefixes, stage directions, and so on). Editorial insertions have been kept to a minimum. However, where the copyist seems to have omitted a word, it is inserted (in square brackets), and omitted letters represented by the macron symbol in Wroth's text have been supplied. The lines of each play are numbered according to the divisions that organize its text. Folio numbers are provided in the right margin in square brackets to help readers identify page breaks in the original. This editorial practice is meant to convey to the modern reader not only the texts of the plays, but also some of their character as dramatic manuscripts, with their idiosyncrasies, untidiness, and inherent ambiguities.

Footnotes identify distinctive manuscript practices, gloss difficult words or passages, and give contextual information. In the case of the two texts that survive in more than one manuscript (*Loves Victorie* and *A Pastorall*), textual notes following the play list variants in wording. An asterisk in those texts indicates the presence of a textual note. Printed text in square brackets indicates words or characters supplied by the editor. For more information on the manuscripts that have been used as copy texts, see the note on the text in the introductions to Wroth (part 1) and Cavendish and Brackley (part 2). Unless otherwise noted,

---

41. In addition to the plays in this volume, only two other manuscripts that include dramatic texts by women from before 1660 have been identified: Lady Jane Lumley's above-mentioned translation of a play by Euripides, *Iphigenia at Aulis*, from around 1550 (British Library MS Royal 15.A.ix), and Rachel Fane's household entertainments from the mid-1620s (*Manuscript of a Masque Performed by the Fane Children*, Centre for Kentish Studies U269/F38/3). On Lumley, see Marta Straznicky, *Privacy, Playreading, and Women's Closet Drama, 1550–1700* (Cambridge: Cambridge University Press, 2004), 19–47; on Fane's works, see O'Connor, "Rachel Fane's May Masque at Apethorpe, 1627."

biblical quotations are from the King James (Authorized) Bible. The abbreviations *OED* and *ODNB* are used for the online versions of *The Oxford English Dictionary* and *The Oxford Dictionary of National Biography* respectively. All dates are in new style.

PART I

MARY WROTH

(1587?–1651)

# Introduction

## Life and Works

Lady Mary Sidney Wroth (1587?–1651) was born into one of the most prominent and distinguished families of the Elizabethan era. The eldest of eleven children of Robert Sidney and Barbara Gamage, she grew up at Penshurst Place, the stately country house of the Sidney family in Kent. Her father held a succession of administrative and diplomatic posts for Queen Elizabeth that frequently took him to the Continent, an absence that was much lamented by his wife and children but that fortunately generated extensive correspondence between him, his family, and his estate agent Rowland Whyte. This correspondence provides us with detailed information about Wroth's upbringing and youth, including her education. In October 1595, when Wroth had just turned twelve, Whyte cheerfully reported to her father that "she is very forward in her learning, writing, and other exercises she is put to, as dancing and the virginals."[1] She herself had been corresponding regularly with her father from at least the age of eight, when he wrote to Whyte that "I thank Malkin [his affectionate name for Mary] for her letter and am exceeding glad to see she writes so well: tell her from me I will give her a new gown for her letter. Kiss all the rest from me."[2] The tenderness of this brief note speaks volumes about the context in which Wroth grew up: unlike the vast majority of young women of her day, she received a wide-ranging secular education and her academic gifts were a joy to her father, the person whose authority over her upbringing could just as easily have denied her these opportunities.

Wroth's father, himself a poet and author of four large volumes of journals, was a member of the Sidney family, whose cultural activities provided Wroth with the models and influences vital to her own development as a writer.[3] Robert's older brother was the legendary Philip Sidney, famed courtier and author of

---

1. Rowland Whyte, *The Letters (1595–1608) of Rowland Whyte*, ed. Michael G. Brennan, Noel J. Kinnamon, and Margaret P. Hannay (Philadelphia: American Philosophical Society, 2013), 67, cited by Margaret P. Hannay, *Mary Sidney, Lady Wroth* (Farnham, UK: Ashgate, 2010), 43. I draw on Hannay's magisterial biography for many of the details in my account of Wroth's life. The biography has significant new information that corrects a number of misconceptions about Wroth's relationship with her husband, her position at court following his death, and the impact of her having had two illegitimate children with her cousin, William Herbert. Hannay summarizes these and other findings in "Sleuthing in the Archives: The Life of Lady Mary Wroth," in *Re-Reading Mary Wroth*, ed. Katherine R. Larson and Naomi J. Miller with Andrew Strycharski (New York: Palgrave Macmillan, 2015), 19–33. See also Mary Ellen Lamb, "Wroth [née Sidney], Lady Mary (1587?–1651/1653)," *ODNB*.

2. Hannay, *Mary Sidney, Lady Wroth*, 43.

3. On Robert Sidney's writings, see Germaine Warkentin, "Robert Sidney's 'Darcke Offrings': The Making of a Late Tudor Manuscript *Canzoniere*," *Spenser Studies* 12 (1998): 37–73, and Robert

several foundational works of English literature (*Astrophel and Stella*, *The Defence of Poetry*, *The Countess of Pembroke's Arcadia*). Their sister, Mary Sidney Herbert, Countess of Pembroke, was also a celebrated literary figure and revered as a model of female learning.[4] In collaboration with her brother Philip she translated the Psalms; she edited and published his works after his death in 1586; and, in the 1590s, she translated from the French Robert Garnier's play, *Antonius: A Tragedie*, as well as Philippe de Mornay's philosophical treatise, *A Discourse of Life and Death*. The latter two works were published together in 1592 under Mary Sidney Herbert's name, and the play was reprinted alone in 1595 with a new title, *The Tragedie of Antonie*. Wroth's aunt was also a distinguished patron of writers, artists, scientists, and other intellectuals; she created a highly respected academic salon at Wilton House, the ancestral estate of the Herbert family in Wiltshire. Philip Sidney famously said he wrote the *Arcadia* at Wilton, under his sister's influence, and Queen Elizabeth was expected there on progress in 1599. That visit never occurred, but Mary Sidney Herbert composed a delightfully wry entertainment for the occasion that displays her mastery of pastoral rhetoric.[5] In her youth, Mary Wroth was frequently at Wilton or at the Herberts' London home, Baynards Castle (where she had been born). Judging by the prominence in her oeuvre of the major genres in which her aunt and uncle wrote (prose romance, sonnets and lyrics, and pastoral drama), it seems very likely, as Margaret Hannay has argued, that Mary Sidney Herbert was a support and inspiration for Wroth in her creative work.[6]

Equally important for Wroth's development as a writer was the time she spent at court or in contact with court culture, from her late teens through her late twenties, a period that coincides with her marriage to Robert Wroth (1604–1614). When King James came to the throne in 1603, Robert Sidney was appointed Lord Chamberlain to James's consort Queen Anne, which put him in charge of managing her household, including organizing the spectacular masques and dances for which her court was famous. During this time, Wroth normally spent the winter season in London. In the Christmas season of 1604–5, Wroth danced at

---

Shephard, "The Political Commonplace Books of Sir Robert Sidney," *Sidney Journal* 21, no. 1 (2003): 1–30.

4. For biographical information on Mary Sidney, see Margaret P. Hannay, "Herbert [née Sidney], Mary, countess of Pembroke (1561–1621)," *ODNB*.

5. On this and other theatrical events at Wilton, see Marta Straznicky, "Wilton House, Theatre, and Power," in *The Intellectual Culture of the English Country House, 1500–1700*, ed. Matthew Dimmock, Andrew Hadfield, and Margaret Healy (Manchester: Manchester University Press, 2015), 217–31.

6. See Margaret P. Hannay, "'Your Vertuous and Learned Aunt': The Countess of Pembroke as a Mentor to Mary Wroth," in *Reading Mary Wroth: Representing Alternatives in Early Modern England*, ed. Naomi J. Miller and Gary Waller (Knoxville: University of Tennessee Press, 1991), 16–34. For biographical information on Philip Sidney, see H. R. Woudhuysen, "Sidney, Sir Philip (1554–1586)," *ODNB*.

court in Ben Jonson's *Masque of Blackness*; as the daughter of the Queen's Lord Chamberlain, she most likely also saw at least some of that season's professionally performed plays, which included Shakespeare's *Othello*, *The Merry Wives of Windsor*, *Measure for Measure*, *The Comedy of Errors*, *Henry V*, and *Love's Labour's Lost*.[7] In 1609, she was a member of the audience for Jonson's *The Masque of Beauty*, his sequel to *The Masque of Blackness*. There are many courtly festivities and entertainments involving women represented in her works, so it is plausible that Wroth participated in other performances at the courts of King James and Queen Anne.[8] Certainly her writings resonate with the pastoral, romantic, and mythological discourses found in Jacobean court entertainments.

Throughout the years when she was at court, Wroth was known not only as a Sidney, but also as the wife of Sir Robert Wroth, the king's forester whose responsibilities included guiding the king's hunting excursions and hosting him and the court at Loughton Hall, the couple's magnificent country house near the royal hunting parks in Essex.[9] They were married at Penshurst on September 27, 1604 and were widely praised as a couple for their gracious hospitality. Although few specifics are known of their married life, they were typical of a couple in royal service in that they moved seasonally from household to household and frequently lived apart.

It was during the early years of her marriage that Wroth began to write poetry, and she circulated enough of it among family and friends to earn the praise of Ben Jonson, one of the family's many *protégés*, long before her prose romance *The Countess of Montgomery's Urania* was printed in 1621.[10] Jonson had probably tutored Wroth's younger brother Will at Penshurst around 1611, so it is conceivable they knew one another personally.[11] Jonson wrote two epigrams to Wroth and dedicated his play *The Alchemist* to her in 1612 (this is the only printed play in the period dedicated to a woman). Although the epigrams were not published until 1616, numerous other tributes to Wroth indicate that she was circulating her

---

7. Hannay, *Mary Sidney, Lady Wroth*, 123.

8. Queen Anne established a tradition of female masquing at the Stuart court to which Wroth would certainly have been exposed; see Clare McManus, *Women on the Renaissance Stage: Anna of Denmark and Female Masquing in the Stuart Court (1590–1619)* (Manchester: Manchester University Press, 2002).

9. On Loughton Hall, see Susie West, "Finding Wroth's Loughton Hall," *Sidney Journal* 34, no. 1 (2016): 15–31.

10. On the relationship between Jonson and Wroth, see Michael G. Brennan, "Creating Female Authorship in the Early Seventeenth Century: Ben Jonson and Lady Mary Wroth," in *Women's Writing and the Circulation of Ideas: Manuscript Publication in England, 1550–1800*, ed. George L. Justice and Nathan Tinker (Cambridge: Cambridge University Press, 2002), 73–93.

11. Hannay, *Mary Sidney, Lady Wroth*, 152.

poetry as early as 1611 and becoming known as an accomplished writer.[12] There is no indication that Wroth's husband in any way objected to or interfered with her writing; indeed, his will refers to her as his "dear and very loving wife" and explicitly bequeaths to her "all her books and furniture of her study and closet," suggesting he was aware of the importance of these belongings and testifying, as Margaret Hannay points out, to "a real affection between husband and wife."[13]

Wroth's husband died in March 1614, only a month after the birth of their first child, James. This was a momentous period in her life. As a widow, Wroth lost much of her income, and with the tragic death of her son only two years later, in July 1616, she also lost her claim to the Wroth properties. We know that King James and later King Charles protected her from her creditors, and although she accrued large debts from the rebuilding of Loughton Hall, she appears to have continued living there in considerable luxury.[14] The period after 1614 is very likely the time when Wroth gained the freedom and opportunity to devote herself to her writing; her only firmly dated work, the vast prose romance *The Countess of Montgomery's Urania*, was printed in 1621.[15] Appended to *Urania* is a series of sonnets and songs purportedly written by the main character, Pamphilia, to her beloved Amphilanthus. These same poems and several others are also found in an autograph manuscript, now at the Folger Shakespeare Library, that was written before the printed edition.[16] Interestingly, the paper used in this manuscript

12. Brennan, "Creating Female Authorship," 79–80. For Jonson's epigrams "CIII. To Mary, Lady Wroth," and "CV. To Mary, Lady Wroth," see *Ben Jonson: The Complete Poems*, ed. George Parfitt (New Haven, CT: Yale University Press, 1982), 71–73. The dedication to *The Alchemist* is addressed "To the Lady, most Deserving Her Name, and Blood: Mary, Lady Wroth"; see Jonson, *The Alchemist*, ed. Alvin B. Kernan (New Haven, CT: Yale University Press, 1974), 19.

13. Hannay, *Mary Sidney, Lady Wroth*, 171, 172.

14. Hannay, "Sleuthing in the Archives," 29.

15. *The Countesse of Mountgomeries Urania* (London: J. Marriott and J. Grismand, 1621). The romance has been edited by Josephine A. Roberts, *The First Part of The Countess of Montgomery's Urania* (Binghamton, NY: Medieval and Renaissance Texts and Studies, 1995). All references to the printed *Urania* are to this edition.

16. Folger Shakespeare Library V.a.104. On the relationship between the manuscript and printed versions of Wroth's poems, see Wroth, *The Poems of Lady Mary Wroth*, ed. Josephine A. Roberts (Baton Rouge: Louisiana State University Press, 1983), 62; and Ilona Bell, "The Autograph Manuscript of Mary Wroth's *Pamphilia to Amphilanthus*," in Larson and Miller with Strycharski, *Re-Reading Mary Wroth*, 171–81. The ordering of the poems in the Folger manuscript is analyzed by Gavin Alexander, "Constant Works: A Framework for Reading Mary Wroth," *Sidney Newsletter & Journal* 14, no. 2 (Winter 1996–1997): 5–32; Heather Dubrow, "'And Thus Leave Off': Reevaluating Mary Wroth's Folger Manuscript, V.a.104," *Tulsa Studies in Women's Literature* 22, no. 2 (2003): 273–91; and Margaret P. Hannay, "The 'Ending End' of Lady Mary Wroth's Manuscript of Poems," *Sidney Journal* 31, no. 1 (2013): 1–22. For an edition of the two versions of the poems, see Ilona Bell and Steven W. May, eds., *"Pamphilia to Amphilanthus" in Manuscript and Print* (Toronto: Iter; Tempe: Arizona Center for Medieval and Renaissance Studies, 2017).

is identical to that in the Penshurst copy of *Loves Victorie,* helping to date that version of the play to the same period.[17] Wroth also wrote a sequel to *Urania* amounting to over 500 pages in two manuscript volumes. The use of different inks and pens indicates that she worked on this text over an extended period,[18] and because the narrative refers to events in Wroth's life from around 1620 and after, it is likely that the second part of *Urania* was written later than the first.[19] Wroth's creative output thus appears to have been concentrated in the decade or so following the death of her husband.

During this decade, too, an intimate relationship developed between Wroth and her cousin William Herbert, third Earl of Pembroke. A distinguished patron and enormously powerful member of the nobility under King James, Pembroke was a notorious womanizer who in his youth had been dismissed from court by Queen Elizabeth for having an affair that led to the birth of an illegitimate child.[20] He was eight years older than Wroth, and they seem to have been close throughout their lives. The birth of twins (a girl, Katherine, and a boy, William) in the spring of 1624 confirms that they were physically intimate by this time at the latest. Throughout Wroth's writing, there is something of an "obsessive repetition" of narratives concerning the forsaken love of a cousin,[21] but considering the sophistication with which she weaves autobiographical references into her fiction (see the section Content and Analysis, below), a longer-term romantic attraction can only be inferred. What is perhaps more important, if not more conclusive, is that writing itself played some role in the development of Wroth and Pembroke's relationship, providing not only a fictional veil for the representation of events and emotions, but also a shared creative activity. Pembroke wrote love lyrics, pastoral songs, and conversational poems that belong to the same Sidnean tradition as the poetry found in Wroth's *Urania, Pamphilia to Amphilanthus,* and *Loves Victorie.* And while his poetry was not published until 1660, it circulated in manuscript decades earlier. Moreover, there is strong evidence that Wroth and Herbert exchanged poems and that some of these, too, circulated widely. For example, one of the sonnets in Wroth's manuscript of the second part of *Urania,* "Had I loved

17. Hannay, *Mary Sidney, Lady Wroth,* 218.

18. Roberts, *Poems,* 65.

19. The manuscript of the second part of the *Urania* is at the Newberry Library in Chicago (Case MS fY 1565. W95). It has been edited by Josephine A. Roberts, completed by Suzanne Gossett and Janel Mueller, *The Second Part of The Countess of Montgomery's Urania* (Tempe: Renaissance English Text Society in conjunction with Arizona Center for Medieval and Renaissance Studies, 1999). All references to the manuscript continuation of Urania are to this edition. On the dating of the second part of Urania, see pages xx–xxi.

20. For biographical information on William Herbert, see Victor Stater, "Herbert, William, third earl of Pembroke (1580–1630)," *ODNB.*

21. Hannay, "Sleuthing in the Archives," 22.

butt att that rate," exists in four other seventeenth-century manuscripts and is attributed to William Herbert in three of them.[22]

When her prose romance *Urania* was printed in 1621, Wroth was known as a writer, but only a limited circle of friends and acquaintances would by that time have read her work. The publication of *The Countesse of Mountgomeries Urania* was a game changer: produced in a large, expensive format, with an elaborately engraved title page boldly identifying the author's heritage as a Sidney and available for sale at two well-known London bookshops, Wroth's book drew attention to itself and its author in a way that made it difficult for her to control its circulation and reception as had been possible with manuscript publication. Presumably this was intended, for there is nothing illegal about the circumstances of its publication: the book was duly registered with the Stationers' Company; its title page was engraved by a prominent Dutch artist, Simon van de Passe, who had painted portraits of royalty and other members of Wroth's family; and Wroth herself states that she sent a copy to the Duke of Buckingham.[23]

Very soon after the book's appearance in print, however, Wroth was accused of libeling the family of a courtier, Lord Denny, in one of the romance's inset narratives.[24] If it had happened today, we might say their quarrel went viral. Denny attacked Wroth in a poem titled "To Pamphilia from the father-in-law of Seralius," calling her a hermaphrodite, a monster, and a fool whose "witt runns madd not caring who it strike."[25] The poem was circulated at court, and perhaps beyond: it survives in three manuscript copies.[26] Wroth responded with an attack poem of her own, mirroring his line for line and accusing him of being so enflamed with rage and passion that he has lost all nobility. Denny and Wroth also exchanged several bitter letters in which they insulted one another and disputed the extent to which *Urania* is or is not a representation of real people and events. These letters, too, were copied and circulated, and they gained enough notoriety that reference is made to them in the correspondence of other courtiers. According to one of Wroth's letters, Denny even went so far as to bring his complaint to King James. In her defence,

22. For bibliographic information on these manuscripts, all of which are in the British Library, see Roberts, *Poems*, 217. On the literary relationship between Wroth and William Herbert, see Mary Ellen Lamb, "'Can You Suspect a Change in Me?': Poems by Mary Wroth and William Herbert, Third Earl of Pembroke," in Larson and Miller with Strycharski, *Re-Reading Mary Wroth*, 53–68.

23. Roberts, *First Part of The Countess of Montgomery's Urania*, cvi; Roberts, *Poems*, 236. On the significance of the frontispiece, see Mary Ellen Lamb, "Selling Mary Wroth's *Urania*: The Frontispiece and the Connoisseurship of Romance," *Sidney Journal* 34, no. 1 (2016): 33–48.

24. For a detailed account of the Denny affair, see Hannay, *Mary Sidney, Lady Wroth*, 235–42.

25. Roberts, *Poems*, 32–33. On the circulation of the hermaphrodite poems and responses to them, see Paul Salzman, "Mary Wroth and Hermaphroditic Circulation," in *Early Modern Women and the Poem*, ed. Susan Wiseman (Manchester: Manchester University Press, 2014), 117–30.

26. The manuscripts are at the University of Nottingham Library, the Huntington Library, and the British Library; see Roberts, *Poems*, 32n82, and 33n83.

Wroth insists that she never intended to represent Denny or his family in any part of *Urania*, that his misreading of the book reflects his own perverse imagination, and that she is prepared to answer his slanders in public. In the year or two following the initial firestorm, Wroth wrote letters to a number of other courtiers seeking their continued support and insisting on her innocence; the affair was an ongoing challenge for her. But while Wroth had offered to have copies of her book removed from sale, whatever effort she made in this regard proved futile: at least twenty-nine copies of *Urania* have survived, and the marks of ownership and marginal annotations on many of them indicate that the book was valued and read with great interest.[27] One surviving copy even has Wroth's own handwritten corrections and revisions, showing that she gave the printed book the kind of ongoing attention evident in her manuscripts.[28] Perhaps she did this while she was at work on the second part of *Urania* in the early 1620s, the latest of her surviving writings.[29]

The 1620s for Wroth were also marked by great personal change: she lost her mother and her aunt Mary Sidney Herbert in the months preceding the publication of *Urania*; she evidently resumed her relationship with William Herbert, for their twins were born in the spring of 1624; her father died in 1626; and her dear friend and sister-in-law, Susan, the Countess of Montgomery named in the title of *Urania*, died of smallpox in January, 1629. William Herbert died on April 9, 1630. Each of these deaths would have been a great personal loss to Wroth, and none of them brought her any relief from the financial problems she had been facing since the death of her son in 1616. Nor is there any evidence that Herbert contributed materially to the upbringing of his children, although it does appear that the children were known by his surname and that Wroth was not stigmatized on account of their illegitimacy.[30]

Thus, throughout the 1620s Wroth was having to adjust to the loss of her closest relatives and the resulting shifts in family networks, while also, from 1624, attending to the upbringing of her two children. It was this responsibility and the management of her complex finances to which she seems to have devoted her remaining years. There are very few surviving documents to chart this period of her

27. For the contemporary reception of *Urania*, see Rahel Orgis, "'[A] Story Very Well Woorth Readinge': Why Early Modern Readers Valued Lady Mary Wroth's *Urania*," *Sidney Journal* 31, no. 1 (2013): 81–100. The details of Wroth's argument with Denny are discussed by Josephine A. Roberts, "An Unpublished Literary Quarrel Concerning the Suppression of Mary Wroth's *Urania* (1621)," *Notes & Queries* 222 (1977): 532–35; and Paul Salzman, "Contemporary References in Mary Wroth's *Urania*," *Review of English Studies*, new series, 29, no. 114 (May 1978): 178–81.

28. This copy is now at the University of Pennsylvania Rare Books and Manuscript Library and available in facsimile online at http://hdl.library.upenn.edu/1017/d/print/3441687, accessed May 6, 2018. For a list and brief descriptions of the known surviving copies of *Urania*, see Roberts, *First Part of The Countess of Montgomery's Urania*, 663–64.

29. Hannay, *Mary Sidney, Lady Wroth*, 263.

30. Hannay, "Sleuthing in the Archives," 25.

life, and it is certainly possible that any later writing she may have produced was destroyed in fires at Loughton Hall and Wilton House.[31] She continued to live at Loughton until her death in March, 1651. Throughout this time, she entertained family and members of the nobility and is referred to by her title in various parish and legal records. It appears she retained her social position and was far from destitute.[32] Her reputation as a writer understandably solidified around *Urania*, this being the only work of hers to have reached print, but later in her life she was also admired as a learned poet and continued to be addressed as the niece of Sir Philip Sidney.[33] The place of her burial is not known.

## *The Huntington Manuscript of* Loves Victorie

*Loves Victorie* (HM600) was acquired by the Henry E. Huntington Library in 1923.[34] It is a folio manuscript consisting of twenty-one leaves and is written in Lady Mary Wroth's handwriting. The physical state of the manuscript suggests a complex process of composition. Wroth used two distinct hands, and the presence of numerous gaps, revisions, and insertions create a striking discontinuity both in the flow and in the materiality of the text.[35] The play is headed with a title, and its final page is written in a very compressed script. There are significantly more lines on this page than on any other page of the manuscript, possibly indicating that Wroth framed the play as it exists even though it ends abruptly with a speech prefix.

31. On the 1836 fire at Loughton Hall and the loss of its library, see Hannay, *Mary Sidney, Lady Wroth*, 309–10. Wilton House suffered a massive fire in 1647.

32. Hannay, *Mary Sidney, Lady Wroth*, 277. Hannay also reveals that Wroth's daughter Katherine married well and moved to Wales with her husband; Wroth's son Will was given an estate in Ireland and a prestigious military commission (287–94).

33. Hannay, *Mary Sidney, Lady Wroth*, 307–8.

34. Portions of this section and the Content and Analysis section of the introduction were published in Marta Straznicky, "Lady Mary Wroth's Patchwork Play: The Huntington Manuscript of *Love's Victory*," *Sidney Journal* 34, no. 1 (2016): 81–92. I thank Iter Press and the Arizona Center for Medieval and Renaissance Studies for permitting early publication of this material. On the date of the Huntington Library's acquisition of the manuscript, see Josephine A. Roberts, "The Huntington Manuscript of Lady Mary Wroth's Play, 'Loves Victorie,'" *Huntington Library Quarterly* 46, no. 2 (1983): 156–74 (162); Arthur Freeman, "*Love's Victory*: A Supplementary Note," *The Library* 19, no. 3 (1997): 252–54, who states that HM600 was acquired "after 1922" (252); and Peter Beal, online *Catalogue of English Literary Manuscripts, 1450–1700*, http://www.celm-ms.org.uk/authors/wrothladymary.html#de-lisle-penshurst-place_id393287, accessed May 6, 2018. On the flyleaf of HM600 is a note stating that the manuscript "was acquired from Rosenbach Company on Sept. 6, 1923."

35. Wroth's hand in HM600 was established by Roberts in her seminal study, "The Huntington Manuscript." In addition, Roberts provides a detailed account of the physical nature of the manuscript, its provenance, and its literary context. For a detailed description of the manuscript, see below, "Note on the Text."

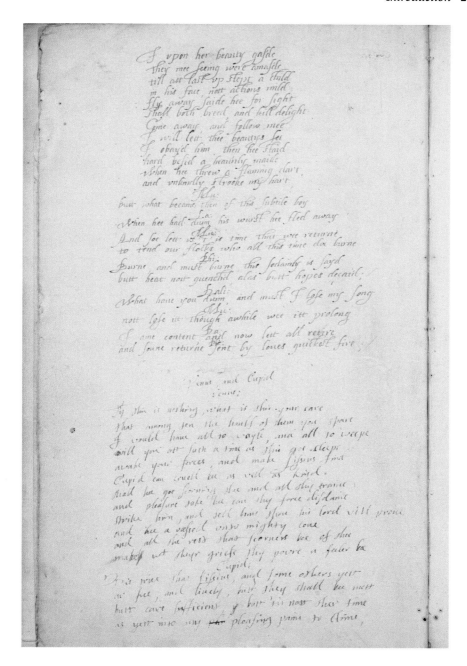

Figure 1. The two hands of *Loves Victorie* in the Huntington manuscript, folio 4v. HM600. © By permission of the Huntington Library, San Marino, California.

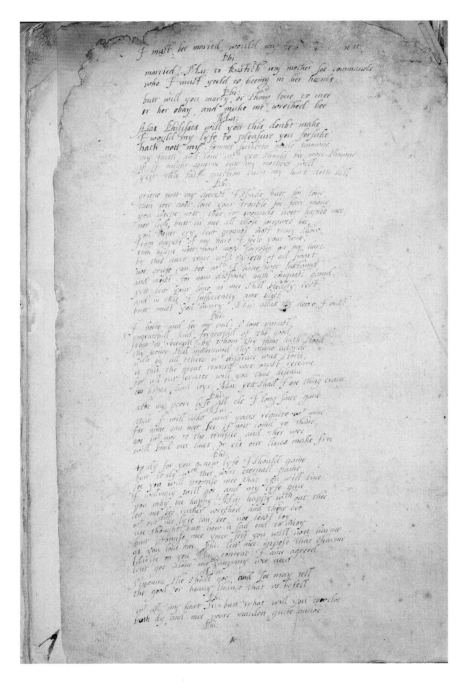

Figure 2. Final page of *Loves Victorie* in the Huntington manuscript, folio 21v. HM600. © By permission of the Huntington Library, San Marino, California.

The two hands in which the manuscript is written correspond to passages of text that appear to be at different stages of composition, with Wroth's formal, italic hand (along with an orderly graphic layout) used for better-developed passages, and her relaxed, cursive hand for passages that appear to be in progress or more recently completed.

The first cursive passage in the play, for instance, is the Venus and Cupid interlude at the end of act 1 (see Figure 1): it ends three-quarters of the way down the page and is followed by a blank page, suggesting that Wroth left it unfinished and went back to add it at a later time. The second interlude, along with some dialogue added to the scene that precedes it, is also written in her cursive hand on two sheets that are roughly half the size used for the rest of the manuscript. These smaller sheets are carefully aligned with the adjacent pages and securely sewn and glued into the manuscript at the correct place in the play. It seems Wroth may have written the play in sections; she certainly made some attempt to assemble the components into a coherent document.[36] Moreover, the pattern of wear on the first and last leaves indicates not only that the manuscript was used, but that it was used for some time in its current makeup.[37]

It is important to notice these characteristics because the Huntington manuscript is often said to be an incomplete, working draft of the play. The argument for its alleged incompleteness rests on a comparison with the longer Penshurst manuscript, which has two additional Venus and Cupid interludes and continues the action of the fifth act through to a conventional ending.[38] The Penshurst manuscript is in a smaller format (quarto) and is written throughout in Wroth's formal italic hand on a single kind of paper. It has many fewer revisions and corrections, and has a red leather binding tooled in gold; it may have been a gift copy.[39] Although neither manuscript has been definitively dated, the longer and more orderly Penshurst version is usually thought to have been written later, and therefore to be more authoritative.[40] A close comparison of the two manuscripts,

---

36. I thank Sara S. Hodson, Curator of Literary Manuscripts at the Huntington Library, for confirming that the smaller sheets are sewn into the manuscript.

37. Playhouse manuscripts from the period frequently show wear on their outer leaves. See, for example, the description of the manuscript of *The Sodderd Citizen* (1628–30) in Paul Werstine, *Early Modern Playhouse Manuscripts and the Editing of Shakespeare* (Cambridge: Cambridge University Press, 2013), 317.

38. A photographic facsimile and transcript of the Penshurst manuscript has been edited by Michael G. Brennan, *Lady Mary Wroth's Love's Victory: The Penshurst Manuscript* (London: Roxburghe Club, 1988).

39. *Love's Victory*, De L'Isle Manuscript, Penshurst Place, Kent. For a description of the manuscript, see Brennan, *Lady Mary Wroth's Love's Victory*, 16.

40. Important counterarguments to this critical consensus have been made by Paul Salzman, *Reading Early Modern Women's Writing* (Oxford: Oxford University Press, 2006), 83–84; and Marion Wynne-Davies, "The Liminal Woman in Mary Wroth's *Love's Victory*," *Sidney Journal* 26, no. 2 (2008): 81.

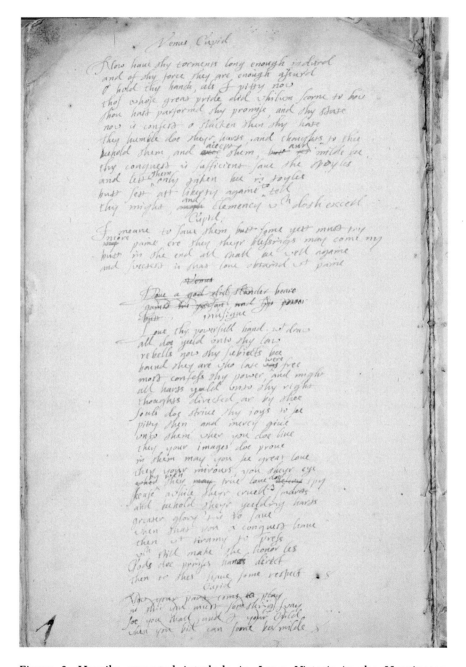

Figure 3. Heavily corrected interlude in *Loves Victorie* in the Huntington manuscript, displaying the *s fermé,* folio 20v. HM600. © By permission of the Huntington Library, San Marino, California.

however, reveals that their chronological relationship with one another is difficult to determine, for while the Penshurst manuscript seems in many places to transcribe the Huntington text, writing out in a continuous flow the revisions that are inserted between lines or otherwise added, there are also hundreds of variants in wording between the two versions, few of which are demonstrably superior to one another and thus do not indicate a straightforward process of revision.

The question of completeness is also more complex than appears at first sight. Although the Penshurst text is longer than the Huntington version, we do not know whether it is more complete because our only basis for this judgment are the two texts themselves. In fact, the Penshurst manuscript itself is demonstrably not complete: it lacks a song in its final act, the absence of which is indicated by nearly a full blank page (fol. 48v). It is not insignificant that the missing text is a song. Tiffany Stern has shown that early modern play manuscripts were often "patchwork" documents, collections of single or folded sheets on which various kinds of text (actors' parts, prologues, epilogues, letters, choruses, interim entertainments) were written and then reassembled, often imperfectly, for archiving, presentation, or print.[41] Song lyrics were particularly prone to being detached or extracted from their plays and circulating separately; many survive outside playbooks in manuscripts or printed books of various kinds.[42] Because songs were frequently lost, removed, altered, added, or written by someone other than the playwright, multiple manuscripts of the same work can differ as to their presence or absence. In light of this practice, the missing song in the Penshurst manuscript may indicate that Wroth was not only copying, but also reassembling separate documents for this presentation copy of the play.

The lacuna in the Penshurst manuscript may seem to be a minor omission but is, in fact, consistent with Wroth's scribal practice generally and thus significant in reassessing the question of the completeness of the Huntington version of *Loves Victorie*. Recent studies of Wroth's literary manuscripts by Gavin Alexander, Heather Dubrow, Margaret Hannay, and Ilona Bell have shown in rich detail that hers was an intricate process of writing, revision, and compilation, working with

---

41. Tiffany Stern, *Documents of Performance in Early Modern England* (Cambridge: Cambridge University Press, 2009), 1–7, 120–73. In *Early Modern Playhouse Manuscripts*, Paul Werstine notes the frequent use of multiple hands and mixed paper stock in playhouse manuscripts and describes numerous examples in which folded sheets, half-sheets, and slips have been inserted, some with considerable precision. It is worth noting that the Penshurst manuscript begins the play proper on fol. 2, with the title "Loues Victory" written above the rule that runs across the page. The opening interlude, then, is not incorporated within the play proper but is positioned outside its boundary. This could suggest it existed as a separate document and explain its absence from the Huntington manuscript.

42. Interestingly, one of the songs in Wroth's manuscript of the second part of her prose romance *Urania* is found in three other manuscripts and attributed there to her cousin William Herbert, and a different song circulated separately and was set to music. See Gavin Alexander, "The Musical Sidneys," *John Donne Journal* 25 (2006): 65–105 (95–96, 99).

groupings and sequences of poems that were rarely in fixed formation.[43] The manuscript of Wroth's poems in the Folger Shakespeare Library (V.a.104), for example, is made up of a number of discrete groupings which are indicated by the use of catchwords, blank pages, internal titles, or the symbol known as "*s fermé*"—resembling a capital S with a diagonal slash through it—which Wroth used in her letters and literary manuscripts to signal closure or termination of some kind.[44] Interestingly, there is a distinctive arrangement of sonnets and songs in this manuscript, the sonnets being consistently linked with catchwords while the songs are not, ending variously with a catchword, a flourish, or the *s fermé*, and thereby signaling that they are not part of a sequence. It appears that Wroth was consulting a number of separate documents and presenting groups of poems in this collection as more or less detached from one another. The afterlife of the poems she gathered here was also varied. Some pieces are only found in this compilation, others circulated in manuscript, and still others were reshaped for print.[45] Although the Folger collection looks very much like a presentation manuscript, a close examination of its internal sequences and what can be glimpsed of its passage through earlier and later documents reveals that it is also a fluid text: if not a work in progress, then a work that gestures both materially and textually to a pattern and process of circulation in which the concept of completeness seems to have had little or no part.[46]

The physical makeup of the Huntington manuscript of *Loves Victorie* reveals this process more visibly than any of Wroth's other manuscripts, particularly in the two-leaf insertion at the end of act 2 that is on paper of roughly half the size as the rest of the volume. These two leaves (fols. 9 and 10) include the entirety of the play's second interlude, which at one time was literally detached from the text and can therefore be presumed to have its own history. The interlude following act 3 is missing entirely, although the initial speech prefix is in the correct place and the remainder of the page (fol. 15) has been left blank, perhaps in order to insert the interlude at a later time. Considering, too, that Wroth used her cursive handwriting only for the interludes and surrounding passages, the Huntington manuscript indicates that these passages were not only written at a different time but were also, at some point, the kind of detachable text that was frequently extracted from playbooks and circulated separately.

43. See Alexander, "Constant Works"; Dubrow, "And Thus Leave Off"; Hannay, "The Ending End"; and Bell, "The Autograph Manuscript."

44. A catchword "is a word that generally appears isolated at the bottom right-hand corner of a page as an aid to continuity, since it anticipates the first word that appears on the next page." Peter Beal, *A Dictionary of English Manuscript Terminology, 1450–2000* (Oxford: Oxford University Press, 2008), 65.

45. On the relationship between the manuscript and printed versions of Wroth's poems, see Bell and May, "*Pamphilia to Amphilanthus.*"

46. Wroth's manuscript of the second part of her prose romance *The Lady of Montgomery's Urania* reveals similar features (Newberry Library, Chicago, Case MS f.Y 1565 W95). For a description of this facet of the manuscript, see Straznicky, "Lady Mary Wroth's Patchwork Play," 85.

The "patchwork" nature of the Huntington manuscript thus reveals that Wroth assembled certain songs, speeches, and even scenes from another source, and that she composed—as her uncle Philip Sidney famously did the *Arcadia*—in "loose" sheets, later compiling these into a more orderly progression.[47] Such a process casts the question of the completeness of the Huntington manuscript in a different light, with possibly quite significant implications for criticism. If we judge its relative completeness based on the physical state of the manuscript rather than the absence of material found in the Penshurst text, there is only one major omission in the Huntington version: the Venus and Cupid interlude meant to be on folio 15. At the top of the page, Wroth wrote the header "The 4 Acte" and the speech prefix "Musella," but then rubbed both out. On a fresh line below them, she wrote the speech prefix "Venus," indicating that an interlude would follow. The remainder of the page is left blank; act 4 begins at the top of the following page (fol. 15v), with the correct header and speech prefix. In the missing interlude, assuming it is the one that ends act 3 in the Penshurst text, we learn that Cupid has planned not only more obstruction for the lovers in act 4, but also a joyous ending. Without this interlude, we proceed directly into the fourth act and the increasingly dire circumstances of the lovers Philisses and Musella, whose union is jeopardized by an arranged marriage. The mood of the play is undoubtedly altered by this gap, and it is a mood that extends right through to the lovers' pact to die together, the shock of which is captured in the final lines of the play, spoken by Simeana: "butt what will you tow doe / both dy, and mee poore maiden quite undoe?" (21v). The speech prefix "Phi:" on the following line, the last line in the Huntington text, suggests a response, but it is also the kind of narrative interruption we find elsewhere in the writings and manuscripts of the Sidney family, not least Wroth's own inconclusive, mid-sentence end to both the first and second parts of her prose romance *Urania*. In the Penshurst manuscript, Philisses responds with a line that immediately recasts the suicide as a triumph ("Dy? Noe, wee goe for euer more to liue, / and to owr loves a sacrifice to giue" [39r]); in the Huntington version, he is silenced, predicting a tragic outcome that is patently different from the ending of the play in the Penshurst text.

As is explored in the Content and Analysis section below, reading *Loves Victorie* in its two textually specific forms enriches our understanding of this remarkable play and its author's creative process. It may also cast light on the question of its performance. The Huntington manuscript was at one time in the possession of Sir Edward Dering (1598–1644), a close acquaintance of the Wroth and Herbert families. Dering owned a large collection of playbooks, among which

---

47. In his dedication of *Arcadia* to his sister, Philip Sidney claims that "Your dear self can best witness the manner, being done in loose sheets of paper, most of it in your presence, the rest by sheets sent unto you as fast as they were done." Sidney, *The Countesse of Pembroke's Arcadia (The Old Arcadia)*, ed. Jean Robertson (Oxford: Clarendon Press, 1973), 3.

are multiple printed copies of individual plays and a manuscript adaptation of Shakespeare's *Henry IV, Part One* for household performance.[48] As Paul Salzman has pointed out, if we view the Huntington manuscript as Wroth's working copy, its ownership by Dering, an avid playgoer and collector of playbooks, is puzzling.[49] But the Huntington text may not be an imperfect draft, as is suggested by its numerous physical traits (its use of formal handwriting, its orderly arrangement on the page, its careful reattachment of the second interlude, and its durable binding). It is possible Wroth was at least partly transcribing from another, *third*, manuscript of the play, no longer extant, and thus preparing a coherent and continuous text for Dering rather than a rough draft for her own use.[50] Even if we put such conjectures aside, approaching the Huntington manuscript as a different version of Wroth's play opens up new avenues for critical, bibliographic, and theatrical research, avenues that are not available in the same terms for the Penshurst version quite simply because the two texts, by virtue of their material differences, have different stories to tell.[51]

## Content and Analysis of Loves Victorie

*Loves Victorie* belongs to the tradition of English pastoral drama, yet Wroth's highly conventional design also demands nuanced attention to structure, style, and theme. Pastoral was ubiquitous in the Renaissance, derived in diverse ways from two of the period's most revered classical authors, Virgil and Ovid, and reimagined in fifteenth- and sixteenth-century European vernacular poetry as a discourse and form almost infinitely adaptable to exploring questions of social, cultural, and political authority, specifically in court settings.[52] Set well away from

48. On Dering as a play collector, see T. N. S. Lennam, "Sir Edward Dering's Collection of Playbooks, 1619–1624," *Shakespeare Quarterly* 16, no. 2 (1965): 145–53. On Dering's ownership of HM600, see Roberts, "The Huntington Manuscript," 163–64, and Freeman, "*Love's Victory*," 252–54. See also S. P. Salt, "Dering, Sir Edward, first baronet (1598–1644)," *ODNB*.

49. Salzman, *Reading Early Modern Women's Writing*, 80.

50. In his edition of the Huntington manuscript, Maxwell notes that the nature of the corrections and omissions in the formal italic passages indicates that these are "certainly a copy." C. H. J. Maxwell, ed., *Loues Victorie*, master's thesis, Stanford University, 1933, xiv. Salzman speculates that Wroth knowingly provided Dering with a "less than satisfactory performance text." *Reading Early Modern Women's Writing*, 80.

51. An excellent tool for exploring these differences is Paul Salzman's online edition of *Love's Victory*, which allows the reader to view images of the Huntington manuscript alongside an old-spelling text, a modern spelling text, and a transcription of the Penshurst text: http://hri.newcastle.edu.au/emwrn/da/index.php?content=lovesvictory, accessed May 6, 2018.

52. For an overview of the pastoral literature in the early modern period, see Walter W. Greg, *Pastoral Poetry and Pastoral Drama* (New York: Russell & Russell, 1959). On the political functions of Elizabethan pastoral, see, among others, Louis Adrian Montrose, "Celebration and Insinuation: Sir

court in a distinctive landscape of fields and meadows,[53] and peopled by shepherds with seemingly endless leisure time, the pastoral mode proved to be the ideal vehicle for representations of power. Many key works of imaginative writing in Wroth's time used pastoral conventions, including two that were at the heart of the literary project that developed around the Sidney family, Edmund Spenser's *The Shepherd's Calendar* (1579) and her uncle Sir Philip Sidney's *The Countess of Pembroke's Arcadia* (1590).[54] The ideological function of these and other pastoral works was complex and well understood: as Sidney himself stated, pastoral is not to be disdained, for "under the pretty tales of wolves and sheep, [it] can include the whole considerations of wrong-doing and patience."[55] Fundamentally allegorical in conception and design, Renaissance pastoral gave voice to the dispossessed and disempowered, while also providing an "imaginative ground-plot" for political thought.[56]

Wroth's use of the pastoral mode in *Loves Victorie* is less explicitly political than many of the models she would have known, but its literary qualities fit squarely within the tradition, especially its dramatic forms such as dialogues, masques, entertainments, and stage plays.[57] The play is about a group of shepherds and shepherdesses who are variously in love with one another and whose desires

Philip Sidney and the Motives of Elizabethan Courtiership," *Renaissance Drama* 8 (1977): 3–35, and "Of Gentlemen and Shepherds: The Politics of Elizabethan Pastoral Form," *English Literary History* 50, no. 3 (1983): 415–59.

53. The place name most commonly associated with the pastoral landscape is Arcadia, derived from classical Greek and Roman literature and denoting "a place of rural bliss conceived as an escape from the stresses of the city and the court." Adam Nicolson, *Arcadia: The Dream of Perfection in Renaissance England* (London: Harper Perennial, 2009), 3. Wroth refers to Arcadia once in *Loves Victorie* as the home of Climeana, who describes herself as a "stranger" to the setting of the play (3.224–25).

54. The political significance of pastoral for the Sidney circle and specifically in connection with Sidney's *Arcadia* is discussed by Alan Stewart, *Philip Sidney: A Double Life* (London: Chatto & Windus, 2000), 227–30.

55. Sir Philip Sidney, *A Defence of Poetry*, in *Miscellaneous Prose of Sir Philip Sidney*, ed. Katherine Duncan-Jones and Jan van Dorsten (Oxford: Clarendon Press, 1973), 95.

56. Sidney, *A Defence*, 103.

57. On Wroth's use of pastoral, see Margaret Anne McLaren, "An Unknown Continent: Lady Mary Wroth's Forgotten Pastoral Drama, 'Loves Victorie,'" in *The Renaissance Englishwoman in Print: Counterbalancing the Canon*, ed. Anne M. Haselkorn and Betty S. Travitsky (Amherst: University of Massachusetts Press, 1990), 276–94; Barbara Kiefer Lewalski, "Mary Wroth's *Love's Victory* and Pastoral Tragicomedy," in Miller and Waller, *Reading Mary Wroth*, 88–108; Josephine A. Roberts, "Deciphering Women's Pastoral: Coded Language in Wroth's *Love's Victory*," in *Representing Women in Renaissance England*, ed. Claude J. Summers and Ted-Larry Pebworth (Columbia: University of Missouri Press, 1997), 163–74; Joyce Green MacDonald, "Ovid and Women's Pastoral in Lady Mary Wroth's *Love's Victory*," *SEL: Studies in English Literature* 51, no. 2 (2011): 447–63. Alison Findlay has written incisively about the different genres of the two versions of *Love's Victory* in "Lady Mary Wroth: *Love's Victory*," in *The Ashgate Research Companion to The Sidneys, 1500–1700*, vol. 2, *Literature*,

are thwarted by the usual obstacles: jealousy, mistrust, self-doubt, ill will, miscommunication, parental constraint, celibacy, and pride. In a cleverly handled dual perspective, these obstacles are actually experienced by the shepherds and shepherdesses and also personified in the mythological figures of Venus and Cupid, who appear in three interludes in which they describe and implicitly control the plot. The plot itself is enacted at the human level through an intricate arrangement of dramatic incident and conversational games.[58] Because the narrative is conveyed almost entirely through dialogue, however, *Loves Victorie* can feel strangely free of action, its drama consisting of the comings and goings of characters in various groupings (solo, duets, trios, and larger clusters) and, quite simply, lots of talking. The play is set within the meadows, woods, and valleys typical of pastoral landscape, but it is unusually simplified in that architectural or indeed any built space is not mentioned, with the possible exception of several references to "paths" and "walks" that may at times evoke a garden rather than a rural setting.[59] The only notable prop is the book carried onstage by Arcas in the second act and handed around from one character to another as they read their fortunes.

In contrast with the quite basic visual and kinetic design of the play, *Loves Victorie* is extraordinarily rich in the intricacy and orchestration of its many verbal components, which include not only dialogue, but also song, riddle, lyric, and narration.[60] These components are written in a variety of metrical forms, but all are highly patterned and steeped in Petrarchan discourse, characterized by its many conventional tropes and images of adoration, sexual passion, insecurity, suffering, and self-pity. With twelve human characters pursuing their loves, and Venus and Cupid determined to throw every conceivable obstacle in their way, it is not surprising that the play has a high degree of verbal uniformity and at times a rather monotonous emotional register. There are, however, some subtle variations to notice in the language of a number of the characters: Dalina and Rustic, for instance, are both feisty and impertinent, and the anger and defiance in Musella's speech in act 5, where the plot makes an unexpected turn toward

ed. Margaret P. Hannay, Mary Ellen Lamb, and Michael G. Brennan (Farnham, UK: Ashgate, 2015), 211–24.

58. Katherine R. Larson gives an insightful comparative analysis of the conversational games in *Loves Victorie* and Shakespeare's *Love's Labour's Lost* in *Early Modern Women in Conversation* (New York: Palgrave Macmillan, 2011), 89–109. For other comparative studies of *Loves Victorie* and Shakespeare, see Paul Salzman and Marion Wynne-Davies, eds., *Mary Wroth and Shakespeare* (New York: Routledge, 2015).

59. On the significance of the garden setting in the play and as a possible performance space (at Penshurst), see Alison Findlay, *Playing Spaces in Early Women's Drama* (Cambridge: Cambridge University Press, 2006), 83–94.

60. On the songs and conversational games in the play as integral to its dramatic design, see Katherine R. Larson, "Playing at Penshurst: The Songs and Musical Games of Mary Wroth's *Love's Victory*," *Sidney Journal* 34, no. 1 (2016): 93–106.

tragedy, is strikingly at odds with her tone elsewhere. Also worth noting is the distinctiveness of Venus's language, especially in the second and third interludes (following act 2 and act 4), where there is a concentration of political references (princes, kings, government, satires, law, rebellion, and tyranny) that add substantially to the range of possible readings of the play.

But it is Wroth's intricate structural arrangement of the many kinds of speech and verbal exchange in *Loves Victorie* that is arguably its most impressive quality. Act 1, for example, is composed in three quite distinct scenes that build in overall complexity—of perspective, mood, and tone—toward the first interlude where Cupid declares that the lovers' pleasures are but "haulfway worne" (1.436). Philisses opens the play with a song mourning the pleasures he has forsaken by falling in love and then explains the reason for his unhappiness and states his intention to hide his feelings. While his song and speech vary in rhetorical stance and metrical form, they are linked with a single voice and literally with the phrase "Joy's lost" (lines 26 and 27), the controlling concept of the entire first act. Following Philisses's soliloquy, his good friend and (to Philisses's mind) rival in love enters, singing his own song that seems to echo Philisses's ("Joyfull pleasant spring") but in fact conveys a completely different spirit of happiness and buoyancy, thus countering the despondent mood with which the play just opened. The dynamic continues as Philisses twice comments cynically on Lissius's state of joy and refocuses our attention on his own misery. Philisses and Lissius are not actually in dialogue at this point, so the effect of this shift of voices is more like counterpoint than conversation, the result being that, at the outset of the play, their discourse is both shared on a number of levels and yet articulated in an oppositional dynamic, suggestive perhaps of the inherently paradoxical nature of desire and the conflict it entails.

The remainder of the first act is similarly orchestrated, with new voices and perspectives being layered upon and interwoven with one another. The next suite of speeches and exchanges comprise a second internal "scene" and introduce two additional ways of being in love: renunciation and infatuation. Silvesta, a rejected lover of Philisses, pronounces in a lengthy soliloquy the virtue of chastity and thus offers a crucial alternative to Philisses's anguish and to Lissius's arrogant rejection of love. She speaks with both passion and wisdom, and her larger perspective makes hers the first voice of authority in the play (1.101–18).[61] Fittingly, it is she

---

61. Lewalski, "Mary Wroth's *Love's Victory*," argues that the play articulates a vision of an egalitarian society in which female protagonists and communities have agency that is not found in male-authored pastoral plays. Silvesta's uniquely authoritative voice is an early indication of this pattern. For a similar line of argument, see Carolyn Ruth Swift, "Feminine Self-Definition in Lady Mary Wroth's *Love's Victorie* (c. 1621)," *English Literary Renaissance* 19, no. 2 (1989): 171–88. Marion O'Connor suggests that Silvesta may represent Lucy Harington Russell; see "'Silvesta was my instrument ordained'?: Lucy Harington Russell, Third Countess of Bedford, as Family Marriage Broker," *Sidney Journal* 34, no. 1 (2016): 49–65.

who extends the play rhetorically to the audience, advising us to turn away from "loves fond desires" (1.104) and embrace freedom instead. Silvesta does not engage with any of the other characters here, so that her speech (the longest in act 1) has a stand-alone quality that sets it on a separate rhetorical plane. Following a short reprise of Philisses's lament, a fourth new character, the Forester, enters and launches into another self-pitying complaint that is sarcastically interrupted by Lissius: "If one may ask; what is th'offence is dunn?" (1.186). The Forester invites Lissius to sit down and proceeds to tell "my sorrowes cause" (1.193) which, we learn, involves both Silvesta and Philisses. Lissius, not surprisingly, makes his own critical response to the Forester's "phant'sie" (1.250). This narrative passage builds the complexity of the plot with admirable control. More importantly, as a storytelling episode including a response from the listener, it introduces a conversational structure in which a multiplicity of perspectives can be synchronized. Act 1 ends with a third scene in which just such a "prety sport" (1.331) occurs, the singing contest in which there is a further display of passions among a still larger group of characters and in response to which Philisses and Musella reveal their attraction to one another.

The sophisticated arrangement of verbal and dramatic elements in act 1 is characteristic of *Loves Victorie* as a whole and has been likened insightfully to choreography or musical orchestration.[62] This is an apt comparison, for Wroth was known as a talented dancer and lute player and performed in at least one court masque.[63] She would have been familiar with the various forms of courtly entertainment and capable of adapting them to her own creative aims. In addition to its intricate depiction of multiple perspectives, *Loves Victorie* shares with masque and other kinds of pastoral entertainments an overall design that is oppositional in nature: the energies of order and disorder are put into an opposing dynamic that leads ultimately and invariably to the triumph of order. This dynamic can be seen on many different levels: the frequent instances of competitive wordplay, debate, and rivalry between speakers; the mirroring of dramatic incidents; the interplay of romantic desire and its impediments, notably the buffoonish character Rustic to whom Musella is forcibly engaged and whose stance opposes the overall momentum of the play; indeed, the paradoxical nature of Petrarchan discourse itself (e.g., "love is a paine w$^{ch}$ yett doth pleasure bring," [2.114]) is inherently oppositional, its forces of desire and frustration producing a rhetorical and performative space in which movement and stasis counterbalance one another.

62. See Katherine R. Larson, "Voicing Lyric: The Songs of Mary Wroth," in Larson and Miller with Strycharski, *Re-Reading Mary Wroth*, 119–36; and Karen L. Nelson, "'Change Partners and Dance': Pastoral Virtuosity in Wroth's *Love's Victory*," in Larson and Miller with Strycharski, *Re-Reading Mary Wroth*, 137–56.

63. On Wroth's performance in Ben Jonson's *Masque of Blackness* at court in 1605, see Hannay, *Mary Sidney, Lady Wroth*, 125–29. For a detailed study of the musical activities of the Sidney family, see Alexander, "The Musical Sidneys."

The oversight and control of events in the play by two mythological figures contributes to this dynamic, creating an overall narrative arc that moves the story from complication toward resolution. Although the play is written in five acts, the three Venus and Cupid interludes in the Huntington manuscript delineate a two-part structure that is strikingly different from the Penshurst play. In the first interlude, following act 1, Cupid assures Venus that while the mortals will at first climb to "pleasing paine," they will in time be cast down and "most humbly creepe" for mercy (1.432, 438). The structural concept at work here is the familiar one of rise and fall, a two-part progression that is also captured in Cupid's reference to there being a "haulfway" point and a sudden reversal in the mortals' experience (1.436). The second interlude, following act 2, is the fulcrum of this design. Venus appears alone in this scene, proclaiming Cupid's triumph and, importantly, breaking out of the narrative to address an audience of "prinses" directly, advising them to subject themselves to love if they wish to reach a state of happiness: "Love command your harts and eyes / and injoy what pleasure tries / Cupid govern, and his care / guard your harts from all dispaire" (2.413–16). Even though the imagined end of the play is "love's victory," the audience is figured as having some impact on that happy outcome.

This is the interlude that is written on half-sheets and glued and sewn into the manuscript precisely at this point in the play. If we look beyond the interlude itself, Venus's speech here appears to be the structural center of the entire play: the half-sheet insertion includes a new ending for act 2, an exchange between Lissius and Philisses where misunderstandings are cleared up and their friendship is restored. We can tell this is a new ending because Wroth has written a six-line speech for Lissius into the margin of the preceding page, in her cursive italic hand, and clearly indicated where in the text it is to be inserted (2.304–8). The sixth line is cropped.[64]

In these lines, Lissius vows to seek Philisses to find out the reason for his "unusiall woe" (2.305). Without this insertion, the scene ends perfectly adequately with Lissius noting the strangeness of Philisses's behavior and with Musella's closing couplet: "well lett's away, and hether soune returne / that sunn to mee whose absence makes mee burne" (2.310–11). With the insertion, a major plot line of the play—the damaged friendship between Lissius and Philisses—is resolved. At the opening of act 3, immediately following Venus's speech, Silvesta and Musella sing a duet and then reach a mutual understanding that mirrors the exchange between Philisses and Lissius.[65] With these four characters newly committed to their

---

64. See Figure 4 and note 174.

65. This structural aspect of the Huntington manuscript jibes with Naomi J. Miller's argument that Wroth represents same-sex friendship as a "sustaining force" in the play; see "Playing with Margaret Cavendish and Mary Wroth: Staging Early Modern Women's Dramatic Romances for Modern Audiences," *Early Modern Women: An Interdisciplinary Journal* 10, no. 2 (2016): 95–110 (104).

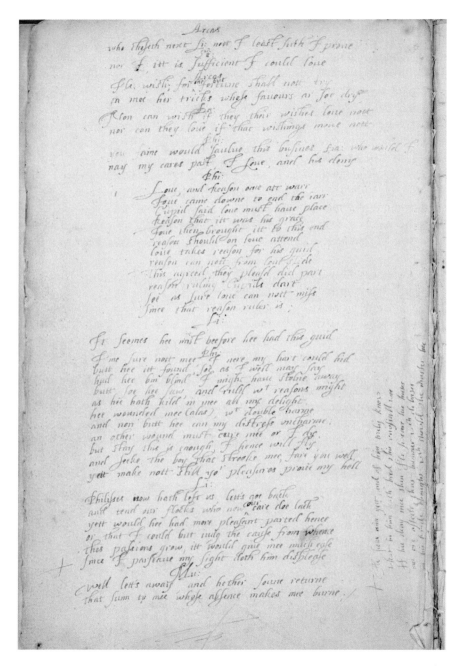

Figure 4. A page showing a significant revision in *Loves Victorie* in the Huntington manuscript, folio 8v. HM600. © By permission of the Huntington Library, San Marino, California.

respective friendships and to the love of Philisses and Musella, the play moves into a new phase where the internal obstacles (fear, jealousy, mistrust) to this central romantic relationship can be overcome, as indeed they are at the beginning of act 4 when Musella and Philisses at last speak honestly to one another.

Act 4, however, introduces a new and more difficult opposing force with the arranged marriage with Rustic, an external obstacle that dominates this part of the play and that the lovers are ultimately powerless to resolve. The question of resolution is a particularly interesting one with respect to the Huntington manuscript because the play ends abruptly only about a hundred lines into act 5, with Simeana's fearful question, "butt what will you tow doe / both dy, and mee poore maiden quite undoe?" (5.117–18). A speech prefix for Philisses suggests further development of some kind, but as is noted in the Huntington Manuscript section above, this page of the manuscript does appear to be complete and final, so it remains to consider whether there is some other way to conceive of this as a workable ending.[66]

One possibility is to return to the idea of a two-part structure, hinging on the interlude at the end of act 2 and concluding not so much with the resolution of the mortals' narrative as with the third of the three interludes, the one that concludes act 4. The strong sense of closure in this interlude is easily overlooked if we read the play expecting it to unfold in five acts of roughly the same length and end with a final choral pronouncement by the mythological characters (or if we have prior knowledge that a "complete" fifth act is to be found in another version of the play). In fact, the interlude has three parts, each of which signals closure in a different way. In the first, Venus pities the lovers and urges Cupid to be merciful, and he replies that there is more pain to come, "butt in the end all shall bee well againe" (4.559). Wroth had intended another speech for Venus at this point, but changed her mind and instead wrote a direction for "musique," the only such cue in the play. The second part of the interlude is a song, not assigned in the manuscript to a particular voice but evidently performed to this "musique." The song is addressed to "Love" and, in both language and sentiment, echoes Venus's earlier appeal to Cupid to act with clemency now that his conquest is certain (4.579). It makes little sense dramatically for Venus to repeat this plea. While its highly politicized language is consistent with her speech in the first interlude, here the

---

66. Significantly, both parts of *Urania* end in mid-sentence: incompletion may have been an intentional rhetorical strategy on Wroth's part, perhaps in imitation of Sidney's *Arcadia*, the revised version of which ends in mid-sentence. On the rhetorical significance of incompletion in Sidney's and Wroth's romances, see Gavin Alexander, *Writing After Sidney: The Literary Response to Sir Philip Sidney, 1586–1640* (Oxford: Oxford University Press, 2006), 35–55, 318–31. Salzman suggests that the Huntington manuscript of *Loves Victorie* is a "*consciously* unfinished text ... a more improvisatory text, more easily adapted." *Reading Early Modern Women's Writing*, 84. On Wroth's ambivalence toward closure as evidenced in the Folger manuscript of *Pamphilia to Amphilanthus*, see Dubrow, "'And Thus Leave Off,'" and Hannay, "The 'Ending End.'"

references to statecraft are more explicit and more concentrated, creating in effect the play's most transparent passage of political allegory: the god of love is the sovereign who shows his greater glory not by conquest and tyranny but by the merciful treatment of his subjects.

This opening up of the ethics and politics of the play to another level of meaning is also found in the third part of the interlude, a four-line speech of Cupid's that Wroth has marked for deletion: "Now your part coms to play / in this you must somthing sway / soe you shall, and I your child / when you bid can soone bee milde" (4.585–88; see Figure 3). As with the preceding song, this speech makes little sense dramatically, for it represents a complete inversion of the power relation between Venus and Cupid that was set out at the beginning of the interlude. What it does do is focus our attention on the present ("Now") and on the "sway" that whoever is being addressed is meant to have over the resolution of the play. Because Cupid refers to himself as "I your child," one obvious referent for "you" is indeed Venus. But the rhetoric, rhythm, and placement of this speech—remembering that the third interlude is the final one in the play—are also suggestive of another possibility, that Cupid here reaches out, as does Rosalind at the end of Shakespeare's *As You Like It* or Prospero in *The Tempest*, to the audience, or to an individual member of the audience, inviting them to play "your part" in subduing Cupid's power and ending the shepherds' torment. This kind of reach from actors to spectators was also present in the second interlude, in which Venus specifically addressed the spectators as "prinses" (2.390), the only other usage of this word in the play.

If Wroth initially wrote Cupid's speech as an invitation to the audience to participate in the resolution, then both of these interludes indicate that she was working very much in the tradition of court masque, which frequently concluded with the merging of spectators and actors in a dance representing a greater harmony than was possible within the world of the fiction alone. Clearly this speech of Cupid's is not correctly positioned in the manuscript to fully substantiate such a reading, but given Wroth's habit in her other manuscripts of moving sections of text around, particularly text that has some kind of metanarrative function, and given that her decision to delete Cupid's speech here leaves open the possibility that it could have been inserted at a later point in the play, it is not unreasonable to view it as an epilogue, in which case the play might have arrived at resolution not within the dramatic narrative, as it evidently does not, but in a masque-like dance of actors and spectators.[67]

While we have no firm evidence of a production of the play in Wroth's own time, many critics have identified layers of biographical and topical meaning that are strongly suggestive of a private performance of some kind, or at least an inner

67. Wroth depicts just such an event in the second part of *Urania*. See note 69.

circle of knowing readers.[68] Philisses and Musella at some level seem to allude to the romance between Wroth's uncle Sir Philip Sidney and Penelope Devereux, the "muse" who inspired his sonnet cycle *Astrophel and Stella* (1591). Extending this line of thinking, it is possible to read Simeana as a figure of Mary Sidney Herbert, Philip's sister, whose own relationship with her physician Matthew Lister ("Lissius") may resonate in the play. Philisses and Musella may also refer to Wroth and William Herbert, and it has been suggested that the play alludes to various other court affairs or family events. Certainly we know from Edward Denny's hostile response to *Urania* that Wroth was no stranger to writing allegorically, and given the numerous echoes between her prose romance and *Loves Victorie*, including the otherwise peculiar use of the word "prinses" to address the audience, it is conceivable that the play arose from a similar mindset.[69] In any event, a private performance of a masque-like pastoral drama for an audience of knowing spectators is entirely consistent with the literary and theatrical practices of the

---

68. Hannay reviews the possible biographical references and performance venues in *Mary Sidney, Lady Wroth*, 213–21. She herself suggests that the play may have been written for Wroth's sister's wedding in 1619 (221). For other biographical readings, see Roberts, "Deciphering Women's Pastoral"; Marion Wynne-Davies, "'Here Is a Sport Will Well Befit this Time and Place': Allusion and Delusion in Mary Wroth's *Love's Victory*," *Women's Writing* 6, no. 1 (1999): 47–64; and Wynne-Davies, "'For *Worth*, Not Weakness Makes in Use but One': Literary Dialogues in an English Renaissance Family," in *'This Double Voice': Gendered Writing in Early Modern England*, ed. Danielle Clarke and Elizabeth Clarke (Houndmills, UK: Palgrave Macmillan, 2000), 164–84. The multilayered resonance of *Loves Victorie* in the contemporary setting of Penshurst Place is explored by Philip Sidney in the introduction to a special issue of *Sidney Journal* on Penshurst and the Sidneys' literary activities; see "Introduction: Penshurst, Place, and Performance," *Sidney Journal* 34, no. 1 (2016): 1–14.

69. One striking parallel between *Urania* and *Loves Victorie* occurs in the unpublished second part of the prose romance, where a "very pretty and pleasant" masque concerning Cupid is presented at court by the visiting knight Rodomandro. The entertainment is acted by twelve masquers, including Rodomandro, and ends with a song by Cupid following which the masquers and audience join in a dance: "This songe ended, the maskers pulld of ther visards, and with the Kings leave tooke … the ladys forthe to dance, and after a daunce ore tow, they made an ende… . Then were they with all that troope conducted to an infinite rich banquett prepared purposely for Rodomandro and his companion maskers, who were all princes in his countrye butt his subjects." Wroth, *The Second Part of The Countess of Montgomery's Urania*, 49. On Wroth's depiction of theatrical events in *Urania*, see Naomi J. Miller, "Engendering Discourse: Women's Voices in Wroth's *Urania* and Shakespeare's Plays," in Miller and Waller, *Reading Mary Wroth*, 154–72; and Gary Waller, "'Like One in a Gay Masque': The Sidney Cousins in the Theaters of Court and Country," in *Readings in Renaissance Women's Drama*, ed. S. P. Cerasano and Marion Wynne-Davies (London: Routledge, 1996), 234–45. Wroth's use of the masque form is discussed by Alexandra G. Bennett, "Playing by and with the Rules: Genre, Politics, and Perception in Mary Wroth's *Love's Victorie*," in *Women and Culture at the Courts of the Stuart Queens*, ed. Clare McManus (Basingstoke, UK: Palgrave Macmillan, 2003), 122–39.

Sidney-Herbert families.[70] It is also consistent with the contents, the materiality, and the provenance of the Huntington manuscript of *Loves Victorie*.

## *Afterlife: Text and Performance*

The Huntington manuscript of *Loves Victorie* was once owned by Sir Edward Dering, a close friend and neighbor of Wroth's in Kent who was an avid theater-goer and playbook collector and whose country house was the site of a flourishing amateur theatrical culture.[71] As is suggested in the Huntington Manuscript section above, it is possible that Wroth herself may have transcribed and assembled the manuscript for Dering. This manuscript was later transcribed, in 1845, by Henrietta Halliwell, wife of the Shakespeare scholar James Orchard Halliwell who published extracts of her transcription in 1853. This was the first appearance of the work in print.[72] The manuscript was reportedly "in private hands" in 1860,[73] advertised for sale in 1899, owned by the American collector William Augustus White in 1901, and acquired by the Huntington Library from White's estate in 1923.[74] Its authorship by Mary Wroth was unknown to its first editor, C. H. J. Maxwell, who prepared an old-spelling text as an M.A. thesis under the supervision of Hardin Craig at Stanford University in 1933.

In 1988, the other known manuscript of the play, in the possession of the Viscount De L'Isle at Penshurst Place, was edited by Michael Brennan and published in a beautiful collectors' facsimile edition by The Roxburghe Club. This version of the play, known as the Penshurst manuscript, appears to have been copied from the Huntington manuscript and/or another interim copy and

70. On Sidney-Herbert theatrical events at Wilton, see Straznicky, "Wilton House, Theatre, and Power"; on Penshurst as a site with unique significance for the play, see Alison Findlay, "*Love's Victory* in Production at Penshurst," *Sidney Journal* 34, no. 1 (2016): 107–21. Findlay's reading draws in part on a professional production of *Love's Victory* held at Penshurst Place in June, 2014. See note 82 for reviews of this production.

71. See note 48.

72. On Henrietta Halliwell's transcription, see Freeman, "*Love's Victory*," and Paul Salzman, "Henrietta's Version: Mary Wroth's *Love's Victory* in the Nineteenth Century," in *Material Cultures of Early Modern Women's Writing*, ed. Patricia Pender and Rosalind Smith (Basingstoke, UK: Palgrave Macmillan, 2014), 159–73. Halliwell's manuscript transcription does not survive. For a printed text of the transcription, see Wroth, "Love's Victorie," in *A Brief Description of the Ancient & Modern Manuscripts Preserved in the Public Library, Plymouth*, ed. James Orchard Halliwell (London: C. and J. Adlard, 1853), 212–36.

73. Brennan, *Lady Mary Wroth's Love's Victory*, 17n32.

74. Roberts, "The Huntington Manuscript," 162–64, and Freeman, "*Love's Victory*," 252. The flyleaf of HM600 has the following note: "HM600 acquired from Rosenbach Company on Sept. 6, 1923. (This information from a letter from Leslie A. Morris of the Rosenbach Museum and Library, August 28, 1989)."

includes material that is not present in HM600. These textual features, in addition to its being available in its entirety in print, has led Wroth scholars to view the Penshurst manuscript as the more complete and authoritative of the two versions.[75] S. P. Cerasano and Marion Wynne-Davies edited a modern-spelling text of the play for their 1996 anthology *Renaissance Drama by Women*.[76] Cerasano and Wynne-Davies note that there are "[s]ignificant differences" between the two versions, and they draw extensively on both in producing their text.[77] To date, theirs has been the version of the play most widely used in scholarship and teaching. An online edition of the Huntington text prepared by Paul Salzman for the *Material Cultures of Early Modern Women's Writing Digital Archive* is set up to facilitate a comparative study of the two manuscripts: the edition is presented in four columns, with images of the Huntington manuscript in one column, alongside an old-spelling transcription, a modernized version of it, and a transcription of the Penshurst text. Salzman has also published a modern-spelling edition of the Huntington text in *Early Modern Women's Writing: An Anthology, 1560–1700*.[78]

Although we do not have firm evidence that *Loves Victorie* was staged in Wroth's lifetime, the material and textual characteristics of the Huntington manuscript are suggestive of a potential performance. The frequent use of exit directions, the scribal differentiation between (and, in one instance, physical detachment of) dialogue, song, and choral interlude, and evidence of the manuscript being written at different times and afterwards assembled into a cohesive document are characteristics also found in early modern performance texts. More broadly, the rich history of private entertainment in the Sidney, Herbert, and Wroth families, including Wroth's own involvement in court masques, raises the possibility of *Loves Victorie* being written with performance in mind. The ownership of the Huntington manuscript by Sir Edward Dering might suggest a performance at Surrenden, his estate in Kent, but scholars have also argued for the suitability of the play to staging either in the Great Hall or the gardens at Penshurst,[79] while Wilton House is also plausible, particularly if the play was written or revised while Wroth and William Herbert were intimate and at some level represents this or

75. Until recently, editorial decisions have been informed by the view that the latest version of a text within the author's lifetime is the most authoritative because it represents the author's "final intentions." Ilona Bell addresses the limitations of this theory as a basis for editing Wroth's manuscript poems in "The Autograph Manuscript," 171–73. A brief comparison of the two manuscripts and others of Wroth's may be found in Ilona Bell, "The Circulation of Writings by Lady Mary Wroth," in Hannay, Lamb, and Brennan, *The Ashgate Research Companion to The Sidneys, 1500–1700*, 77–85 (80–81).

76. S. P. Cerasano and Marion Wynne-Davies, eds., *Renaissance Drama by Women: Texts and Documents* (London: Routledge, 1996).

77. Cerasano and Wynne-Davies, *Renaissance Drama by Women*, 95.

78. For the online edition, see above, note 51; for the print edition, see Salzman, *Early Modern Women's Writing: An Anthology, 1560–1700* (Oxford: Oxford University Press, 2000), 82–103, 437–38.

79. Findlay, *Playing Spaces*, 90–94; and Hannay, *Mary Sidney, Lady Wroth*, 221.

other relationships among members of the Sidney and Herbert families.[80] There is no reason to consider these venues as mutually exclusive; other early modern plays that survive in multiple texts, either in print such as Shakespeare's *Hamlet* or in manuscript such as the anonymous *The Humorous Magistrate*, are believed to have been performed at different venues or at different times.[81]

A performance of *Loves Victorie* occurred in the Great Hall at Penshurst Place in 2014 in conjunction with the conference "Dramatizing Penshurst: Site, Script, Sidneys." This was a production of the Penshurst text by Shakespeare's Globe company in their "Read Not Dead" series, a program of staged readings (performances using scripts) of neglected early modern plays.[82] The actors arrived at Penshurst on the day of the performance and rehearsed on the grounds while the estate was open to the public. The performance occurred in the evening, for an audience of scholars and members of the Sidney family. The Great Hall proved to be ideal: the elaborately carved wooden screen at one end of the Hall gave the main action a practical framework, with two doors serving to indicate the different locations in which the action occurs and the balcony above the screen offering a separate performance space used exclusively for the Venus and Cupid

80. It was usual for members of the aristocracy to move frequently between their estates. Wroth and her family were almost constantly moving between Penshurst, Baynards Castle, Wilton House, Loughton Hall, Durance, and other houses. There is only one direct reference to Wroth's being at Wilton House, in 1588, but her family was often there in her youth and presumably she visited at other times, at least to attend major festivities and royal visits (Hannay, *Mary Sidney, Lady Wroth*, 148). Hester Lees-Jeffries has suggested that the Jacobean gardens at Wilton resemble certain of Wroth's landscape descriptions in *Urania*; see "Pictures, Places, and Spaces: Sidney, Wroth, Wilton House, and the *Songe de Poliphile*," in *Renaissance Paratexts*, ed. Helen Smith and Louise Wilson (Cambridge: Cambridge University Press, 2011), 185–203. Wilton House was a favorite retreat of King James, who moved the court there to escape the plague in 1603 and also visited in 1615, 1618, and 1620. A planned visit in August 1623 has not been documented, but one contemporary writer records having seen rooms at Wilton a short while later, "richly adorned with Costly and sumptuous hangings" from when the king "dined there with most magnificent Entertainment." See John Taylor, *A New Discovery by Sea, with a Wherry from London to Salisbury* (London: Edward Allde, 1623), sig. C2. On King James's visits to Wilton, see Straznicky, "Wilton House, Theatre, and Power," 224–25. Intriguingly, this event is within one year of the birth of Wroth's two children by William Herbert and coincides with King James's protection of Wroth from her creditors, so it is possible she was present at Wilton around this time, if not for this particular occasion.

81. *The Humorous Magistrate* survives in two manuscripts that place it within the theatrical and social network of several leading families and estates in the Midlands, a network that overlaps with the Cavendish family. See M. J. Kidnie, "Near Neighbours: Another Early Seventeenth-Century Manuscript of *The Humorous Magistrate*," *English Manuscript Studies, 1100–1700* 13 (2007): 187–211.

82. For reviews of the Globe Education performance, see Marta Straznicky, "Lady Mary Wroth's *Love's Victory*," *Early Modern Women: An Interdisciplinary Journal* 9, no. 2 (2015): 166–70; and Marion Wynne-Davies, "Performance of Lady Mary Wroth's *Love's Victory*: A Review," *Sidney Journal* 34, no. 1 (2016): 123–26. For a discussion of this performance in relation to contemporary critical interest in Wroth, see Naomi J. Miller, "Playing with Margaret Cavendish and Mary Wroth."

interludes. As Katherine Larson has written, the large windows in the Great Hall provided not only a view to the gardens but also a threshold across which the play's many conventional allusions to the natural environment were literally grounded in the gardens and landscape surrounding Penshurst.[83] As a non-amateur production, this performance was an important "first" in the reception history of *Loves Victorie*, revealing not only that the play has considerable power on stage, but also that it is suited to multiple sites of reading and performance.

## Note on the Text

This edition of *Loves Victorie* is based on the autograph manuscript of the play in the Huntington Library (HM600). The manuscript is a folio measuring 31.5 cm x 18.5 cm and containing twenty-one leaves; folios 9 and 10 are smaller sheets (folio 9 measures 19.8 cm x 15.2 cm; folio 10 measures 20.1 cm x 15.5 cm), stitched and tipped (that is, glued along their left edges adjacent to the spine) into the manuscript. The manuscript is written by Wroth and is "bound in parchment boards, with two slits each near the fore-edge on the front and back cover, originally for ribbon ties over the fore-edge."[84] The ribbon is not extant. The watermark is similar to Heawood 1721A.[85] Wroth has used two distinct hands in writing the play, which are represented in this edition by two fonts, roman for her formal italic hand and *italic* for her cursive italic hand. Missing speech prefixes are supplied in the present edition in square brackets. The symbol known as *s fermé*, a slashed capital S used by Wroth to mark sections of text, is represented with a dollar sign ($).[86] The abbreviation "*ex*" for exit is standardized in italic font throughout the text. The abbreviations H and P in the notes are used for the Huntington and Penshurst manuscripts, respectively. The Huntington text is divided into five acts; lines in this edition are numbered continuously through each act. An asterisk (*) indicates the presence of a textual note, referred to by line number.

---

83. Larson, "Playing at Penshurst," 104.

84. I thank Sara S. Hodson, Curator of Literary Manuscripts at the Huntington Library, for providing this description of the binding and the adhesion of folios 9 and 10.

85. Edward Heawood, *Watermarks, Mainly of the 17th and 18th Centuries* (Hilversum, Holland: Paper Publications Society, 1950).

86. See above, page 30, for a discussion of the *s fermé*.

Philisses[87]
you pleasant floury meade[88]
  w$^{ch}$ I did once well love
  your pathes noe more I'le tread           5
  your pleasures noe more prove
  your beauty more[89] admire
  your coulers more adore
  nor gras w$^t$ daintiest store
  of sweets to breed desire,[90]          10

Walks once soe sought for now
  I shunn you for the darcke,
  birds to whose song did bow
  my* eares your notes nere mark;
  brooke w$^{ch}$ soe pleasing was        15
  upon whose banks* I lay,
  and on my pipe[91] did play
  now, unreguarded pass,

Meadowes, pathes, grass, flouers
  walkes, birds, brooke, truly finde    20
  all prove butt as vaine[92] shouers
  wish'd wellcome els unkind:
  you once I loved best
  butt love makes mee you leave
  by love I love deseave         25
  Joy's lost for lives[93] unrest

Joy's lost for lives unrest indeed I see
alas poore sheapheard miserable mee

---

87. The placement of the first three stanzas in a central column indicates that they are to be sung. Wroth uses this practice throughout H. In P, this opening is preceded by a masque-like interlude featuring Venus and Cupid. For the text of the interlude, see Textual Notes.

88. Meadow.

89. Wroth wrote "more" twice and deleted the second instance.

90. Wroth wrote "desyre," crossed it out, and wrote "desire" above the line.

91. A woodwind instrument conventionally played by shepherds.

92. "Unprofitable, useless" (*OED*).

93. Life's.

yett faire Musella love, and worthy bee
I blame thee nott, butt mine owne miserie          30
live you still hapy, and injoy your love,
and lett loves paine* in mee destressed move
for since itt is my freind thou doest affect
then wrong him once my self I will neglect,
and thus in secrett will my passion* hide          35
till time, or fortune doth my feare deside
making my love apeere as the bright morne,
w<sup>th</sup> out, or mist, or cloud, but truly borne,

    Lissius
Joyfull pleasant spring          40
w<sup>ch</sup> comforts to us bring
    flourish in yo<sup>r</sup> pride
never lett decay
your delights alay
    since joye is to you ti'de,          45

    Phi:
Noe joye is tide to you, you t'is doe prove
the pleasure of your freinds unhapy love
t'is you enjoy the comfort of my paine,
t'is I that love, and you that love obtaine,          50

    Lissius
Lett noe frost nor wind
your dainty* coulers blind
    butt rather cherish
your most pleasing sight          55
lett never winter bite
    nor season perish[94]

    Phi:          [1v]
I cannott perish more then now I doe
unless my death my miseries undoe          60
Lissius is hapy, butt philisses curst
love[95] seekes to him, on mee hee doth his wurst,

---

94. Wroth wrote "Phi:" at the bottom of fol. 1r and also at the top of fol. 1v.

95. In Roman mythology, the god of love is Cupid, son of Mercury and Venus, conventionally depicted as a blind boy.

and doe thy wurst on mee still froward[96] boy
more ill thou can'st nott, butt poore lyfe destroy
w^ch doe, and glory in thy conquest gott                    65
all men must dy, and love drew my ill lott


      Lissius,
My deare Philisses what alone, and sad,


      Phi:
nether, butt musing Why the best is bad                     70
butt you were merry I'le nott marr yo^r song
my thoughts ar tedious, and for you to long        *ex:*[97]


      Li:
Alas what meanes this, surely itt is love
that makes* in him this alteration move,                    75
this is the humor[98] makes our sheapheards rave
I'le non of this, I'le souner* seeke my grave
love, by your favour, I will non of you
I rather you should miss, then I should sue
yett Cupid, poore Philisses back restore                    80
to his first witts, and I'le affect[99] thee more;   *ex:**


      Silvesta.
Faire shining day, and thou Apollo[100] bright
w^ch to these pleasant vallys gives thy light,*
and w^t sweet shoures mixt w^th golden beames               85
inrich these meadowes, and these gliding streames
Wherin thou seest thy face like mirrour faire
dressing in them thy curling, shining haire;
this place w^th sweetest flouers still doth deck
whose coulers show theyr pride, free from the check         90
of fortunes frowne soe long as spring doth last

---

96. "Disposed to go counter to what is demanded or what is reasonable" (*OED*).

97. When she indicates an exit, Wroth uses the abbreviation "ex:" and usually places it in the right margin, as here.

98. A fluid of the human body, the quantity of which was thought to determine a person's mental and physical health. In Wroth's time, unrequited love was thought to produce an excess of black bile, one of the four chief humors, and lead to a state of unsociability, dejection, and sadness.

99. "To incline, like" (*OED*).

100. In Roman mythology, the god of light and sun, frequently depicted with a head of golden hair.

butt then feele chang, wherof all others tast
as I for one, who thus my habitts[101] chang
once sheapherdess, butt now in woods must rang,
and after the chaste Godess[102] beare her bowe,                    95
though service once to Venus[103] I did owe,
whose servante then I was, and of her band
butt farewell folly, I w^th Dian stand
against loves changings,* and blind foulery
to hold w^th hapy, and bles'sd chastity                    100
for love is idle hapines ther's none
when freedomes lost, and chastity is gone,
and wher, on earth most blessednes their is
loves fond desires never faile to miss,
and this beeleeve mee you will truly find                    105
lett nott repentance therfor chang yo^r mind
butt chang befor, yo^r glory wilbee most
When as the waggish[104] boy can least him bost;
for hee doth seeke to kindle flames of fire
butt never thinks to quench;* a chaste desire                    110
hee calls his foe; hee hates non more then those
who strives* his lawe, to shunn, and this have chose =[105]
All vertu hates, his kingdomes wantonnes                    [2r]
his crowne desires, his septer idlenes
his wounds hott fires,* his helps like frost                    115
glad to hurt, butt never heales; think's time lost
if any gaine theyr long sought joye w^t bliss,
and this the government of folly is:
Butt heere Philisses cōmes, poore sheapheard lad
w^t loves hott fires, and his owne made mad,                    120
I must away, my vowe allowes noe sight
of men, yett must I pitty him poore wight[106]
though hee rejecting mee this change have* wrought

101. "Fashion or mode of apparel, dress" (*OED*).

102. Diana, Roman goddess of chastity, twin sister of Apollo; also the goddess of the hunt and as such associated with the woods.

103. Roman goddess of love, sexuality, and fertility and the mother of Cupid, the "waggish boy" of line 108 below.

104. "Playfully mischievous" (*OED*).

105. Wroth occasionally marks the end of a page with two short horizontal lines, similar to an equal sign.

106. "A living being in general; a creature" (*OED*).

hee shalbee noe less worthy in my thought;
yett wish I doe hee were as free as I                                125
then were hee hapy now feels misery;
for thanks to heaven, and to the Gods above
I have wunn chastity in place of love;
now love's as farr from mee as never knowne,
then bacely tied, now freely ame mine owne;          130
slavery, and bondage w[th] mourning care
was* then my living, sighs, and teares my fare,
butt all these gon now live I joyfully
free, and untouch'd of thought but chastitye,     *ex:*

       Phi:                                                        135
Love beeing mist[107] in heaven att last was found
lodg'd in Musella's faire though cruell brest
cruell alas, yett wheron I must ground
all hopes of joye, though tired w[th] unrest;
O deerest deere, lett plaints[108] which true felt are          140
gaine pitty once, doe nott delight to prove
soe mercyles, still killing w[th] despaire
nor pleasure take soe much to try[109] my love;
yett if your triall, will you milder make,
try, butt nott long, least pitty come to late;          145
butt Ô. she can nott, may nott,* will nott take
pitty on mee, she loves, and lends mee hate,

       Li:
Fy my Philisses will you ever fly
my sight that loves you, and your good desires          150

       Phi:
Fly you deare Lissius no, butt still a cry
I heere that sayes I burne in scorners fires
farwell good Lissius, I will soune returne
butt nott to you, a rivall like to burne;     *ex:*          155

       Liss:
Ah poore phi: would I knew thy paine

---

107. Missed.
108. Laments.
109. Test.

that as I now lament might help obtaine
butt yett in love they say non should bee us'd
butt self desarts[110] least trust might bee abus'd;                    160

A Forester:
Did ever cruelty itt self thus showe?*
did ever heaven our mildnes thus farr move?[111]
all sweetnes, and all beauty to orethrow                    [2v]
all joy deface, and crop in spring time love?                    165
could any mortall brest invent such harme?
could living creature think on such a loss?
noe, noe (alas) itt was the furies[112] charme
who sought by this our best delights to cross,
and now in triumph glory in their gaine,                    170
Wher was true beauty found if nott in thee
O deere Silvesta? butt accursed swaine[113]
that caus'd this chang, ô miserable mee
that* live to see this day, and days bright light
to shine when pleasure's turn'd into dispite;[114]                    175

Li:
An other of loves band ô mighty love
that can thy folly make in most to move;

Fo:
Accursed sheapheard why wert thou ere borne                    180
unles itt were to bee true Vertues scorne
curst bee thy days, unlucky ever bee
nor ever live least hapynes to see,
butt wher thou lov'st lett her as cruell prove
as thou wert to Silvesta, and my love,                    185

Li:
If one may ask; what is th'offence is dunn?

110. Self-directed rewards.

111. Wroth wrote the catchword "all =" in the bottom right corner of fol. 2r.

112. "Avenging deities … dread goddesses with snakes twined in their hair, sent from Tartarus to avenge wrong and punish crime: in later accounts, three in number" (OED).

113. "A country gallant or lover; hence gen. a lover, wooer, sweetheart, esp. in pastoral poetry" (OED).

114. "Contempt, scorn, disdain" (OED).

Fo:
that curst Philisses hath mee quite undunn

    Li:             190
Undunn as how; Fo: sitt downe, and you shall know,
for glad I am y$^t$ I my griefe may tell
since t'is some ease my sorrowes cause to show
disburdning my poore hart w$^{ch}$ griefe doth swell;
then know I lov'd (alas) and ever must    195
Silvesta faire, sole m$^{rs}$: of my joy
whose deere affections were in surest trust
laid up in flames, my hopes cleane to destroy:
for as I truly lov'd, and only shee,
she for philisses sigh'd who did reject    200
her love, and paines, nor would (she cruell) see
my plaints, nor teares butt followed his neglect
w$^{th}$ greater passion; I, her followed still
she rann* from mee, hee flew* from her as fast
I after both did hy[115] though for my ill    205
who thus doe live all wrechednes to tast;
long time this lasted, still she constant lov'd;
and more she lov'd, more cruell still hee grew;
till att the last,* thus tiran[116] like hee prov'd,
forcing that chang w$^{ch}$ maks my poore hart rue;  210
For she parseaving hate soe farr to guide
his settled hart to nothing butt disdaine
having all fashions,* and all manners* tride
that might give comfort to her endles paine,
butt seeing nothing would his favor turne    215
from fondly flying of her truest love,
led by those passions w$^{ch}$ did firmly burne
so hott as nothing could those flames remove
butt still increase, she, for the last, resolv'd    [3r]
to kill this heat this hopeles course to take    220
making a vow w$^{ch}$ can nott bee desolv'd,
As[117] nott obtaining love, will love forsake;
for she hath vowed unto Diana's lyfe
her pure virginitie, as she who could

---

115. "Haste, speed" (*OED*).

116. Tyrant.

117. Wroth wrote something that is now indecipherable and reshaped it into "As."

noe more then[118] once love, nor an others wyfe          225
consent to bee, nor his now if hee would;
this hath hee dunn by his ungratfullnes;
would itt might turne to his owne wrechednes

       Li:

Ô curse him nott, alas itt is his ill          230
to feele soe much as doth his sences kill,
and yett indeed this cruelty, and course
is somwhat hard* for sheapheards heere to use,
yett see I nott how this can prove the wurse
for you, whose love she always* did refuse,          235
butt much the better since your suffer'd paine
can bee noe glory to an others gaine;

       Fo:

Would itt could bee to anys gaine the most
of glory, honor, fortune, and what more          240
can added bee, though I had ever lost,
and hee had gain'd* the chiefe of beauties store,
for then I might have her somtimes beheld
butt now am bar'd, for my love placed was
in truest kind wherin I all excel'd          245
nott seeking gaine, butt losing did surpass
those that obtaine, for my thoughts did assend
no higher then to looke, that was my end;

       Li:

What strang effects doth phant'sie[119] 'mong us prove          250
who still brings forth new images of love,
butt this of all is strangest to affect
only the sight, and nott the joys respect
nor end* of whining[120] love, since sight wee gaine
w[t] smale adoe, the other w[th] much care*          255
doubling the pleasure having left dispaire*[121]

---

118. Wroth wrote "thene" and deleted the final "e."

119. "Mental apprehension of an object of perception; the faculty by which this is performed" (*OED*).

120. Probably winning rather than whining, or complaining, considering the reference in line 258 to gaining the "fruictfull ends of love."

121. Wroth appears to have made a transcription error at line 255, mistakenly writing "care" for "paine" and thus failing to complete the couplet. The following line occurs in P between this edition's

and sure if ever I should chance to love
the fruictfull ends of love I first would move,

       Fo:
I wish you may obtaine yo<sup>r</sup> harts desire,          260
and I butt sight who wast in chastest fire,     *ex:*

       Li:
Thes tow to meete in one I ne're did finde
love, and chastity link'd in one[122] mans mind
butt now I see love hath as many ways        265
to winn, as to destroy when hee delayes;

       Philisses, Dalina,
       Rustick, Lacon, and Lissius,

       Da:
The sunn growes hott 'twer best wee did retire[123]    270

       Li:                          [3v]
Ther's a good shade, phi: butt heer's a burning fire

       La:
never did I see man soe chang'd as hee

       Da                         275
truly nor I what can the reason bee

       Phi:
Love, love itt is, w<sup>ch</sup> you in time may know
butt happy they can keepe their love from show

       Da:                      280
Musella wellcom to our meeting is
of all our fellowes you did only miss

---

lines 256 and 257: "and fauor wun w<sup>ch</sup> kills all former care."

122. Wroth inserted "link'd" above the line and crossed out the "s" in "ones."

123. Wroth wrote "=" in the lower right corner of fol. 3r. She also wrote the speech prefix "Li:" both at the bottom of fol. 3r and at the top of fol. 3v.

Mu:
smale loss* of mee for often'st when I'me heere,
I am as if I were another wher                                        285
butt wher is Fillis seldome doe I find
her, or Simeana missing, yett the blind
god Cupid late hath strooke her yeelding brest,
and makes her lonely walk to seek for rest

Phi:                                                                   290
yett when the paine is greatest t'is some ease
to lett a freind partake his freinds disease

Mu:
That were no frindly part in this you miss
impart unto yo freind no harme, butt bliss;                           295

Phi:
some freinds will redy bee to ease on's smart

Mu:
so to beefreind your self, you'l make them smart,*

Da:                                                                   300
Now wee ar mett what sport shall wee invent
while the suns fury somwhat more bee spent

La:
Lett each one heer their fortune* past relate
ther loves, ther froward chance, or their good fate                   305

Mu:
And soe discource the secretts of the mind
I like nott this, thus mirth* may crosses find,

Phi
Let one beginn a tale Da: nor that I like                             310

La:
then what will please wee see what doth dislike

Phi:
dislike is quickly knowne, pleasure is scant

Mu:                                                               315
And wher joy's seeme to flow alas ther's want

Climena $[124]
O my eyes how* do you lead
my poore hart thus forth to rang
from the wounted[125] course to strang              320
unknowne ways, and pathes to tread

Lett itt home returne againe
free untouch'd of gadding thought
and your forces back bee brought
to the ridding of my paine                          325

Butt mine eyes if you deny
this smale favor to my hart,
and will force my thoughts to fly
know yett you governe butt your part;

Li:                                             330        [4r]
Climena hath begunn a prety sport
lett ech one sing, and so the game is short

Ru:
Indeed well sayd, and I will first begin

Da:                                                            335
And who=so=evers out, you'll nott bee in

Phi:
sing they who have glad harts, or voice to sing
I can butt patience to this pleasure bring

Mu:                                                            340
then you, and I will sitt, and judges bee

---

124. "Climena" appears twice on this line; the second instance is deleted and the line thus ends with the *s fermé*.

125. "Accustomed, customary, usual" (*OED*).

Phi:
'Would faire Musella first would judg of mee

Mu:
will you then sing, Phi: noe, I would only say                345

Mu:
chuse some time els, who will beegin this play

Ru:
why that will I, and I will sing of thee

Mu:                                                          350
sorry I ame I should your subject bee,

[Ru:]*126
When I doe see
thee, whitest thee
Yea whiter then lambs wull                                   355
how doe I joy
that thee injoy
I shall w^t my hart full

Thy eyes do play
like goats w^th hay,                                         360
and skip lik kids flying127
from the sly Fox
soe eye lids box
shutts up thy sights priing

Thy cheecks as* red                                          365
as* okar spred
On a fatted sheeps back
thy paps128 are129 found
as* aples round
noe prayses shall lack,                                      370

---

126. The speech prefix for Rustick is omitted in H.
127. Wroth reshaped an "i" into the "y" in "flying."
128. "A woman's breast" (*OED*).
129. Wroth reshaped "as" into "are."

Mu:

Well, you have prayses given enough, now lett
an other come some other[130] to commend,

Ru:

I had much more to say but thus I'me mett,                    375
and staid, now I will*[131] hearken, and attend,

La:

By a pleasant rivers side
hart, and hopes on pleasures ti'de
might I see w^t in a bower                                    380
proudly[132] drest w^t every floure
w^ch the spring can to us lend
Venus, and her loving freind[133]
I upon her beauty gas'de                                     [4v]
they mee seeing were amas'de                                  385
till att last up stept a child
in his face, nott actions mild
fly away saide hee for sight
shall both breed, and kill delight
Come* away, and follow mee                                    390
I will lett thee beautys see
I obay'd him, then* hee staid
hard besid a heav'nly maide
When hee threw a flaming dart,
and unkindly strooke my hart,                                 395

Mu:

butt what became then of this subtile* boy

La:

When hee had dunn his wurst hee fled away

Mu:                                                           400

And soe lett us 't'is time that wee* returne
to tend our flocks who all this time* doe burne

130. Wroth deleted the "s" in "others."

131. Wroth inserted "will" above the line.

132. Wroth inserted "u" above the line in "proudly."

133. Wroth wrote the catchword "I upon=" at the bottom right corner of fol. 4r.

Phi:

Burne, and must burne this sodainly is sayd

butt heat nott quench'd, alas butt hopes decai'd; /     405

Dali:

What have you dunn, and must I lose my song.

Mu:

nott lose itt though awhile wee itt prolong

Da:     410

I ame content, and now lett* all retire

Phi:

and soune returne sent by loves quickest fire; /

~ ~ ~ ~ ~ ~[134]

*Venus, and Cupid**

*Venus;*     415

*Fy this is nothing, what is this your care*

*that among ten the haulf of them you spare*

*I would have all to wayle, and all to weepe*

*will[135] you att such a time as this goe sleepe*

*awake your forces, and make Lissius find*     420

*Cupid can cruell bee as well as kind*

*shall hee goe scorning thee and all thy traine*

*and pleasure take hee can thy force disdaine*

*strike him, and tell him thou his lord will prove*

*and hee a vassell unto mighty love*     425

*and all the rest that scorners bee of thee*

*make[136] w^t theyr griefe thy powre a feeler bee**

*Cupid;*

*T'is true that Lissius, and some others yett*

*ar free, and lively, butt they shall bee mett*     430

134. Wroth frequently used a flourish to mark the end of a section of text. Together with the semicolon and slash at the end of line 413, the flourish gives this scene an emphatic close.

135. Wroth reshaped an "a" into the "w" in "will."

136. Wroth deleted the "s" in "makes."

butt* care sufficient,[137] butt* 'tis nott ther time
as yett into my[138] pleasing paine to clime,
lett them alon, and lett themselves beeguile                               [5r]
they shall have torments when they thinke to smile
they are nott yett in pride of all theyr scorne                        435
butt er'e they have theyr pleasures haulfway worne
they shall both cry, and waile, and weepe*
and for our mercy shall most humbly creepe
love hath most glory when as greatest sprites
hee downeward throwse unto his owne delights                          440
then take noe care loves victory shall shine
when as your honor shall bee raisd by mine

    Venus
Thanks Cupid if thou doe parform thy* othe
and needs you must for gods must want[139] noe trothe                  445
lett mortalls never think itt od or vaine
to heere[140] that Love can in all spiritts raine
prinses ar nott exempted from owr mights
much[141] les should sheapheards scorne us, and owr rights
though they as well can love, and like affect                         450
they must nott therfor owr commands reject*

    Cu:
Nor[142] shall, and mark butt what my vengance is
I'le miss my force or they shall want theyr blis
and arrows heere I have of purpose fram'd                              455
w^ch as they* qualities soe are they namd
Love, jealousie, malice, feare,[143] and mistrust
yett all thes shall att last incounter just
harme shall bee non, yett shall they harme* indure
for som small season then of joy bee sure                             460
like you this mother, ve: sunn I like this well

137. Wroth deleted a "y" preceding "butt 'tis nott ther time."

138. Wroth began to write another word after "my" but deleted it.

139. Lack.

140. Wroth first wrote "knowe," deleted it, and then wrote "heere."

141. Wroth changed her mind twice. She wrote "much," deleted it, wrote "and" above the line, deleted it, and then wrote "much" again, this time above the line.

142. Wroth began to write another word, crossed out the intial letter, and wrote "Nor."

143. Wroth first wrote "hate," deleted it, and then wrote "feare."

*and faile nott now in least part of this\* spell;*     $*
$*144


[blank page]                                                    [5v]


The Secound Act;145                                             [6r]

Musella, Dalina, Simena, Philisses,
Lissius, Rustick, Lacon; Silvesta
and a forester*146

       Da:                                                    5
My\* thinks wee now to silent ar, let's play
att somthing while wee yett have pleasing147 day,


       Li
heer's sport enough, viewe butt her new atire,
and see her slave who burns in chast desire          10


       Da:
Mark but theyr greeting, Li: shee I'me sure will fly
and hee poore foole will follow still, and cry.


       Mu:
What pleasure do you take to mock att love          15
ar you sure you can nott his pouer prove
butt looke he kneels, and weepes, Li:, and cries ay mee
sweet Nimph have pitty or hee dies for thee


       Fo:
Alas deere nimph, why fly you still my sight          20
can my true love, and firme affection
so litle gaine mee as your fairest light
must darckned bee for my affliction

---

144. Two *s fermés* conclude the first Venus and Cupid interlude; the remainder of the page is blank, and all of fol. 5v is blank.

145. Wroth drew a line between this heading and the massed entry direction.

146. Wroth wrote "and a forester" between the massed entry and the first speech prefix.

147. Wroth inserted "pleasing" above the line between "have" and "day."

Ô looke on mee, and see if in my face
true griefe, and sorrow show nott my disgrace;          25
If y<sup>t</sup> dispaire doe nott by sighs apeere
if felt disdaine doe nott w<sup>th</sup> tears make show
my ever wailing, ever saddest cheere,
and mourning w<sup>ch</sup> noe breath can e're o'reblowe
pitty mee nott; els judg w<sup>t</sup> your faire eyes          30
my loving soule w<sup>ch</sup> to you captive lies

        Sill:
Alas fond forester urge mee noe more
to y<sup>t</sup> w<sup>ch</sup> now lies nott w<sup>t</sup> in my might
nor can I grant, or you to joye restore          35
by any meanes to yeeld you least delight
for I have vow'd w<sup>ch</sup> vowes I will obay
Unto Diana what more can I say

        Fo:
Ô this I know yett give mee butt this leave          40
to doe as birds, and trees, and beasts may doe,
doe nott ô doe nott mee of sight beereave
for w<sup>th</sup> out you I see nott, ah! undoe
nott what is yo:<sup>rs</sup> o'rethrowe nott what's your owne
lett mee though conquer'd nott bee quite or'ethrowne;          45
I know you vowed have, and vowes must stand,
yett though you chaste must bee I may desire
to have your sight, and this the strictest band
can nott refuse, and butt this I require
then grant itt mee w<sup>ch</sup> I on knees doe seeke,          50
bee nott to nature, and yo<sup>r</sup>self unlieke

        Sill:                                                    [6v]
Noe noe, I ne'r beeleeve your fond made othe
I chastity have sworne then noe more move
I know what t'is to sweare, and breake itt both          55
what to desire, and what itt is to love;
protest you may that theyr shall nothing bee
by you imagin'd 'gainst my chastitie,
butt this I doubt; your love will make you curse
(if you soe much doe love) that cursed day          60
when I this vow'd, attempt itt may bee wurse,

then follow nott thus hopeles your decay,
butt leave of loving, or some other chuse
whose state, or fortune need nott you refuse;

       Fo:                              65
Indeed deere* nimph t'is true that chastity
to one who* loves may justly raging move
yett loving you, those thoughts shall banish'd bee
since t'is in you, I, chastitie will love,
and now depart since such is yo$^r$ pleasure         70
depart (ô mee) from lyfe from joy,* from ease
goe I must, and leave behind that treasure
w$^{ch}$ all contentment gave,* now to displease
my self w$^t$ liberty I may free goe,
and w$^{th}$ most liberty most grievd,* most woe;    *ex*:[148]   75

       Mu:
Lissius I hope this sight doth somthing move
in you to pitty soe much constant love

       Li:
yes thus itt moves that man should bee soe[149] fond     80
as to bee ty'de t'a womans faithles bond*
for wee should woemen love butt as our sheepe,
who beeing kind, and gentle gives us ease,
butt cross, or straying, stuborne, or unmeeke[150]
shun'd as the woulf w$^{ch}$ most our flocks disease,     85

       Mu:
Wee litle ar beeholding unto you,
in[151] kindnes less, yett you these words may rue;
I hope to live to see you waile, and weepe,
and deeme your griefe farr sweeter then your sleepe     90
then butt remember this, and think on mee
who truly told, you could nott still live free,

---

148. This exit direction is written in a slightly darker ink and placed further to the right of the dialogue than the other exits.

149. Wroth inserted "soe" above the line between "bee" and "fond."

150. "Unkind, harsh, cruel" (*OED*).

151. Wroth first wrote "and," deleted it, and then wrote "in."

Li:
I doe nott know, itt may bee very well
butt I beleeve I shall uncharme loves spell,                    95
    And Cupid if I needs must love
    take yo<sup>r</sup> aime, and shute your wurst[152]
    once more rob your mothers dove
    all your last shafts sure were burst
    those you stole, and those you gave                    100
    shute nott mee till new you have; /

    Phi:                                                                    [7r]
Rustick faith tell mee hast[153] thou ever lov'd

    Ru:
what call you love, I have bin to trouble mov'd                 105
as when my best cloke hath by chance binn torne
I have liv'd wishing till itt mended were
and butt soe lovers do, nor could forbeare
to cry if I my bag, or bottle lost
as lovers doe who by theyr loves ar crost                       110
and grieve as much for thes, as they for[154] scorne,

    Phi:
Call you this love, why love is noe such thing
love is a paine w<sup>ch</sup> yett doth pleasure bring
a passion w<sup>ch</sup> alone in harts doe move                         115
and they that feele nott this they can nott love;
t'will make one Joyfull, merry, pleasant, sad
cry, weepe, sigh, faste, mourne, nay somtimes starck mad
if they parseave scorne, hate, or els desdaine
to wrap their woes in store for others gaine                    120
for y<sup>t</sup> (butt jealousie) is sure the wurst,
and then bee jealous better bee accurst
but ô some are,* and would itt nott disclose
though* silent love, and loving feare, ah those
deserve most pitty, favor, and reguard                          125
yett are they answered butt w<sup>th</sup> scorns reward
this theyr misfortune, and the like may fall

---

152. Following line 97, Wroth wrote and struck out "all your last shafts," which occurs two lines later.

153. Wroth first wrote "didst," deleted it, and then wrote "hast."

154. Wroth inserted "for" above the line between "they" and "scorne."

to you, or[155] mee who waite misfortunes call
butt if itt doe take heed, bee rul'd by mee,
though you mistrust, mistrust not that shee see      130
for then shee'lle smiling say allas poore foole
this man hath learn'd all parts of follys skoole;
bee wise, make love, and love though nott obtaine
for to love truly is sufficient gaine,

        Rustick;      135
sure you doe love you can soe well declare
the joys, and pleasures, hope and his[156] dispare,

        Phi:
I love indeede; Ru:[157] butt who is she you love

        Phi:      140
she who,[158] best thoughts, must to affection move
if any love, non neede ask who itt is
wthin thes plaines, non loves that loves nott this
delight of sheaphards, pride of[159] this faire place
noe beauty is that shines[160] not in her face      145
whose whitnes whitest Lillys doth excell
match'd w^{th}[161] a rosie morning to compell
all harts to serve her, yett doth she affect
butt only vertue, nor[162] will quite neglect
those who doe serve her in a modest* fashion      150
w^{ch} sure doth more increase, then decrease passion;

        Arcas      [7v]
Heere are they mett wher beauty only raines

---

155. Wroth wrote "ore" and deleted the "e."

156. Wroth deleted the "s" in "hopes." Also on this line, she wrote "theyr," deleted it, and then wrote "his."

157. There is an apparent mix-up in the speech prefixes for these two lines, with "Ru:" and "Phi:" being crowded together and occupying nearly the same line. The sense is easily restored by separating the prefixes to precede the appropriate line.

158. Wroth wrote "whose," deleted it, and then wrote "who."

159. Wroth wrote and then deleted "all" between "of" and "this."

160. Wroth wrote "flowes," deleted it, and then wrote "shines."

161. Wroth wrote "with," deleted it, and then wrote "w^{th}" above the line.

162. Wroth wrote "yett," deleted it, and then wrote "nor."

whose presence brings* the excellentest light,
and brightnes dimming[163] Pheabus[164] who butt faines;      155
to outshine thes itt is nott in his might
Faire troope heere is a sport will well beefitt
this time, and place if you will lisence itt

Phi:
What is't good Arcas; Ar: why stay, and you shall see      160
heer is a booke wherin each one shall draw
a fortune, and therby their luck shall bee
conjectur'd, like you this, you ne're itt sawe

Rustick:
itt is noe matter t'is a prety one      165
Musella you shall drawe Mu: though chuse alone

Phi:
I never sawe itt butt I like itt well

Liss:
then hee chiefs best of all must beare the bell      170

Ru:
pray thee good[165] Arcas lett mee hold the book

Arcas
w$^t$ all my hart, yett you'll nott some lotts brooke

Rus:      175
Fairest, sweetest, bonny las
you that love in mirth to pas
time delightfull come to[166] mee,
and you shall your fortune see,

Mu:      180
you tell by booke then sure you can nott miss
butt shall I know what shalbee, or what is

163. Wroth wrote "moveth," deleted it, and then wrote "dimming."
164. "Apollo as the god of light or of the sun" (*OED*).
165. Wroth inserted "good" above the line.
166. Wroth wrote "come to" above a deleted word that is indecipherable.

Ru:
what shalbee, nay never* feare
Rustick doth thy fortune beare,                                    185
draw, and when you chosen have
prais mee who such fortune gave

Mu:
And soe I will if good, or if untrue
I'le blame my owne ill choise, and nott blame you        190

Phi:
'pray,[167] may I see the fortune you did* chuse

Mu:
yes, and if right I will itt nott refuse

Phi:                                                                       195
non can bee cross to you except you will

Mu:
read itt, Phi: I will although itt were my ill
    Fortune can nott cross yoʳ will
        though your patience much must bee          200
    feare nott that your luck is ill
    you shall your best wishes see
Refuse, beeleeve mee noe, you have no cause
Thus hope brings lingring,* patience passion drawes

Da                                                                        205
I'le try what mine shalbee good Rustick hold

Arcas,                                                             [8r]
A man must follow, Da: I ame still to bold

Phi:
then I will try though sure of cruelty                        210
and yett this promises some joy* att last
that though I now feele greatest misery
my blessed days to come[168] ar nott all past

167. Wroth abbreviated "I pray" to "'pray," which preserves the meter.
168. Wroth inserted "to come" above the line.

Da:
come this fond lover knowes nott yett the play          215
hee studdies while our fortunes runn away
what have you gott, lett's see, do you this love

Phi
Read itt, butt heavn grant mee the end to prove

Da:                                                     220
you doe live to be much crost
yett esteeme no labour lost
since you shall w<sup>th</sup> joy obtaine
pleasure for yo<sup>r</sup> suffer'd paine,
truly I can nott blame you, like you this              225
so I att last might gaine I well could mis

Mu:
After a raine the sweetest floures doe grow
soe shall yo<sup>r</sup> hap bee as this book doth show

Da.                                                     230
now I may* draw, sweet fortune bee my guide

Mu:
she can nott see, yett must yo<sup>r</sup> chance abide

Da:
blind, or nott I care nott this I take, and            235
if good my luck, if bad* a luckles hand

Phi:
If Fortune guide she will direct to love
they can nott parted bee; what* now, do'st move?

Da:                                                     240
move? did you ever see the like; phi: nott I

Da:
nay read itt out itt showes my constancie

Phi:
They that can nott stedy bee                            245

  to them selves; the like must see
  ficle pæple, ficly chuse
  slightly like, and soe refuse
  this your fortune who can say
  heerin justice bears nott sway       250
In troth Dalina fortune is prov'd curst
to you w<sup>t</sup> out desert, Da: this is the wurst
that she can doe t'is true, I'have fickle binn
and soe is[169] shee. t'is then the lesser sinn,
lett her prove constant, I will her observe,    255
and then as shee[170] doth mend, I'le good deserve; /

    Arcas              [8v]
who choseth next, Li: nott I least such I prove

    Si:
nor I, itt is sufficient I could love      260

    Arcas
I'le wish, for one but[171] fortune shall nott try
on mee her tricks whose favours ar soe dry

    Da:
Non can wish if they their wishes love nott   265
nor can they love if that wishings* move nott

    Phi:
you faine would saulve this busines, Da: who would I
nay my cares past, I Love, and his deny

    Phi:             270
  Love, and Reason once att warr
  Jove[172] came downe to end the jarr
  Cupid said love must have place
  Reason that itt was his grace
  Jove then brought itt to this end     275
  reason should on love attend

---

169. Wroth inserted "is" above the line.

170. Wroth inserted "shee" above the line.

171. Wroth inserted "one but" above the line.

172. "A poetical equivalent of *Jupiter*, name of the highest deity of the ancient Romans" (*OED*).

love takes reason for his guid
reason can nott from love slide
This agreed, they pleasd did part
reason ruling Cupids dart                                    280
soe as sure love can nott miss
since that reason ruler is;

        Li:
It seemes hee mist beefore hee had this guid

        Phi:                                                 285
I'me sure nott mee, I nere my hart could hid
butt hee itt found, soe as I well may say
had hee bin blind I might have stolne away
butt soe hee saw, and rul'd w^t reasons might
as hee hath kild in mee all my delight,                      290
hee wounded mee (alas), w^t double harme
and non butt hee can my distress uncharme;
an other wound must cure mee or I dy,
but stay this is enough, I hence will fly,
and seeke the boy that strooke mee, fare you well,           295
yett make nott still yo^r pleasures prove my hell

        Li:
Philisses now hath left us, lett's goe back
and tend our flocks who now our[173] care doe lack
yett would hee had more pleasant parted hence                300
or that I could but judg the cause from whence
thes passions grow, itt would give mee much ease
since I parseave my sight doth him displease[174]
*I'le seeke him yett, and of him truly know*
*what in him hath bred this unusiall woe*                     305
*If hee deny mee then I'le swear hee hates*
*mee ore affects that humour w^ch debates*
*in his kinde thought w^ch showld the master bee*[175]

---

173. Wroth inserted "our" above the line.

174. The following five lines are written in Wroth's cursive italic hand in the right margin and marked with an X for insertion in Lissius's speech at this point. They are written vertically rather than horizontally across the page. See Figure 4. This is also where the smaller folios (9 and 10) are inserted.

175. One line of the inserted passage is missing in H but occurs in P: "butt who the freind is, I will quickly see; ex:" (fol. 15v). The missing line may have been cropped in the process of binding H.

Mu:

well lett's away, and hether soune returne                310
that sunn to mee whose absence makes* mee burne;[176] /*

~ ~ ~ ~ ~ ~*

Li:[177]                                                      [9r]

*Ô. plainly deale w^t mee my love hath bin*
*still firme to you then lett us nott beegin*
*to seeme as strangers if I have wrongd you speake*        315
*and I'le forgivnes ask, els doe nott breake*
*that band of freindship of our long held love*
*w^ch did[178] thes plaines to admiration move*

Phi

*I can nott change, butt love thee ever will*                320
*for noe cross shall my first affection kill,*
*butt give mee leave that sight once lov'd to shunn*
*since by the sight I see my self undunn*

Li:

*When this opinion first possest thy hart*                   325
*would death[179] had strooke mee w^t his cruell dart;*
*live I to bee mistrusted by my freind?*
*'tis time for mee my wreched days to end*
*but what begann this change in thee; Phi: mistrust*

Li:                                                          330

*mistrust of mee; Phi: I ame nott soe unjust*

Li:

*what then? pray tell, my hart doth long to know[180]*

---

176. A flourish following this speech marks the end of this section of the play. The next two leaves in the manuscript (fols. 9 and 10) are smaller sheets, pasted and sewn in, containing the play's second Venus and Cupid interlude. The interlude is written in cursive italic. See the introduction to this part of the volume for comments on the significance of this interlude in the play's structural design.

177. In P, Lissius's speech prefix is preceded by the entry direction "Philisses, Lissius."

178. Wroth wrote "all," deleted it, and then wrote "did."

179. Wroth wrote "it," deleted it, and then wrote "death."

180. Wroth wrote the "w" in "know" above the word. It was evidently cropped when the sheet was cut for binding, and she seems to have taken care to restore it.

*Phi:*
*Why then the change and cause of all my woe*                    335
*proceeds from this, I feare Musellas love*
*is placed on\* you, this doth my torment\* move,*
*for\* if she doe, my freindship bound to you*
*must make mee leave for*[181] *love, or joy to*[182] *sue,*
*for though I love her more then mine owne hart*         340
*if you affect her I will nott\* impart*
*my love to her; soe constant freindship binds*
*my love wher truth such faithfull biding finds*
*then truly speake, good Lissius plainly say*                    [9v]
*nor shall a love make mee your trust betray*            345

*Li:*
*O my Philisses, what was this the cause*
*alas see how misfortune on mee drause*
*I love butt vowe t'is nott*[183] *Musellas face*
*could from my hart*[184] *my freer thoughts displ[ace]*[185]    350
*although I must confese she worthy is*
*butt she allas can bring to mee noe bliss*
*it is your sister who must end my care*
*now doe you see you need noe more dispai[re]*[186]

*Phi:*                                                                         355
*yett shee may love you can you that deny;*

*Li:*
*and sweare I never yett least show could spy*
*butt well assurd I ame that she doth love*
*and you I venter dare doth her hart move*              360
*t'is true she speaks to mee, butt for your sake*
*els for good looks from her I might leave take*
*her eyes can nott dissemble though her toungue*
*to speake itt, hasards nott a greater wrong,*

181. Wroth wrote "my," deleted it, and then wrote "for."

182. Wroth wrote "for," deleted it, and then wrote "to."

183. Wroth inserted "nott" above the line.

184. Wroth wrote "thou," deleted it, and then wrote "hart."

185. The last three letters of "displace" are illegible because they are written on the edge of the paper that was bound into the manuscript.

186. Ditto the last two letters of "dispaire."

her cheeks can nott command the blood, butt still                365
itt must[187] appeere allthough against her will
thus have I answerd, and advise doe give
tell her your love if you will happy live
she can nott, nether will she you deny
and doe as much for mee or els I dy                              370

    Phi:
what may I doe that you shall nott command
then heere I gage my word, and give my hand
if w^t my sister I butt power have                               [10r]
she shall requite you, and the love you gave*                   375
soe freely to her* butt once more say this
from faire Musella hope you for noe blis

    Li:
Non butt her freindship w^ch I will require
from both as equall to my best desire                           380

    Phi:
Then thus assurd that freindship still* remaine
or lett my soule indure endles* paine;            ex =

    Venus;*
Cupid blessed bee thy might                                     385
lett thy triumph see noe night
bee thou justly god of love
who thus can thy glory move
harts obay to Cupids sway
prinses non of you say nay                                      390
eyes, lett him direct your way
for w^t out him you may stray
hee your secrett thoughts can spy
beeing hid els from each eye
lett your songs bee still of love                               395
write noe satirs w^ch may prove
least offensive to his name
if you doe you will butt frame
words against your selves, and lines
wher his good, and your ill shines                              400

187. Wroth wrote "will," deleted it, and then wrote "must."

*like him who doth sett a snare*
*for a poore betrayed hare*
*and that thing hee best doth love*                                    [10v]
*lucklesly the snare doth prove,*
*Love the king is of the mind*                              405
*please him, and hee will bee kind*
*cross him you see what doth com*
*harmes w^{ch} make your pleasures tomb*
*then take heed, and make your blis*
*in his favour, and soe miss*                              410
*noe content, nor\* joy nor pease*
*butt[188] in[189] hapines increase; /[190]*
*Love command your harts and eyes*
*and injoy what pleasure tries*
*Cupid govern, and his care*                              415
*guard\* your harts from all dispaire; $\**
                          $\*


~ ~ ~ ~ ~ ~


The 3\* Act; /                                    [11r]


          Silvesta;
Silent woods[191] w^t desarts shade
          giving peace
wher all pleasures first ar made                      5
          to increase
give your favor to my mone
now my loving time is gone

Chastity my pleasure is
          folly fled                              10
from hence now I seeke my blis

---

188. Wroth inserted "still" above the line between "butt" and "in," then deleted it.

189. Wroth deleted "all" between "in" and "hapines."

190. The unusual combination in mid-speech of a semicolon and slash suggests that the speech may originally have ended here. The following four lines are written in a slightly smaller script. They end emphatically with a semicolon, two *s fermés*, and a flourish.

191. Wroth inserted "woods" above the line.

    cross love dead
       In your shadows I repose
       you then love I now have* chose

       Mu:                         15
Choise ill made were better left
    beeing cross
of such choise to bee bereft
    were no loss
chastity you thus commend            20
doth proceed butt from loves end

And if love the fountane was
    of your fire
love must chastitie surpas
    in desire                     25
love lost bred your chastest thought
chastity by love is wrought

       Sill:
Ô poore Musella, now I pitty thee
I see thou'rt bound who most have made unfree    30
t'is true disdaine of my love made mee turne,
and hapily I think, butt you to burne
in loves faulce fires your self, poor soule take heed
bee sure beefor you too[192] much pine to speede
you know I loved have, behold my gaine,        35
this you dislike I purchas'd w$^t$ loves paine
and true felt sorrow, yett my answer was
from (my then deere) Philisses you[193] must pas
unlov'd by mee, and for your owne[194] good leave
to urg that w$^{ch}$ most urgd, can butt deseave    40
yo$^r$ hopes, for know Musella is my love
as then of duty I should noe more move
and this his will hee gott, yett* nott his minde
for yett itt seemes you ar noe less unkind

192. Wroth inserted "too" above the line.
193. Wroth wrote "y," erased it, and then wrote "you."
194. Wroth inserted "owne" above the line.

Mu:                                                           45
Wrong mee nott chast Silvesta t'is my greif
that from poore mee hee will nott take reliefe

Sill:
What, will hee lose what hee did most desire

Mu:                                                           50
Soe is hee led away w$^t$ jealous fire
And this Sillvesta butt to you I speak,
for souner should my hart w$^t$ silence break
then any els should heere mee thus much say
butt you, who I know will nott mee betray        55

Sill:                                                    [11v]
betray Musella, souner will I dy
noe I do love you, nor will help deny
that lies in mee to bring your care to end
or service w$^{ch}$ to your content may tend              60
for when I lov'd Philisses as my lyfe
parseaving hee lov'd you, I killd the strife,
w$^{ch}$ in mee was, yett doe I wish his good,
and for his sake love you, though I wthstood
good fortunes this chast lyfe well[195] pleaseth mee     65
and yett joy most* if you tow hapy bee
few would say this, butt fewer would itt doe
butt th'one I lov'd, and love the other too,

Mu:
I know you lov'd him, nor could I the less             70
att time* love you, soe did hee posses
my hart as my thought all harts sure must yeild
to love him most, and best, who in this field
doth live and have* nott had[196] some kind of touch
to like him, butt ô you, and I to much                 75

Sill:
Mine is now past tell mee now what yo$^{rs}$ is
and I'l wish butt the meanes to work yo$^r$ blis

---

195. Wroth inserted "lyfe well" above the line.

196. Wroth inserted "had" above the line.

Mu:

Then know Silvesta I Philisses love,        80
butt hee allthough (or that because) hee loves
doth mee mistrust (ah) can such mischief move
as to mistrust her who such passion proves;
butt soe hee doth, and thinks I have Lissius made
master of my affections w<sup>ch</sup> hath staid        85
him ever yett from letting mee itt know
by words allthough hee hid's itt nott from show,
some times I faine would speake then straite forbeare
knowing itt most unfitt; thus woe I beare

Sill:        90

indeed a woman to make love is ill
butt heere, and you may all<sup>197</sup> thes sorrowes kill;
hee poore distressed sheapherd evr'y morne
befor the sunn to our eyes new is borne
walks in this place, and heer alone doth cry        95
against his lyfe, and your great cruelty;
now, since you love soe much, come butt,* and find
him in thes woes, and show your self butt kind
you soune shall see a hart soe truly wunn
as you would nott itt miss to bee undunn;        100

Mu:

Sillvesta, for this love I can butt say<sup>198</sup>
that peece of hart w<sup>ch</sup> is nott given away
shalbee your owne, the rest will you observe
as savor<sup>199</sup> of tow harts, w<sup>ch</sup> tow* will serve        105
you ever w<sup>t</sup> soe true, and constant love
yo<sup>r</sup> chastity itt self shall itt aprove

Sill:        [12r]

I doe beleeve itt; for in soe much worth
as lives in you vertue must needs spring* forth;        110
and for Philisses I love him &<sup>200</sup> will
in chastest service hinder still his ill,

197. Wroth inserted "all" above the line.
198. Following line 102, Wroth wrote and then deleted a full line, most of which is indecipherable.
199. Saver.
200. Wroth inserted the symbol "&" above the line.

then keepe your time alas lett him nott dy
for whom soe many sufferd misery

       Mu:                                   115
Lett mee noe joy receave if I neglect
this kind advise, or him I soe respect

       Sill:
farewell musella, love, and hapy bee          *ex,*

       Mu:                                   120
And bee thou blest that thus doth comfort mee  *ex,*

       Philisses
O wreched man: and thou all conquering love
w$^{ch}$ showst thy pouer still on haples mee
yett give mee leave in thes sweet shades to move     125
rest, but to show my killing miserie;
and bee once pleasd to know my wreched fate,
and somthing pitty, my ill, and my state
Could ever Nature,[201] or the heavns e're frame*
soe rare a part so like them selves devine         130
and yett that work be blotted w$^t$ the blame
of cruelty, and dark bee, who should shine;
To bee the brightest star, of deerest prise,
and yett to murder harts w$^{ch}$ to her cries
Cry, and even att the point of death for care     135
yett have I nothing left mee butt dispaire,
despaire, ô butt dispaire, alas hath hope
noe better[202] portion, nor a greater scope
well then dispaire w$^t$ my lyfe coupled bee,
and for my soddaine end doe soune agree,       140
ay! mee unfortunate, would I could dy.
butt soe soune as this company I fly          *ex*:

       Dalina, Climena,
        Simena, fillis

---

201. The "N" in "Nature" was originally written in lower-case.

202. The "b" in "better" was originally a "p."

       Dalina[203]                            145
Now wee're alone lett every one confese
truly to other what our lucks have binn
how often lik'd, and lov'd, and soe express
our passions past shall wee this sport beegin,
non can accuse us, non can us betray,             150
unles our selvs, our owne selves will bewray,[204]

       Fillis
I like this, butt will each one truly tell

       Cli:
trust mee I will, who doth nott, doth nott well[205]    155

       Si:
I'le plainly speake butt who shalbe the first[206]

       Da:                           [12v]
I can say least of all yett I will speake
A sheapherd once ther was, and nott the wurst   160
of those were most esteem'd whose sleepe did breake
w<sup>t</sup> love for-southe[207] of mee, I found itt thought
I might have him att leasure, lik'd him nott,
then was ther to our house a farmer brought
rich, and lively butt those bought nott his lott   165
for love; tow Jolly youthes att last ther came
w<sup>ch</sup> both mee thought I very well could love
when one was absent t'other had the name,
in my staid hart hee present did most move
both att a* time in sight I scarce could say   170
w<sup>ch</sup> of the tow I then would wish away
butt they found how to chuse, and as I was
like changing, like unsertaine lett mee pass,

203. Wroth originally wrote this speech prefix flush left but erased it.

204. "To accuse, malign, speak evil of" (*OED*).

205. Following line 155, Wroth wrote and then deleted a line that is mostly indecipherable but appears to have some similarities with line 159.

206. Wroth wrote the catchword "Dalina=," centered, at the bottom of fol. 12r and then repeated the speech prefix "Da:" at the top of fol. 12v.

207. Forsooth. "In truth, truly" (*OED*).

Si:

I would nott this beeleeve if other tongue                    175
should this report butt think itt had bin wrong
butt since you speake this could nott you agree
to chuse some one butt this unchosen bee

Da:

truly nott I, I plainly tell the truth                        180
yett doe confess t'was folly in my youth
w<sup>ch</sup> now I'le mend the next that comes I'le have*
I will noe more bee foulish, nor* delay
since I do see the lads will labor save
one answere rids them, I'le noe more say nay                  185
but if hee[208] say Dalina will you love,
and thank you I'le say if you will prove;
the next go on, and tell what you have dunn

Si:

I am the next, and have butt losses wunn                      190
butt yett* I constant was, thoug still rejected
lov'd, and nott lov'd I was, lik'd, and neglected
yett now some hope revives* when love thought dead
doth[209] like the spring-young bud* when leaves ar fled,

Fillis                                                        195
yo<sup>r</sup> hap's the better, would mine were as good
though I as long as you dispised stood,
for I have lov'd, and lov'd butt only one,
yett I disdaind could butt receave y<sup>t</sup> mone
w<sup>ch</sup> others doe for thousands soe unjust              200
is love to those who in him most doe trust
nor did I ever lett my thoughts bee showne
butt to Musella who all els hath knowne
w<sup>ch</sup> was long time I had Philisses lov'd,
and ever would though hee did mee dispise                     205
for then allthough* hee ever cruell prov'd
from him, nott mee the fault must needs arise,
and if Simena thus your brother deere
should bee unkind my love shall still bee cleere;

208. Wroth inserted "hee" above the line.

209. In this line, "doth," "the," and the letter "w" in "when" are written over erased words and letters.

Si:                                                              210        [13r]
T'is well resolv'd but how lik'd she you yo<sup>r</sup> choyse*
did she or blame or els your mind commend


Fi:
Niether she seem'd to dislike or rejoise
nor did commend I did this love intend                            215
butt smiling said* t' were best to bee advis'd
comfort itt were to winn but death dispis'de


S
I doe beeleeve her; butt climena yett
hath nothing said wee must nott her forgett              220


Cli:
Why you have said enough for you, and mee
yett for your sakes I will the order keepe
who though I* stranger heere by birthe I bee,
and in Arcadia ever kept my sheepe                              225
yett heere itt is my fortune w<sup>th</sup> the rest
of you to like, and loving bee oprest;
for since I came I did a lover turne,
and turne I did indeed when I lov'd heere
since for an other I in love did burne                            230
to whom I thought I had bin held as deere
butt was deseav'd when I for him had left
my freinds and country was of him bereft,
and all, butt that you kindly did imbrace,
and welcome mee into this hapy place                           235
wher for your sakes I ment to keep<sup>210</sup> some sheep
nott doubting ever to bee more deseav'd<sup>211</sup>
butt now alas I am anew beereav'd
of hart, now time itt is my self to keepe,
and lett flocks goe, unles Simeana please                       240
to give consent, and soe give mee some ease


210. Wroth originally wrote "to keepe" at the end of the line, deleted it, and then wrote "to keep" above the line between "ment" and "some."

211. This line is squeezed between lines 236 and 238. It is integral to the rhyme scheme and seems therefore to have been overlooked while copying.

Si:
Why what have I to do w<sup>t</sup> whom you love

Cli:
beecause t'is hee who doth your passion move,*                245

Si:
The les* I fear the wining of his love
since all my faith could never so much move,
yett can hee nott soe cruell ever bee
butt hee may live my miserie to see,                          250

Cli:
And when his eyes to love shall open bee
I trust hee will turne pitty unto mee,
and lett mee have reward w<sup>ch</sup> is my due

Si:                                                           255
W<sup>ch</sup> is your due, what pitty's due to you
dreame you of hope? ô you to high aspire
think you to gaine by kindling an old fire?

Cli:
My love wilbee the surer when I know            260
nott love alone, butt how love to bestow,

Si:
you make him yett for all this butt to bee
the secound in your love,* soe was nott hee
in mine, butt first, and last of all, the chiefe       265
that can to mee bring sorrow, or reliefe[212]

Cli:                                                    [13v]
This will nott winn him, you may taulke and hope
butt in loves passages ther is larg scope

Si:                                                     270
T'is true, and you have scope to chang, and chuse
to take, and dislike, like, and soune refuse,

212. Wroth wrote the speech prefix "Cli:" at the bottom of fol. 13r and then repeated it at the top of fol. 13v.

Cli:

My love as firme is to him as is thine

Si:                                                      275

yett mine did ever rise, never decline
noe other mov'd in mee the flames of love,
yett you dare hope, as much as I to move
folly indeed is provd, and only vaine
and[213] you his servante feeds wt hope of gaine,          280

Cli:

I love him most, Si: I love him best can you
chaleng reward, and can nott say you'r true

Cli:

In this you wrong mee, faulce I have nott binn          285
butt chang'd on cause Si: well now you hope to winn
this secound, yett, I like those lose noe time
butt can you thinke yt you can this way clime
to your desires, this showes you love have trid,
and that you can both chouse,[214] and choise devide        290
butt take yor course, and winn him if you can
and I'le proseed in truth, as I began

Da:

Fy what a lyfe is heere about fond love[215]
never could itt in my hart thus much move                295
this is the reason men ar growne soe coy
when they parseave wee make their smiles our joy
lett them alone, and they will seeke, and sue,
butt yeeld to them, they will* wt scorne poursue;
hold awhile of they'll kneele, nay* follow you,          300
and vowe, and sweare, yett all their othes untrue;
lett them once see you coming; then they fly
butt strangly looke, and they'll for pitty cry,
and lett them cry ther is noe evill dunn
they gaine butt that wch you might els have wunn,        305

213. Wroth rewrote "and," which is heavily inked, and deleted a word ending in "gh" which she had written above the line.

214. Wroth inserted the "u" in "chouse" above the word, having originally written "chose."

215. Wroth wrote "fond love" over something she deleted and is now indecipherable.

Si:

is this your counsell why butt now you said
your folly had your loves, and good betraid,
and that heerafter you would wiser bee
then to disdaine such as have left you free,                         310

Da:

't'is true, that was the course I ment to take
butt this must you doe, your owne ends[216] to make
I have my fortunes lost, yours doe beginn
and to cross those could bee noe greater sinn               315
I know the world, and heare mee, this I' advise
rather then to soune wunn, bee too presise
nothing is lost by beeing carefull still,                                    [14r]
nor nothing soe soune wunn as lovers ill,
heer Lissius comes, alas hee[217] is love strooke          320
hee's even now learning love w^t out the booke

Lissius

Love pardon mee I know I did amiss
when I thee scorn'd or thought thy blame my bliss
Ô pitty mee, alas I pitty crave                                                325
doe nott sett trophies on my luckles grave,
though I, poore slave, and ignorant, did scorne
thy blesed name, lett nott my hart be torne
w^th thus much torture, ô butt looke on mee
take mee a faithfull servant now to* thee,                    330

Cli:

Deere Lissius, my deere Lissius fly mee nott
lett nott both scorne, and absence bee my lott,

Liss:

'pray lett mee goe you know I can nott love              335
doe nott thus farr my pasience stirive to move,

Cli:

Why cruell Lissius wilt thou never mend
butt still inrease thy frounes for my sad end,

216. Wroth wrote "good," deleted it, and wrote "ends" above the line.
217. Wroth originally wrote "thee" and struck out the "t."

Li:                                          340
Climeana t'is enough that I have saide
bee gon, and leave mee, is this for a maide
to follow, and to haunt mee thus, you blame
mee for disdaine butt see nott your owne shame
fy, I doe blush for you, a woman woo,           345
the most unfittest,* shamfullst thing to doo

Cli:
Unfitt, and shamefull, I indeed t'is true
since sute is made to hard relentles you
well I will leave you, and restore the wrong   350
I suffer for my loving you too* long,
noe more shall my words trouble you, nor I
er'e follow more if nott to see mee dy;        *ex:*

Liss:
farewell you now doe right, this is yᵉ way     355
to winn my wish, for when I all neglect
that seek mee she must needs something²¹⁸ respect
my love the more, and what though she should say
I once denide her, yett my true felt paine
must needs from her soft brest some favor gaine 360

Da:
Lissius is taken, well said Cupid, now
you partly have parform'd your taken vow
of all our sheapheards I ne're thought that hee
would of thy foulish troupe a follower bee;    365
butt this itt is a goddess to dispise,
and thwart a wayward boy who* wants his eyes;
come lett's nott trouble him, hee is distrest
enough hee neede²¹⁹ nott bee wᵗ us oprest,

Si:                                          370      [14v]
Ile stay, and aske him who t'is hee doth love

Da:
do nott a pensive hart to passion move

218. Wroth inserted "something" above the line.
219. Wroth inserted "neede" above the line.

Si:
to passion would I could his passion find                    375
to answere my distressd,* and grived mind

Da:
Stay then, and try him, and yo<sup>r</sup> fortune try
itt may bee hee loves you, come letts goe by*

Liss:                                                         380
Ô Sweet simena looke butt on my paine
I grieve, and curse my self for my disdaine
now butt have pitty love doth make me serve,
and for yo<sup>r</sup> wrong, and you I will reserve
my lyfe to pay, your love butt to deserve,                   385
and for your sake I doe my lyfe* preserve,

Si:
preserve itt nott for mee I seeke nott now,
nor can I creditt this, nor* any vow
w<sup>ch</sup> you shall make, I was to long dispis'd             390
to bee deaseav'd, noe, I will bee advis'd
by my owne reason,* love shall noe more blind
mee, nor make mee beeleeve more then I find,

Li:
beleeve butt that, and I shall have the end                  395
of all my paine, and wishes, I pretend
a vertuous love, then grant mee my desire
who now doe wast in true, and faithfull fire,

Si:
how can I this beeleeve; Li: my faith shall tell             400
that in true love I will all els excell,
butt then will you love mee as I doe you

Si:
I promise may, for you can nott bee true,

Li:                                                           405
then you will promise breake, Si: nott if I find
that as your words are, soe you'll make yo<sup>r</sup> mind,

Li:

lett mee nor speach, nor mind have, when that I
in this or any els doe faulssefy                           410
my faith, and love to you; Si: then bee att rest
and of my true affection bee possest

Li:

Soe deere Simeana bee of mee, and mine
now doe my hopes, and joys together shine,           415

Si:

nor lett the least cloud rise to dim this light
w^ch love makes to apeere w^t true delight; /        *ex**


~ ~ ~ ~ ~ ~²²⁰


Venus;* /²²¹                                              [15r]


The 4* Acte;                                             [15v]


Musella:

This is the place Silvesta 'pointed mee
to meete my joy, my sole felicitie
and heere Philisses is (ay mee) this showes            5
the wounds by love given ar noe childish blowes

Phi:

you blessed woods into whose secrett guard
I venter dare my inward wounding smart
and to you dare impart the crosses hard               10
w^ch harbour in my love destroyed hart
to you, and butt to you I durst²²² disclose

220. The scene closes emphatically with a flourish. The rest of the page is blank.

221. At the top of fol. 15r Wroth wrote and then erased a heading, which is centered and appears to
have been "The 4 Acte," followed by the speech prefix "Musella." Below the scratched out words, she
wrote another heading, "Venus; /," indicating that this is where the next Venus and Cupid interlude
was to go. The interlude does not follow, and the remainder of fol. 15r is blank. See Textual Notes,
below, for the Venus and Cupid interlude that occurs at this point in P.

222. "To be so bold as" (*OED*).

these flames, thes paines, thes griefs w^ch I do find
for your true harts soe constant are to those
who trust in you as you'll nott chang your mind          15
Noe Echo shrill shall yo^r deere secretts utter,
or wrong yo^r silence w^th a blabing tongue
nor will your springs against your private mutter
or thinke that counsell keeping is a wrong;
then since woods, springs, echoses, and all are true,     20
my long felt woes I'le tell, shew, write in you:
Alas Musella, cruell sheapherdess
who takes no pitty on mee in distress
for all my passions, plaints, and all my woes
I am soe farr from gaine, as outward showes          25
I never had could feede least hope to spring
or any while least comfort to mee bring;
yett pardon mee deere m^rs of my soule,
I doe recall my words, my tongue controle,
for wronging thee, accuse my poore sterv'd hart        30
w^ch wither'd is w^t loves all killing smart,
since truly I must say I can nott blame
thee, nor condemne* thee w^th a scorners name,
noe, noe (alas) my paines thou dost nott know
nor dare I wrech to thee my torments* show,          35
why did I wrong thee then, who all must serve,
and happy hee by thee thought to deserve,
Who heaven hath fram'd to make us heere beelow
deserne²²³ they strive all worth in thee to show,
and doth these vallies, and these meads disgrace      40
when thou art present w^th excelling grace
as now; who att this time doth show more bright
then faire Aurora²²⁴ when she lends best light;
Ô that I might butt now have hart to speake,
and say I love, though after hart did breake          45

      Mu:
I faine would comfort him, and yett I know*
nott* if*²²⁵ from mee 't' will comfort bee or noe

---

223. Discern. "To perceive or recognize" (*OED*).

224. In Roman mythology, goddess of the dawn.

225. Wroth wrote two indecipherable words at the beginning of this line, deleted them, and then wrote "nott if" above the line.

since causles jealosie hath soe possest
his hart, as noe beeleefe of mee can rest;                    50
yett* why stay I, I came to give reliefe
should I then doubt, no I may ease his griefe,
and help will seeke, none should ones good neglect
much more his blis who for mee joys reject[226]
How now Philisses, why do you thus grieve              55      [16r]
speake, is ther non that can your paines relieve

        Phi:
yes faire Musella, butt such is my state
reliefe must come from her who can butt hate;
What hope can* I wrech have least good to move         60
wher scorne doth grow for mee, for others love;

        Mu:
butt are you sure she doth your love disdaine,
itt may bee for your love she feels like paine,

        Phi:                                          65
like paine for mee, I would nott crave soe much,
I wish noe more butt that love might her tuch,
and that she might deserne by love to know
that kind reguard* is fitt for her to show;

        Mu:                                           70
sure this she knowes; Phi: prove itt, and I may live

        Mu:
tell mee who 't'is you love, and I will give
my word I'le winn her if she may bee wunn

        Phi:                                          75
aŷ[227] mee that doubt in mee made mee first runn

226. Wroth does not formally mark the end of fol. 15v, but there is a semantic shift in Musella's speech with her coming forward to speak directly to Philisses: this is accentuated with a capital "H" in "How," the first word on fol. 16r. By comparison, in P the speech does not run over a page break, and "how" is not capitalized (see P, fol. 27r).

227. Wroth's use of a circumflex over the "y" in "ay" may indicate that some attention is being paid to pronunciation: the *OED* notes that the circumflex may be "placed … over long vowels having a particular accent or 'tone'" (*OED*). By comparison, P has "Ay."

into this labourinth of woe, and care
w<sup>ch</sup> makes mee thus to wed my* owne dispaire

      Mu:

butt have you made itt knowne to her you love      80
that for her scorne you doe these torments prove

      Phi:

yes now I have, and yett to ease some paine
I'le plainlier speake, though my owne end I gaine,
and soe to end itt were to mee a bliss,      85
then know for your deere sake my sorrow is,
itt may bee you will hate mee, yett I have
by this some ease though w<sup>t</sup> itt come my grave,
yett deere Musella since for you I pine,
and suffer welcom paine,* lett favor shine      90
thus far, that though my love you doe neglect
yett sorry bee I died; w<sup>t</sup> this respect
I shalbee satisfied, and soe content
as I shall deeme my lyfe, soe lost, well spent,

      Mu:      95

Sory (alas Philisses) can itt bee
butt I should grieve, and mourne, nay dy for thee,
yett tell mee, why did you thus hide your love,
and suffer wrong conseits[228] thus much to move
now 't'is allmost to late your wish to gaine      100
yett you shall pitty, for your[229] love obtaine

      Phi:

Pitty, when helples t'is, is endless given
am I to this unhapy bondage driv'n
yett truly pitty, and t'will bee some ease      105
unto my griefe though all els doe* displease,
butt doe nott yett unles you can affect
for forced pitty's wurse then is neglect,
and to bee pitty'd butt for pitty* sake[230]
and nott for love do never pitty take      110      [16v]

---

228. Conceit. "A notion, conception, idea, or thought" (*OED*).

229. Wroth wrote "and my," deleted it, and wrote "for your" above the line.

230. Wroth wrote the catchword "and=" in the bottom right corner of fol. 16r.

Mu:
Well then I love you, and soe ever must
though time, or Fortune should bee still unjust;
for wee may love, and both may constant prove
butt nott injoy unless ordaind above                                    115

Phi:
Dost thou love mee, o deere Musella say
and say itt still to kill my late dismay

Mu:
More then my self, or love my self for thee                             120
the better much; butt wilt thou love like mee?

Phi:
My only lyfe, heer doe I vow to dy
when I prove faulce, or show inconstancy,

Mu:                                                                      125
All true content may this to both procure

P[hi]:[231]
and when I breake lett mee* all shame indure

Mu:
nor doubt you mee, nor my true hart mistrust,                           130
for dy I will befor I prove unjust;
butt heere comes Rustick whose incombred[232] braine
wᵗ love, and jealousie must our loss gaine
for since hee hops,[233] nay says that I am his
I can nott absent bee butt hee'l mee miss                               135
butt when that is, lett day no longer shine,
or I have lyfe, if live nott truly thine
butt now least that our love should be found out
lett's seeke all meanes to keepe him from this doubt,
and lett non know itt butt your sister deere                            140
whose company I keepe, soe hold all cleere;

231. There is a blot over the "hi" in "Phi," but the colon is spaced correctly for the three-letter speech prefix.
232. Encumbered. "Hampered, burdened" (*OED*).
233. Hopes.

then lett him wach, and keepe what hee can gett;
his plotts must want ther force our joys to lett;
I'le step awhile aside,* till you doe meet
this wellcom man,[234] whose absence were more sweet        145
for though that hee pour thing can litle find
yett I shall blush w$^t$ knowing my owne mind,
fear, and desire still to keepe itt hid
will[235] blushing show itt when t'is most forbid,

       Phi:                                        150
Non can have pouer against a[236] pouerfull love
nor keep the blood butt in the cheeks t'will move
butt nott for feare, or care itt ther doth show
butt kinde desire makes you blushing know
that joy takes place, and in your face doth clime     155
w$^t$ leaping hart, like lambkins in the prime;
butt sweet Musella since you will away
take now my hart and lett yours in mee stay, Mu: *ex:*
could I express the joy I now conseave
I were unworthy soe much* to receave               160
butt soe much am I thine, as lyfe, and joy
are in thy hands to nurse, or to destroy;
how now Rustick, whether away soe fast?[237]

       Rus:                                    [17r]
To seeke Musella; phi: now that labour's past       165
see wher she comes: Mu: Rustick wher were you
I sought butt could nott find you:[238] Ru: is that true[239]
faith I was butt the truth to you to tell
marking som kattle, and asleepe I fell

       Mu:                                        170
and I was seeking of a long lost lamb
w$^{ch}$ now I found ev'n as along you came

234. Wroth wrote "man" over an indecipherable word.

235. Wroth wrote "wi," deleted it, and wrote "will" above the line.

236. Wroth inserted "a" above the line.

237. Wroth did not mark the end of this page except by the use of a question mark.

238. Wroth inserted "nott" and "you" above the line, which originally read "I sought butt could find:"—phrasing that is both nonsensical and ungrammatical and thus possibly a copying error.

239. Wroth deleted "and" before "is that true."

Ru:

I'me glad you found itt; Mu: truly soe am I

Ru:                                                            175

now lett us goe to finde our company

Phi:

see wher some bee, Mu: itt seemes to soune, alas
that love dispis'd should com to such a pas

Li:                    :Simena:[240]                       180
Loves begining like the spring
   gives delight in sweetnes flowing
   ever pleasant flourishing
   pride in her, brave coulers showing
Butt love ending is att last                               185
   like the stormes of winters blast

Mu:

Lissius mee thinks you ar growne sad of late,
and privately w^t your owne thoughts debate
I hope you ar nott fal'ne in love, that boy            190
can nott I trust your settled hart injoy

Li:

'T'is well; you may bee merry att my fall
rejoise, nay doo, for I can lose butt all;

Simena:                                                       195

and soe to much; *ex*:[241] Mu: sure some strang error is

Phi:

learne you itt out, Ru: wee'll leave you, and bring blis*

Mu:

Come Lissius tell mee whence proseeds this griefe      200
discover[242] itt, and you may find reliefe

240. Note the unusual placement of the entry for ":Simena:" The entry is written in a darker ink, suggesting that Wroth inserted it at a different time. In P, "Simeana" is similarly positioned, flush right on the same line as the speech prefix for Lissius.

241. Unusually, this exit direction is positioned at mid-line (as also in P). See also 4.523.

242. "To disclose, reveal, etc., to others" (*OED*).

Li:
Noe I'le goe seeke Philisses, hee I'me sure
will comfort mee who doth the like indure;
yett faire Musella do thus much for mee                    205
as tell* Simena she hath murder'd mee,
and gaine butt this that she my end will bless
w^th some (though smalest griefe) for my distress,
and that she will butt grace my haples tombe
as to beehold mee dead by her hard dombe;²⁴³            210
this is a smale request, and 't'is my last,
who* to obay, to my sad end will haste

Mu.
Nay Lisius heere mee, tell mee ere you²⁴⁴ goe
what sodaine matter moves in you this woe              215

Li:
Alas t'is love of one I did disdaine,
and now I seeke, the like neglect I gaine
yett att the first she answerd mee w^t love,                    [17v]
w^ch made my passions more increase, and move,    220
butt now she scorns mee, and tells mee I give
my love in equall sort to all, and drive
my sighs, and plaints butt from an outward part
of fained love, and never from my hart,
and when on knees I doe her favor crave              225
she bids mee seeke Climena, wher I gave
as many vowes as then to her I did,
and therupon her sight did mee forbid,
Vowing that if I ever more did* speake
of love, she would nott only speaches breake          230
butt ever more her sight; and would bee blind
rather then in my sight her self to find;
this is the cause, and this must bee my end
w^ch my sad days to saddest night must lend,

Mu:                                                                          235
When grew this chang: Li: Alas to late, to day
and yett to soune to bring* my joys decay,

243. Doom.

244. Wroth wrote "I," crossed it out, and wrote "you" above the line.

Mu:

Have nott some made some false report of you,*

Li:                                                                              240

I know nott butt my hart was ever true
since first I vow'd, and that my death shall tell
w<sup>ch</sup> is my last hope that will please her well,

Mu:

soft, I will speake w<sup>th</sup> her and know her mind,          245
and why on such a soddaine[245] she's unkind,
and truly bring you answere what she says,
till then bee quiett, for itt can noe praise
bring to your death when you shall wayling dy
w<sup>th</sup> out soe just a cause as to know why,                      250

Li:

Butt will Musella do thus much for mee
shall I nott of all freinds forsaken bee,

Mu:

Never of mee, and heere awhile butt stay                    255
and I shall comfort bring your care t'allay,          *ex:*[246]

Li:

Ô noe, I know she will nott pitty mee,
unfortunate, and haples must I bee,
and now thou conquering, pourefull* god of love    260
I doe butt thus much crave, thy forces prove,
and cast all stormes of thy just caused rage
upon mee vassell, and noe heat asswage
of greatest fury since I doe deserve
noe favour, or[247] least grace, butt heer to sterve    265
fed butt w<sup>t</sup> tortures;* lett mee live to see
my former sinn in* soe much slighting thee
death yett more wellcome were itt nott soe meete*
I oft should dy who knew nott souer from sweet;*

245. Suddenly.

246. This exit direction is written in a more upright script and darker ink than the surrounding dialogue.

247. Wroth wrote "nor" and deleted the "n."

Simeana comes, ah most ungratefull maide                    270
who answers love, as one would welcome death
the neerer that itt comes the more flys, stayd
ne're butt by lims that tire wanting breath
Soe flys* she still from mee whoes love is fixt                    [18r]
in purest flames w<sup>t</sup> justest<sup>248</sup> meaning* mixt                    275

      Mu:

Simena this can bee no ground to take
soe great dislike upon one mans report,
and what may well prove faulce, as thus to make
an honest, loving hart dy in this sort                    280
say that hee useth others well, and smiles
on them who't may bee<sup>249</sup> love of him beeguiles,
or that hee us'd Climeana well, what then,
t'is all poor soule she getts, who did contemn
and raile att her; Si: t'is true beefor my face                    285
hee did revile her w<sup>th</sup> words of disgrace
my back butt turnd she was his only joy
his best his deerest lyfe, and soune destroy
him self hee would if she nott lovd him still
and just what hee had vow'd his hart did kill                    290
for my disdaine, hee shamles did protest
w<sup>th</sup> in one houer to her causd his unrest;
can I beare this, who liv'd soe long disdaind
now to bee mock'd, I thought I love had gaind,
and nott more scorne, butt since thus much I find                    295
I ame glad the joy sunk nott deepe* in my mind

      Mu:

fy, fy Simeana leave thes doubts to farr
all reddy growne to breede soe great a jarr,
t'was butt his dutty kindly once to speake                    300
to her who for him would her poore hart breake,
would you nott thinke itt sinn quite to undoe
a silly mayd w<sup>t</sup> scorne, butt lett thes goe
thinke you if I did love, and that I saw
hee us'd more well, would I my love w<sup>th</sup> draw                    305
from him for that, Ô! noe great cause may bee

248. Wroth originally wrote "iustest" but reshaped the "i" into a "j."
249. Wroth wrote "his," crossed it out, and wrote "may bee" above the line.

to move good lookes, mustrust nott butt bee free
from this vild humor of bace jealousie
w<sup>ch</sup> breedeth nothing butt self miserie;
for this beeleeve while you your self are just                              310
you can nott any way your love distrust,*
lett him discourse, and smile, and what of this
is hee the liklier in his fayth to miss
noe, never feare him for his outward smiles
't'is private freindship that our trust beguiles,                          315
and therfor lett nott Arcas flattering skill
have pouer in your brest his deserts to spill
Lissius is worthy, and a worthy love
hee bears to you, then thes conceits remove,

        Si:                                                                     320
Arcas did see them sitt too privately
and kiss, and then imbrace, Mu: well if hee did

        Si:
and in her eare discource familliarly
when they did thinke itt should from bee*250 hid                           325

        Mu:
Lord how one may conjecture if one feare
all things they doubt to bee the same they feare
though private must itt follow hee's untrue,
or that they whisper'd must bee kept from you,                             330
fy leave thes follys, and beegin to think
you have your love brought to deaths river brinck,
repent you have him wrong'd, and now cherish
the diing lad who els soune will perish                                    [18v]
goe aske him pardon; Si: pardon why, that hee                              335
the more may brag hee twise hath cousend mee

        Mu:
nay hee is past all braging, mend your fault,
and sorry bee you have his torment wrought
see wher hee lies, the truest signe of woe                                 340
goe haste, and save him, loves wings are nott slowe,

250. P has "from mee bee hid" (fol. 32r).

Si:

Ô deerest Lissius looke butt up, and speake
to mee most wreched, whose hart now must breake
w^th self accusing of a cursed wrong                    345
w^ch rashly bred, did winn beeleefe to strong,
ah cast butt up thyn eyes, see my true teares
and view butt her, who now all torment beares;
doe butt looke up, and thou shalt see mee dy
for having wrong'd thee w^t my jealousie                350

Li:

To see thee dy? alas I dy for thee
what pleasure can thy death[251] then bring to mee
yett if love make you say this, then poor I
shall much more happy, and more blessed dy              355

Si:

Nay lett mee ende, beefor thy ende I see
alas I love you, and 't'was love in mee
bred this great ill; by jelousie abus'de*
I brought your harme, and my best love abus'd,          360

Li:

Ô joy, w^ch now doth swell as much as griefe,
and pleasing, yett doth make mee seeke reliefe,
ame I my self? noe I am only joy,
nott Lissius, griefe did lately him destroy,            365
I am Simeanas love, her slave revived,
late hopeles dead, now have dispaire surviv'd

Mu:

All care now past, lett joy in triumph sitt
this for such lovers ever is most fitt,                 370
this doth beecome that happy loving paire
who seeke to nurse the joys that kill all care;*
lett those fall out, mistrust, wrangle, and jarr
who love for fashion nott for love, butt warr
nott you, the couple Cupid best doth love               375
whose troubled harts his Godheads self did move

---

251. Wroth wrote "griefe," crossed out the "g," and reshaped the word to read "death."

Li:

Musella you have turnd this cloudy day
to sweet, and pleasant light, nor can I say
soe much as in my hart this kindnes breeds                         380
for now delight all forme, and speech exceeds
butt lett us happy now, unhappy bee
when in us least unthankfullnes you see

Si:

Lett mee my self, nay my deere Lissius leave                       385
when I in service, or in faith deceave
Musella, sole restorer of this joy,
and jeaLosie²⁵² anew strive to destroy
our lovs, and hopes if I forgettfull bee
of this increase of lost felicitie;                                390         [19r]
butt now my Lissius have you mee forgiv'n
my last offence by love, and fearing driv'ne

Li:

Thou lov'st mee, t'is enough, and now injoy
all blis, bring noe doubts now* to cross our joy                   395
I all forgett, and only hold thee deere
and from you,* all faults past my love doth cleare

Si:

Soe lett us ever doubtles live, and love
and noe mistrust in least sort our harts move                      400

Li:

noe doubt of thee shall ever stirr in mine,

Si:

nor breed in mee; soe wholy I ame thine;

Mu:                                                                405

Happy this time, and blessed bee your loves,
and most accursed they that other moves;
live both contented, and still live* as one,
never devided till your lives bee dunn; /

252. The use of a capital letter in mid-word is highly unusual.

Fillis, Dalina, Philisses, Arcas                    410
Climeana, Rustick,

Mu:
Heere comes the flock; Ru: wee're all heer now; Mu: 'tis true
wee all are heere, and one to much by you

Da:                                                 415
Heere bee our fellowes now lett us beeginn
some pretty pastime pleasures for* to winn
sweetest Musella what think you is best

Mu:
That wherunto your phantsie is adrest              420

Da:
mine is to ridling, Si:, and indeed that's good

Cli:
butt mee thinks nott least[253] they bee understood

Si:                                                 425
understood, why soe shall all bee that I make

Cli:
tush you'l say one thing, and an other take

Si:
you'll still bee wrangling; Da: I, and for a man   430
would I might live till quarell I beegan
on such a cause, butt pray now quiett bee,
and faire Musella, first beeginn w$^t$ mee,

Fillis:
butt must the riddles bee expounded; Da: noe       435

Mu:
Then I'le beeginn though scarce the play doe* know

That I wish w$^{ch}$ w$^t$ most paine

253. Lest.

I must gaine
that I shun w^ch w^t such ease                                      440
cannott please
that most easy, still I fly;
bar'd I fainest would come ny;*

     Da:²⁵⁴
I ame the next marke then what I will say              445              [19v]
'best is my lovers can nott mee beetray

What I seeke can never bee
found in mee
faine I would that try, and find
w^ch my mind                                                       450
ever yett from my hart kept
till away my luck was stept

     Phi:
Lett them alone the woemen still will speake
Rustick come you, and I this course will breake        455

Late I saw a starr to shine
whose light mee thought was only mine
till a cloude came, and did hide
that light from mee wher light doth* bide
yett tell mee how can thes agree                             460
that light though dimmd, that light I see,

     Li:
Now Rustick, fortune's falling on your head,
bring forth your riddle, fy, in love, and dead
to such a sport, think nott upon the day                   465
ther is noe danger in't I dare well say,

     Ru:
truly I can nott ridle, I'was nott taught
thes triks of witt, my thoughts noe* higher wrought
then how to marke a beast, or drive a Cowe              470
to feed, or els w^t art to hold a plowe,

254. This is the only instance in H where Wroth wrote a speech prefix at the bottom of one folio without repeating it at the top of the next.

w<sup>ch</sup> if you knew, you surely soune would finde
a matter more of waight* then thes od things
w<sup>ch</sup> never profitt butt some laughter brings,
thes others bee of body, and of minde                            475

       Phi:
spoke like a husband, though you yett are non
butt come, what is this sport allredy dunn

       Ru:
I can nott riddle: Da: whistle, t'is as good                     480
for you sufficiently are understood

       Ru:
What meane you: Da: nought, butt that you are
an honest man, and thrifty, full of care;

       Ru:                                                485
I thought you had ment wurse: Da: ment wurse, what I
fy, this doth show, your doubt, and jealousie;
why should you take my meaning wurse then 't'is

       Ru:
Nay I butt smile to see how all you miss                         490
butt some shall finde when I doe seeme to smile,
and showe best pleas'd I oftnest, doe beeguile

       Da:
your self you meane, for few els doe respect
your smiles, or frownes, therfor doe nott neglect                495
your pleasant youth, ill will is too soune gott,
and once that rooted, nott soe soune forgott;

       Phi:
you grow too wise, dispute noe more, heere bee
others who will lett us ther hearers bee,                        500    [20r]
and give this sport some lyfe againe w<sup>ch</sup> you
allmost made dead; Da: I have dunn lett joy insue;

       Li:
Guess you all what this can bee,

a snake to suffer fire I see,                                          505
a fogue, and yett a cleere bright day,
   a light w<sup>ch</sup> better were away,
tow sunns att once both shining cleere,
and w<sup>th</sup> out envy hold each deare,

    Fillis:                                        510
A spring I hop'd for butt that di'de
then on the next my<sup>255</sup> hopes relide
butt sommer past the latter spring
could mee butt former losses bring
I di'de w<sup>t</sup> them, yett still I live                         515
while autume can noe comfort give; /

    Mu:
Unmanerly I must your presence leave
sent for in haste unto mother,* butt<sup>256</sup>
I hope in this sweet place soune to receave                            520
your most lov'd companies, and soe to putt
good Rustick into better humours say
will you bee merry; *ex:*<sup>257</sup> Ru: I'le nott after stay; /*

    Phi:
noe follow; shadowes never absent bee                                  525
when sunn shines, in w<sup>ch</sup> blessing<sup>258</sup> you may see
your shadow'de self, who nothing in truth are
butt the reflection of her too great care
what will you farder<sup>259</sup> doe; Da: lett us depart

    Ar:                                            530
come* lett's away, butt some ere long will smart

    Phi:
when shall wee meet againe, Da: when day apeers,

---

255. Wroth wrote "I," crossed it out, and then wrote "my."

256. Wroth wrote "soune," crossed it out, and then wrote "butt." This seems to be a simple transcription error, since "soune" appears in the following line.

257. This is one of two mid-line exits in the play. See also 4.196.

258. Wroth wrote "butt soe," crossed it out, and then wrote "in w<sup>ch</sup> blessing" above the line.

259. Farther.

Li:
noe nott till sunn who all foule mists still cleers,                    535

Phi:
why then att sunn, and who shall then miss heare
a punishment by us ordainde must* beare,

Da:
lett itt bee soe; Fillis; for mee I'me well agreed;*              540

Lissius;
soe are wee all, and sunn appeere²⁶⁰ wᵗ speede $*


~ ~ ~ ~ ~ ~²⁶¹


*Venus, Cupid**                                              [20v]

*Now have thy torments long enough indurd*
*and of thy force they are enough assur'd*                   545
*O hold thy hande, als I pitty now*
*thos whose great pride did whilum* scorne to bow*
*thou hast parformd thy promise, and thy state*
*now is confest o slacken then thy hate*
*they humble doe theyr harts, and thoughts to thee*          550
*beehold them, and accept²⁶² them, and²⁶³ milde bee,*
*thy conquest is sufficient save the spoyles*
*and lett them²⁶⁴ only taken bee in toyles*
*butt sett att liberty againe to²⁶⁵ tell*
*thy might, and²⁶⁶ clemency wᶜʰ doth excell*                 555


260. Wroth wrote "must show," crossed it out, and then wrote "appeere" above the line.

261. Wroth ended this section of the play with an *s fermé* and a flourish.

262. Wroth began to write "axce," crossed it out, and then wrote "accept" above the line.

263. Wroth wrote "butt" and another indecipherable word, crossed out both words, and then wrote "and" above the line.

264. Wroth inserted "them" above the line.

265. Wroth inserted "to" above the line.

266. Wroth wrote "augh," crossed it out, and then wrote "and" above the line.

*Cupid;*

*I meane to save them, butt some yett must try*
*more[267] paine ere they theyr blessings may come ny*
*butt in the end all shall bee\* well againe*
*and sweetest is that love obtaind w$^t$ paine*          560

*musique\*[268]*
*Love thy powerfull hand w$^t$ draw*
*all doe yeeld unto thy law*
*rebells now thy subjects bee*
*bound they are who late were[269] free*          565
*most confess thy power, and might*
*all harts yeeld unto thy right*
*thoughts directed ar by thee*
*souls doe strive thy joys to see*
*pitty then, and mercy give*          570
*unto them\* wher you doe live*
*they your images doe prove*
*in them may you see great love*
*they your mirours, you theyr eye*
*by w$^{ch}$[270] they[271] true love doe spy[272]*          575
*scease\* awhile theyr cruell smarts*
*and beehold theyr yeelding harts\**
*greater glory 'tis to save*
*when that you a\* conquest have*
*then w$^t$ tiranny to press*          580
*w$^{ch}$ still make\* the honor les*
*Gods doe prinses hands\* direct*
*then to thes have some respect, \$\**

267. Wroth wrote "my," crossed it out, and then wrote "more" above the line.

268. Wroth wrote the speech prefix "Venus" and the lines "Love a god did slander beare / gainst his person, and his power / butt," crossed out the speech prefix and these lines, and then restarted with the direction for "musique." Given that the speech prefix was deleted, the speech itself is not necessarily assigned to Venus. In fact, Cupid's final lines in the interlude are also deleted, so that this speech stands outside the dramatic frame. See the discussion of this passage in the Content and Analysis section of the Wroth introduction.

269. Wroth wrote "was," crossed it out, and wrote "were" above the line.

270. Wroth wrote "wher," crossed it out, and wrote "by w$^{ch}$" above the line.

271. Wroth wrote "may" between "they" and "true," and deleted it.

272. Wroth wrote "descry," deleted it, and wrote "doe" above the line and "spy" to the right of the deleted word.

*Cupid*
~~Now your part coms to play~~                                                585
~~in this you must somthing sway~~
~~soe you shall, and I your child~~
~~when you bid can soone bee milde~~ $[273]

$*

The 5* Act; /                                                                 [21r]
Musella, Simena;*

Mu:
O eyes that day can see, and can nott mend
what my joy's poyson, must my wreched end                                     5
proseed from love, and yett my true love crost,
neclected for bace gaine, and all worthe lost
for riches, then 't'is time for good to dy
when wealth must wed us to all misery;

              Si:                                                             10
if you will butt stoutly tell your mother
you hate him, and will match w[t] any other
she can nott, nor will goe about to cross
your liking, soe to bring your endless loss;

              Mu:                                                             15
Alas I have urg'd her, till she w[t] teares
did vowe, and grieve she could nott mend my state
agree'd on by my fathers will, w[ch] beares
sway in her brest, and duty in mee; Fate
must have her courses,[274] While most* wreched I               20
wish butt soe good a fate as now to dy,

              Si:
wish nott such ill[275] w[ch] all wee suffer must

---

273. Cupid's final speech is deleted in the manuscript, but the speech prefix remains. The deleted lines are printed here in strikethrough so as to make sense of the otherwise dangling speech prefix. Notably, Wroth wrote three *s fermés* at the end of this scene. See Figure 3.

274. "Onward movement in a particular path" (*OED*).

275. Wroth inserted "ill" above the line.

butt take some hope, the Gods ar nott unjust,
my minde doth give mee[276] yett, you shall bee blest,          25
and seldome doe I faile,* then quiett rest

    Mu:

rest quiett, (o! heavens) have you ever knowne
the paines of love, and bin by him orethroune
to give this counsell, to advise your freind          30
to impossibilities, why to what end
speake you thus idly,* can itt ere bee thought
that quiett, or least rest can now bee[277] brought
to mee, while deere Philisses thus is crost
who missing, all my hapines is lost,          35

    Si:

you have nott mist, nor lost him yett, Mu: I must,
and that's enough, did I my blessings trust
in your kind brests you fatall sisters,[278] now
by your decree[279] to bee beestowd, and bow          40
to bace unworthy riches, o! my hart
that breaks nott, butt[280] can suffer all this smart;

    Si:

have patience, Mu: I can nott, nor I will nott,
patient bee, ay mee, and beare this hard* lott          45
noe, I will grieve in spite of greife, and mourne
to make those madd who now to pleasurs* turne

    Philisses.

My deere Musella what is itt doth grieve
your hart thus much, tell mee, and still beleeve          50
while you complaine I must tormented bee
your sighs, and tears (alas) doe bleed in mee,

---

276. Wroth inserted "mee" above the line.

277. Wroth inserted "bee" above the line.

278. The Fates.

279. Wroth wrote "hard harts," crossed out both words, and then wrote "decree" above the line.

280. Wroth wrote "yett," crossed it out, and then wrote "butt" above the line.

Mu:

I knowe itt, t'is your loss I thus lament;
I must bee maried, would my days [   ]ent,[281]       55       [21v]

Phi:

married! Mu: to Rustick my mother soe commands
who I must yeeld to beeing in her hands

Phi:

butt will you marry, or show love to mee       60
or her obay, and make me wreched bee

Mu:

Alas Philisses will you this doubt make
I would my lyfe to pleasure you forsake
hath nott my firmnes hetherto made knowne       65
my faith, and love w$^{ch}$ yett should bee more showne
if I might governe butt my mothers will
yett this last question even my hart doth kill

Phi:

grieve nott my deerest, I spake* butt for love,       70
then lett nott love your trouble soe farr move,
you weepe nott, that itt wounds nott haples mee,
nor sigh, butt in mee all those sorrowes bee,
you never cry, butt groanes most truly show
from deepest of my hart I feele your woe,       75
then heape nott now more sorrows on my hart
by thes deere tears, w$^{ch}$ tasteth of all* smart,
noe griefe can bee w$^{ch}$ I have nott sustaind,
and must for now dispaire hath conquest gaind;
yett lett your love in mee still steddy rest,       80
and in that I sufficiently ame blest
butt must you marry; Mu: allas my deere, I must*[282]

---

281. The top right corner of fol. 21v, the last leaf in the manuscript, is considerably worn, to the point of having made the final words of line 55 illegible. The pattern of wear on this folio, as also on fol. 1r, indicates these were the outer leaves of the manuscript before it was sewn into its current binding. P has "days were spent" (fol. 37v). See Figure 2.

282. Wroth made a significant change here. See Textual Notes, below, for a six-line speech by Musella that is not in H. The change appears to have been deliberate, since the rhyme scheme is maintained in both versions.

     Phi:
I heere, and see my end. O love unjust,\*
ungratefull, and forgettfull of the good             85
from us\* receav'd, by whom thy fame hath stood,
thy honor still\* maintaind, thy name adorde,
w<sup>ch</sup> by all others w<sup>t</sup> disgrace was stor'd,
is this the great reward wee must\* receave
for all our\* service, will you thus deseave     90
our\* hopes, and joys; Mu: yett shall I\* one thing crave

     Phi:
aske my poore lyfe all els I long since gave\*

     Mu:
that I will\* aske, and yours requite w<sup>t</sup> mine     95
for mine can nott bee if nott joind to thine,
goe w<sup>t</sup> mee to the temple, and ther wee
will bind our lives, or els our lives make free

     Phi:
to dy for you\* a new lyfe I should gaine        100
butt to dy w<sup>th</sup> thee were eternall paine
soe you will promise mee that you will live
I willingly will goe, and my lyfe give,
you may bee happy; Mu: happy w<sup>th</sup> out thee
lett mee bee\* rather wreched, and thine bee     105
w<sup>t</sup> out thee[283] noe lyfe can bee, nor least joy
noe\* thought butt how a sad end to injoy
butt promise mee your self you will nott harme
as you love mee, Phi: lett mee impose that charme
likwise on you Mu: content I ame agreed       110

     Phi:[284]
lett's goe alone noe company wee need

     Mu:
Simeana she shall goe, and soe may tell

283. Wroth wrote "thee" above the line.

284. This speech prefix is written in the single space between lines 110 and 112, which form a couplet. The couplet would not have been written for Musella alone, since she expresses the opposite sentiment in lines 114–15. The omission seems therefore to have been a transcription error.

the good, or heavy chance that us befell*[285]                    115

        Phi:
w[t] all my hart Si: butt what will you tow doe*
both dy, and mee poore maiden quite undoe?

       Phi:*[286]

285. P has two lines following line 115 that are not present in H; see Textual Notes.

286. H ends here. See Textual Notes for the P ending. Whether the play is unfinished is a matter of critical debate, as is discussed in the introduction, above. The last page of H is written in a far denser script than any other page of the manuscript (sixty-five lines, as compared with a median of fifty-five for all other fully inscribed folios in Wroth's formal italic hand) and becomes more dense partway through line 11, possibly to fit a set amount of text within the remaining space. The number of differences between the H ending and the P ending suggest fairly extensive revision. See Figure 2.

The following notes record variants in wording between the Huntington (H) and Penshurst (P) manuscripts. In the numbered list below (corresponding to the line numbers of the text) the H text precedes the square bracket; the P text follows the square bracket. Included in the these notes are the opening and closing interludes that appear in P, but not in H. The P text is based on the photographic facsimile of the manuscript published in Brennan, *Lady Mary Wroth's Love's Victory*. The P text has not been edited.

[*not in H*]

> Venus, and Cupid w$^t$ her in her
>     Temple, her Priests attendinge
>         her,

>         Venus /
> Cupid me thinks wee haue too long bin still
> and that thes people growe to scorne owr will
> mercy to those vngratefull, breeds neglect
> then lett vs growe owr greatnes to respect
> make them acknowledg that owr heaunly power
> can nott theyr strength butt euen themselues deuowre
> Lett them nott smile and laugh beecause thine eyes
> are couer'd as if blind or loue dispise
> noe thou y$^t$ scarse shallt from thine eyes take of
> w$^{ch}$ gaue them cause on thee to make this scoff
> thou shalt discerne theyr harts, and make them knowe
> that humble homage vnto thee they owe;
> take thou the shaft w$^{ch}$ headed is w$^t$ steele
> and make them bowe whose thoughts did lately reel
> make them thine owne, thou who didst mee once harme
> can nott forgett the fury of that charme
> wound them butt kill them nott, so may they liue
> to honor thee, and thankfullnes to giue,
> shun noe great cross w$^{ch}$ may theyr crosses breed
> butt yett lett blest inioying them succeed,
> griefe is sufficient to declare thy might,
> and in thy mercy glory will shine bright;

> Cupid,
> Mother I will noe cross, noe harme forbeare
> of iealousie for loss, of griefe or feare
> w^ch may my honor, touchd againe repaire,
> butt w^th theyr sorrows will my glory reare
> freinds shall mistrust theyr freinds, louers mistake,
> and all shall for theyr folly woes partake
> some shall loue much yett shall noe loue inioye
> others obtaine when lost is all theyr ioye
> this will I doe your will, and minde to serue,
> and to your triumph will thes rites preserue

> Venus,
> Then shall wee haue againe owr ancient glory,
> and lett this called bee loues victory
> triumphs vpon theyr trauells shall assend,
> and yett most hapy ere they come to end,

> Cu:
> Joy, and inioying on some shalbee sett
> sorrow on others caught by Cupids nett; /

[Act One]

| | |
|---|---|
| 1 | $] *not in P* |
| 14 | my] mine |
| 16 | banks] bank |
| 32 | loves paine] loue paines |
| 35 | passion] passions |
| 53 | dainty] daintiest |
| 75 | makes] doth |
| 77 | souner] rather |
| 81 | ex:] *not in P* |
| 84 | pleasant vallys gives thy light] vallies giust thy pleasant sight |
| 99 | changings] changinge |
| 110 | quench] heale |
| 112 | strives] striue; have] life |
| 115 | fires] fires are |
| 123 | have] hath |
| 132 | was] were |
| 134 | ex:] *not in P* |
| 146 | can nott, may nott] may nott, cannott |

| | |
|---|---|
| 155 | *ex*:] *not in P* |
| 162 | ever cruelty itt self thus showe] cruelty itt self thus euer show |
| 174 | that] Who |
| 204 | rann ... flew] flew ... ran |
| 209 | last] length |
| 213 | fashions ... manners] manners ... fashions |
| 233 | hard] strang |
| 235 | always] euer |
| 242 | had gain'd] obtaind |
| 254 | end] ends |
| 255 | care] paine |
| 256 | *not in H*] and fauor wun w^ch kills all former care, |
| 284 | loss] miss |
| 299 | you'l make them smart] they showld bear part |
| 304 | fortune] fortunes |
| 308 | mirth] sport |
| 318 | my eyes how] mine eyes why |
| 352 | *not in H*] Ru: |
| 365 | as] are |
| 366 | as] like |
| 369 | as] like |
| 376 | I will] will I |
| 390 | Come] Fly |
| 392 | then] when |
| 397 | this subtile] the cruell |
| 401 | that wee] wee doe |
| 402 | time] while |
| 411 | lett] lett's |
| 414 | *Venus, and Cupid*] Venus, and Cupid apeering / in the clowds |
| 427 | *thy powre a feeler bee*] of thy might feelers bee |
| 431 | *butt ... butt*] w^th ... for |
| 437 | *and waile, and weepe*] and sigh, and wayle, and weepe |
| 444 | *thy*] thine |
| 451 | *reject*] neglect |
| 456 | *they*] theyr |
| 459 | *yett shall they harme*] yett all shall harme |
| 462 | *this*] thy; $] *not in P* |
| 463 | $] *not in P* |

[Act Two]

| | |
|---|---|
| 4 | and a forester] a Forester |
| 6 | My] Mee |

| 66 | deere] sweet |
|----|----|
| 67 | who] that |
| 71 | from lyfe from joy] from ioy, from lyfe |
| 73 | gave] giues |
| 75 | grievd] griefe |
| 81 | bond] band |
| 123 | are] bee |
| 124 | though] they |
| 150 | a modest] an honest |
| 154 | brings] giues |
| 184 | nay never] you need nott |
| 192 | did] doe |
| 204 | lingring] longing |
| 211 | promises some joy] lott doth promise good |
| 231 | I may] must I |
| 236 | bad] nott |
| 239 | what] how |
| 266 | wishings] theyr wishings |
| 308 | *not in H*] butt who the freind is, I will quickly see; ex: |
| 311 | makes] make; *not in H*] ex; *not in H*] Philisses, Lissius |
| 337 | *on*] in; torment] torments |
| 338 | *for*] since |
| 341 | *nott*] ne're |
| 375 | *the love you gave*] your sorrow saue |
| 376 | *soe freely to her*] wᵗ gift of her loue |
| 382 | *still*] shall |
| 383 | *endles*] eternall |
| 384 | *Venus*] Venus Priests to Loue, or his prayes / the Goddess, and her Sonne / apeering in glory |
| 411 | *nor*] noe |
| 416 | *guard*] guide; $] *not in P* |
| 417 | $] *not in P* |

[Act Three]

| 1 | 3] third |
|----|----|
| 14 | now have] rather |
| 43 | yett] butt |
| 66 | yett joy most] would ioy more |
| 71 | att time] att that time |
| 74 | have] hath |
| 97 | butt] heere |
| 105 | tow] too |

| | |
|---|---|
| 110 | spring] break |
| 129 | heavns e're frame] bright heauns frame |
| 170 | a] one |
| 182 | w^ch now I'le mend the next that comes I'le have] the next that coms this fault I'le mend, and haue |
| 183 | nor] or |
| 191 | butt yett] yett still |
| 193 | hope revives] hopes remaines |
| 194 | doth like the spring-young bud] proues like the spring's young bud |
| 206 | allthough] though |
| 211 | you yo^r choyse] yo^r choyce |
| 216 | said] told mee |
| 224 | I] a |
| 245 | move] proue |
| 247 | les] lesser need |
| 264 | love] choyce |
| 299 | they will] and they'll |
| 300 | nay] and |
| 330 | now to] vnto |
| 346 | unfittest] vnfittingst |
| 351 | too] soe |
| 367 | who] that |
| 376 | distressd] desire |
| 379 | *not in H*] ex: |
| 386 | lyfe] self |
| 389 | nor] or |
| 392 | my owne reason] reason now, my |
| 418 | *ex*] *not in P* |
| 419 | *Venus*] Venus, and Cupid; *not in H*] |

Cu:
Is nott this pretty? who doth free remaine
of all this flock that waits nott in owr traine?
will you haue yett more sorrow? yett more woe?
shall I an other bitter arrow throwe?
speak if you will, my hand now knows the way
to make all harts your sacred power obay;

Venus
T'is pretty, butt 't'is nott enough, some are
to slightly wounded, they had greater share

in scorning vs. Lissius to soone is blest,
and w^t too little paine hath gott his rest
scarce had hee learn'd to sigh beefor hee gaind,
nor shed a teare, e're hee his hopes obtain'd,
this easy wining breeds vs more neglect
w^t out much paine, few doe lous ioys respect,
then are they sweetest purchas'd w^th felt griefe
to floods of woe sweet looks giues full reliefe
a world of sorrow is easd w^t one smile,
and hart wounds cure'd when kind words rule, the while
that foregon wailings in forgotten thought
shall wasted ly disdaind, once deerly bought
one gentle speach more heals a bleeding wound
then baulms of pleasure, if from other ground,
strike then to fauor him, and lett him gaine
his loue, and blis by Loues sweet pleasing paine;

       Cu:
That shalbee dunn, nor had hee this delight
beestow'd butt for his greater harme, and spite,
you shall beefor this Act bee ended see
hee doth sufficiently taste miserie
t'is farr more griefe from ioye to bee downe throwne
then ioy to bee aduanc'd to pleasurs throuene,

       Venus:
Lett mee see that, and I contented ame
such gratious fauor, wowld butt gett thy shame,

       Cu:
    Hee and others yett shall taste
    such distress as shall lay waste
    all ther hopes, theyr ioys, and liues,
    by such loss owr glory thriues;
    fear nott then all harts must yeeld
    when owr forces come to field; $

[Act Four]
1       4] Forth
33     condemne] accuse
35     to thee my torments] my torments to thee

| | |
|---|---|
| 47/48 | know / nott] doe nott know |
| 48 | if] whether |
| 51 | yett] butt |
| 60 | can] may |
| 69 | reguard] respect |
| 78 | my] mine |
| 90 | paine] death |
| 106 | els doe] things els |
| 109 | pitty] pittys |
| 128 | lett mee] may I |
| 144 | awhile aside] aside awhile |
| 160 | soe much] such blis |
| 198 | and bring blis] Mu: I'le know this |
| 206 | as tell] tell fierce |
| 212 | who] whom |
| 229 | ever more did] did more moue or |
| 237 | soune to bring] erly for |
| 239 | nott some made some false report of you] no ill tongues reported fauls of you |
| 260 | conquering, pourefull] powrfull, conquering |
| 266 | butt w$^t$ tortures] w$^{th}$ sharpe tortures |
| 267 | in] for |
| 268 | soe meete] in dispit |
| 269 | I oft should dy who knew nott souer from sweet] to punnish mee who knew nott day from night |
| 274 | flyes] hast's |
| 275 | w$^t$ justest meaning] wthout all bacenes |
| 296 | nott deepe] noe deeper |
| 311 | distrust] mistrust |
| 325 | from bee] from mee bee |
| 359 | by jelousie abus'de] w$^{th}$ iealousie confus'd |
| 372 | all care] dispaire |
| 395 | blis, bring noe doubts now] rest, nor bring new doubts |
| 397 | you] thee |
| 408 | still live] liue still |
| 417 | for] sport |
| 437 | doe] I |
| 443 | ny] by |
| 459 | doth] did |
| 469 | noe] ne're |
| 473 | waight] worth |

| | |
|---|---|
| 519 | unto mother] vnto my mother |
| 523 | *not in H*] ex: |
| 531 | come] I |
| 538 | must] shall |
| 540 | for mee I'me well agreed] I'me very well agreed |
| 542 | $] *not in P* |
| 543 | *Cupid*] and Cupid |
| 547 | *whilum*] lately |
| 559 | *all shall bee*] most shalbee |
| 561 | *musique*] The Musique, or song / of the Priests |
| 571 | *unto them*] to those harts |
| 576 | *cease*] Ease |
| 577 | *theyr yeelding harts*] humble harts |
| 579 | *a*] the |
| 581 | *make*] makes |
| 582 | *hands*] harts |
| 583 | $] *not in P* |
| 584 | *Cupid*] *not in P* |
| 589 | $] *not in P* |

[Act Five]

| | |
|---|---|
| 1 | 5] fift |
| 2 | Simena] and Simena |
| 20 | most] that |
| 26 | faile] miss |
| 32 | idly] madly |
| 45 | hard] ill |
| 47 | pleasurs] pleasure |
| 70 | spake] speak |
| 77 | tasteth of all] taste of endles |
| 82 | Mu: allas my deere, I must] Phi: Ô those words deny / or heere beehold your poore Philisses dy: |
| 82 | *not in H*] |

Mu:

I wowld I could deny the words I spake
when I did Rusticks mariage offer take
hopeles of you I gaue, my ill consent;
and wee contracted were w^ch I repent,
the time now curse, my toungue wish out w^ch gaue
mee to that clowne w^t whom I wed my graue;

84      *not in H*] and careles of my hart putt in your trust.
86      us] mee
87      still] binn
89      wee must] I shall
90      our] my
91      our] my; shall I] lett mee
93      I long since gave] long since I gaue
95      I will] will I
100     you] thee
105     lett mee bee] Ô lett mee
107     noe] nor
115     *not in H*]

            Phi:
I ame content your will shall bee obayd
till this lyfe chang, and I in earth am layd;

117     Phi: / w^t all my hart Si: butt what will you tow doe] Si: / I feare the wurst;
            butt what will you tow doe
119     *not in H*]

Dy? noe, wee goe for euer more to liue,
and to owr loues a sacrifies to giue

            Mu:
Our tears, and sorrows wee will offer ther,
and of owr offrings you shall wittnes beare,
the truest and most constant loue ther shall
in your sight end, and yett shall neuer fall,

            Phi:
such faith wee'll sacrifies as non can touch
w^th once reporting ther could bee too much

            Si:
I know nott what you meane, butt I'le along;

            Phi:
Lett's haste for heere com som may doe vs wrong; ex:

            Lissius, Dalina, Arcas,
                Rustick.

Li:
Arcas ist possible itt is to day?

Ar:
Itt is, Musella now can beare noe sway
Rustick shall haue her, hee's the blessed man
yett cannott gett her loue doe what hee can;

Da:
I'me sorry for Philisses; Li: truly soe am I
what then a lost loue is more misery;

Ru:
Lissius, Dalina, Arcas well mett to day
I must bee maried, pray bee nott away
butt see vs ioin'd, and after dine w$^t$ vs.
Wher is Philisses? I hope hee'll nott miss
this is a iolly day, this my day is.

Li:
I will nott faile; must wee nott fech the bride

Ru:
yes marry from her mothers wher w'abide, ex:

Da:
How well this busines doth beecom this man?
how well hee speaks word mariage? and began
in as good forme his nieghbours to inuite
as if hee studied maners, yett att night
I'le vndertake much mirth will nott apeere
in faire Musella, she'll showe heauy cheere;

Ar:
This t'is to looke soe high, and to dispise
all loues that rose nott pleasing in her eyes
now she that soar'de aloft all day, att night
must roost in a poore bush w$^t$ small delight;

Li:
I neuer knew this in her; butt t'is true
she lik'd nott of the loue proferd by you,

and for refusing that she could nott like
noe man aught blame her; or her mind dislike
butt you haue other qualities to moue
a iust dislike, you loue cross baites in loue:
I was beeholding to you when time was
butt I inioy her now: Da: com lett that pas,
Arcas in knowne, and I dare lay my lyfe
you haue bin meddling, and haue caus'd some stryfe
lately about Musella, butt take heed,
if itt proue soe parchance you'll want your meede,

       Li:
Iff itt bee found thou shallt noe longer liue
then while thou dost her satisfaction giue,

       Arcas:
Bee nott soe cholerick, till you know the truthe,
I haue left that foule error of my yuthe;

       Da:
Hardly I doubt for I saw you last day
sneaking, and priing all along this way,
t'was for noe goodnes that I'me very sure
for from a childe you cowld nott that endure; / ex:

       Climena, Lacon;

       Cli:
Lacon how fare you now? Musella must
this day bee marie'd is nott loue vniust
to suffer this distastefull mach to bee
against her choyse, and most against poore thee?

       La:
Nott against mee I neuer hop'd then how
doth Cupid wrong mee though she marry now,
yett thus is loue vniust to lett her wed
one who she neuer see's, butt wisheth dead,
soe I, although for her I oft haue dide
grieue for her loss, nott that I was deni'de;
I was vnworthy of her, and she farr
too worthy for this clowne; Ô she, the starr

of light, and beauty, must she, louely she?
bee mach'd to Rustick bace, vnworthy hee?

      Silluesta,
Musella to bee forc'de, and made to ty
her faith to one she hates, and still did fly:
itt showld nott bee, nor shall bee, noe noe I
will rescue her, or for her sake will dy,
haue you yett seene Musella heere to day?

      Cli:
Noe butt I heere she passed by this way
w^(th) faire Simeana both by breake of morne
w^(th) humble minds farr from theyr wounted scorne
to offer theyr last rights of maiden thought
to your chaste Mistress Venus now hath bought
theyr future time, how thinke you of this chang?
t'is better sure then still alone to range;

      Sill:
Itt's well you think soe, yett my thinks you can
make a cleane shift to liue w^(th) out a man; ex:

      Philisses Musella offring
        in the Temple of Loue;

Venus, and great Cupid heere
take owr sacrifices cleere
wher nott rights wee only giue
butt our harts wherin you liue,
those true reliques of firme loue
on yo^(r) allter still to moue,
wher non such; non soe sincere
to your triumph light did beare,
yours they liu'd while ioye had lyfe
dying, heere will end all strife
truer loue, or truer harts
neuer perish'd by your darts; /

Phi: to Venus;
Venus only Queene of Loue
take thes passions w^(ch) I proue

take thes tears, this vowe take
w<sup>ch</sup> my death shall perfect make
butt Musella my hart lou'd
her loss hath my ioye remou'd,
hers I liu'd, hers now I dy
crown'd w<sup>t</sup> fames eternity
thus your force shall glory haue
by Philisses louing graue;

  Mu: to Cupid;
Cupid Lord of loue, and harts,
king of thoughts, and louing smarts,
take thes offrings w<sup>ch</sup> I giue,
and my lyfe w<sup>ch</sup> new shall liue
Earthe to meane for such a truthe
shall in death haue lasting yuth,
noe decay, noe strife, noe fate
shall disturb that during state
Lyfe I offer to true loue
then accept this end I proue
Time non such did know, nor shall,
see soe willingly to fall,
In Philisses I did liue,
hee departing lyfe I giue;

  Phi: Mu:
Fame heerafter swell w<sup>th</sup> pride,
neuer loue thus liu'd, thus died;

  Phi:
Now my Musella, and in death butt mine
take this last farwell in w<sup>ch</sup> glorys shine,
Loue butt to you could neuer bee soe true
and death then lyfe I chuse since t'is for you,
my lyfe in you I had, my ioye, my blis,
and now for you, and by you my end is,
yett keepe your promise, euer happy bee
you may bee fortunate, and outliue mee,

  Mu:
That I beeleeue, when I doe thee outliue
shame shall insteed of fame my triumph giue;

I lou'd as firmly as thou could'st mee loue,
and can as willingly a deaths wound proue;
butt you forgett the promise you did make,
and since condition made, yo<sup>r</sup> self first brake
I ame releas'd, your word forgott, and broke
my hand shall first conclude that blessed stroke
vnto thy loue, and mine since itt is thus
farewell poore world lifs liuing bides in vs;

    Silluesta:
O hold your hands, I knew your minds, and haue
brought fitter meanes to wed you to yo<sup>r</sup> graue,
lett nott those hands bee spotted w<sup>th</sup> your blood
butt since your desteny is nott w<sup>th</sup> stood
drink this sweet potion then take leaue, and dy
imbracing thus you dead shall buried ly;

    Phi:
Freindship what greater blessing then thou art
can once desend into a mortall hart;
Siluesta freind, and priest doth now apeere
and as our loues, lett this thy deed shine cleere;

    Mu:
Neuer more fitt did freindship meet w<sup>th</sup> need
blest bee thy days, most blessed bee this deed;

    Sim:
What haue you kil'd them for this you must dy,

    Sill:
And dying for them, I dy happyly
who would outliue them? who would dying fly
that heere beheld loue, and loues tragidy,
butt first vpon loues alter lett's them lay
ther to abide till theyr new mariage day,
then lead mee to those who my lyfe must take
butt ere I dy some ioyfull hart shall ake; ex:

      Rustick w<sup>th</sup> sheapherds, and
      sheapherdesses redy to fetch
      the bride; / Ru:

Now is the time aproch'd; what think you now?
ist nott a trim day? what clowd showes a brow?
all att my fortune cleere, all smile wᵗ ioye
sheepe, goates, and Cattle glad that I inioye

        Da:
I neuer lou'd him, now I hate him fy
to thinke Musella by this beast must ly

        Ru:
Come lett's alonge, and quickly fetch the bride
mee thinks I long to haue her by my side
how now? what, stumble t'is nott fatall ist!

        Li:
good luck that you to his the grownd haue mist;

        Da:
A farr wurse signe then this itt doth foretell
butt yett haue courage all things may proue well,

        Ru:
Nay 'pray resolue mee I beegin to feare

        Li:
To feare; fy man can trips make hope forbeare
on, on, haue mettle will you now wax fainte
you who to vs a hapy lyfe must paint

        Ru:
This is nott all this morne a Cowe did low,
and that ill luck foretells I truly know,

        Da:
had she nott lost her caulf; Ru: her caulf fy noe
she had a dainty one as I will showe
att my returne, and they together cam,
and while she low'd the youngling suck'd her dam;

        Li:
And soe might hurt her wheratt she did cry
and for your help did low soe bitterly,

Ru:

Well come what will wee now may nott goe back

Da:

yes very well for her consent you lack;

Ru:

Come then, away, the pretious time doth wast

Simeana, Silluesta:

Sim:

Heere first my newes for itt may stay your haste,
yo$^r$ bride a bridegroome new, w$^{th}$ ioy hath gain'd,
and both for wedding bed a tombe obtain'd,
heere is the prist that marrie'd them to death,
and I the wittnes of theyr passing breath;

Ru:

How, is she married, and thus coussend mee,
and dead, and buried, how can all this bee?

Sill:

Fetch forth her mother, and you then shall know
the cause, and actor of this cruell blowe,

Li:

O heau'n was she too rare a prize for earth,
or were wee only hapy in her birth?

Da:

Only made rich inioying of her sight;
she gon, expect wee nothing butt sad night;

Fyllis:

What glory day did giue vs was to show
the vertu in her beauty seem'd to grow;

Cli:

Sweet loue, and freindship in her shined bright,
now dim'd ar both since darkned is her light

La:
Noe worthe did liue w<sup>ch</sup> in her had nott spring,
and she thus gon to her graue worth doth bring:


Ru:
I lik'd her well, butt she nere car'd for mee,
yett ame I sorry wee thus parted bee:


Sim:
Now heere of mee the mournfull'st end, of loue
that hart for hart could finde, and hartles proue: /
Philisses, and Musella had lou'd long,
and long vnknowne w<sup>ch</sup> bred ther only wrong,
att last discouer'd to theyr greatest ioy
this mach came cross theyr deere hopes to distroy,
for she (alas) dispairing of her blis
agreed to marry Rustick and to miss
noe cross, nor froward happ, w<sup>ch</sup> sure w<sup>t</sup> him
she must incounter if in this streame swim,
when this was dun they knew each others hart,
and by itt knew the thred w<sup>ch</sup> led to smart
they yett awhile reioiced in theyr loue
butt too too soone ther followd this remoue;
her mother hasty to conclud her will
apointed this sad day showld y<sup>t</sup> fulfill
w<sup>ch</sup> hath indeed fulfild a greater harme
then spite itt self could purchace w<sup>t</sup> her charme,
Musella finding that her giu'n consent
prou'd thus her hell, her soule did then lament
yett could nott gaine release butt that she must
looke as her mother lik'd (O force vniust),
yett soe itt was, and this procur'd her end
her mother growne her foe, and death her freind
her freind she chose; Philisses who did loue
as much as she, and she as much did proue
of loue, and paine as hee who felt all smart
vow'd since they might nott ioine butt rather part
they yett as most vnfained louers wowld
louingly dy, and soe firme louers showld;
vnto the Temple then they tooke theyr way,
together wept, together did they pray

together offred; now Silluesta you
must tell the haples end w^ch did ensue;

Sill:

And soe I will; ther loues they gaue, and liues
w^ch showld haue finisht bin by too sharp kniues
prouided closely those too to haue kild
who haue the world w^t loue and wounder fill'd
butt I came in, and hindred that sharp blow
though nott theyr wills more honor I did owe
to that (in loue alone) vnhapy paire
and brought theyr ends more quiett, and more faire,
a drink I gaue them made theyr soules to meete
w^ch in theyr clayie cages could nott, sweet
was theyr farewell while sorrow then vs'd art
to flatter ioye till they noe more should part,
theyr bodys likwise ioin'd by vs, ar place'd
vpon loues alter, nor from thence displac'd
by vow must bee till all you louers lay
this loue kild couple in theyr biding, clay,
this I haue dunn, and heere ame I to dy
if soe you please, and take itt willingly,

Ru:

Nay if she lou'd an other farwell she
I'me glad she by her death hath made me free

Li:

Is this your care, O clownish part, can you
for shame nott sorrow, when owr harts doe rue

Ru:

I'me free I care nott; Sill: the like is she then now

Ru:

she is for mee, and heere I disauow
all promises w^ch haue beetweene vs past
or haue bin made by her, att first, or last
to mee, and thus I doe release her, now
may I seeke one and please my self in loue
I'le non but such whose hart my loue shall moue; ex

Si:
she's hapy yett in death that she is free
from such a worthles creature; can this bee
such vertu should in her faire brest abound,
yett to bee ti'de wher noe worthe could bee found;

Li:
Thus haue your yeers your hapines outwourne,
and brought vntimely death to your first borne
can you indure this change, and heere vs say
your forced mariage brought her funerall day;

The Mo:
If the true grief I feele could bee exprest
by words, or sighs I showld my self detest
sorrow in hart, and soule doth only bide
and in them shall my woe bee iustly tride,
yett iustice doe I craue of this vild paire
w^{ch} were the founders of my endles care
Arcas first plotted itt w^t skillfull art
to ruin mee, and liuing eat my hart
hee told mee that Musella wantonly
did seeke Philisses loue, alas only
the speach of that did inly wound mee soe
as stay I could nott, nor the time lett goe
butt sent for her and forc'd her to consent
to finish that w^{ch} makes vs all lament,
and mee to dy, O mee w^{th} grief, and shame
that thus deseruedly I beare this blame;
Silluesta who theyr liues brought to an end
must also suffer, death alone my freind
shall mee release, thes things I hope you'l doe
w^{ch} dunn w^t age, and griefe I'le suffer too; /

Li:
Thes must, and shall bee dunn, and rites
parformd to theyr deer bodys, and theyr sprits
now to the Temple, and theyr bodys view
then giue thes, iudgment, biding ioye adue; ex:

The Forester;
Vnder a hedg all dead, to rest I lay'd

my body by dispaire wholy decay'd
when sleepe noe sooner did my eye lids close
butt haulf distracted w^t a dreame, I rose,
my thought I sawe Siluesta's faire hands ty'de
fast to a stake wher fire burnt in all pride
to kis w^t heat those most vnmached limms
wher vertu w^th her shape like habitts trims
her self w^t her; while she, alas faire she
should to those flames a sacred ofring bee,
this dreame parswaded mee to seeke her out,
and saue her, or to free mee from the doubt,
and ther I see her to the Temple goe
I'le after, and my lyfe att her feete throwe,

> The Temple, and the dead
> bodys on the Aulter; the
> sheapherds, and sheapherdesses
> casting flowers on them, & while
> Venus apeers in glory they sing
> this song; /

> Sorow now conclude thy hate
> more can nott bee dunn by fate
> Griefe abandon thy curst skill
> loue hath now found means to kill
> Louers heere example take;
> faith in loue showld neuer shake
> Only death hath force to part
> louers bodys by his dart
> butt theyr spiritts higher fly
> death can neuer make them dy
> butt ther soules w^t pure loues fire
> will to heaunly blis aspire; /

> The Priests

Now must wee iudg the'offenders for this deed
and each one punnish, thus itt is decreed,
Silluesta greatest in the fault must bend
her spiritt first vnto her owne sought end;
W^th flames of fire, as she w^th flames of zeale
did act this, she must now her last day seale,
death she procur'd, and for death, lyfe shall giue

Sill:
T'is iustice, thus by death a=new I liue;
my name by this will win eternity
for noe true hart will lett my meritt dy;

Fo:
I must inioye my death e're this bee dunn;
bright Venus I beeseech thee, and thy sunn
to looke on mee, your true, though luckles slaue
and view the hart my faith to firm loue gaue
saue sweet Siluesta, whose youth fram'd this deede
lett nott her Vertu, as offences speed,
or though by law she haue deseru'd this dombe
lett mee for her obtaine her pointed tombe,
I am more fitt to dy, and suffer farr
lyfe w$^t$ my sorrows are att endles warr,
besids the law allowes if one will dy
for others fault, his death may theyr lyfe buy,
lett mee first beg itt, pay itt then w$^{th}$ lyfe
death for her sake shall please, and end the stryfe

Venus,
Poore Forester thy loue deserueth more
for in thy hart true firmnes liu'd in store,
butt since you will her lyfe w$^{th}$ your lyfe buy
you must inioye death wee can non deny
that thus doe claime itt, she's by you made free,
and you for her must now my offring bee,

Fo:
Godess of harts you thus haue dun mee right
now shall my faith to honor you shine bright,

Sill:
Thanks is your due for sauing mee from death
did I nott rather hate then loue this breath,
yett shall this bounty gaine in my chast hart
to yo$^r$ desarts a kind, and thankfull part;

Fo:
death, hapy death, since she for whom I dy,
doth pitty mee, and weighs my constancy,

could I liue ages 't' would nott bee soe good
as now to dy w^th thanks giu'n for my blood.
Then farwell world; death wellcom as new lyfe,
Silluesta thanks mee, and giues mee this wyfe

Mo:
you sacred Priests parforme the latest due
to theyr dead bodys, and my ioys adue

Pri:
Rustick before vs heere disclaime the right
in lyfe was tyde to you now to her sprit,

Ru:
I loue noe sprites nor those affect nott mee
she lou'd Philisses, therfor she is free
were she aliue she were her owne to chuse
thus heer to her all claime I doe refuse

Pri:
Philisses of vs take Musella faire
wee ioine your hands, rise and abandon care
Venus hath causd this wounder for her glory,
and the Triumph of loues Victory;

Venus
Louers bee nott amas'd this is my deed
who could nott suffer yo^r deere harts to bleed
come forth, and ioy your faith hath bin thus tride
who truly would for true loues sake haue dyde,
Silluesta was my instrument ordaind
to kill, and saue her freinds by w^ch sh'hath gaind
immortall fame, and bands of firmest loue
in theyr kind brests wher true affections moue; /
Then all reioyce, and w^th a louing song
conclude the ioye hath bin kept downe to long; /

The mo:
Ioy now as great as was my former woe
shutts vp my speach from speaking what I owe
to all butt mine, for mine I ioye you are

and loue, and blis maintaine you from all care
pardon my fault, inioye, and blessed bee,
and children, and theyr childrens children see

      Mu:

pardon mee first who haue your sorrow wrought
then take owr thanks whose good yo$^r$ care hath brought,
Silluesta, next to you owr liues ar bound
for in you only was true freindship found

      Phi:

Mother, for soe your gyfte makes mee you call
receaue my humble thanks w$^{ch}$ euer shall
w$^t$ faithfull loue, and duty you attend
till death owr liues bring to a finall end,
and chast Siluesta take my lyfe when I
vngratefull proue to your worth=binding ty; /

      Sil:

Venus the prayse must haue whose loue to you
made her desend on earth, and your cares view
she sent the drink hath weded you to ioye,
and in ioye liue, and hapines inioye,
chaste loue relieu'd you in chaste loue still liue
and each to other true affections giue;
For you kind Forester, my chast loue take,
and know I grieue now only for your sake; ex

      Fo:

My ioys encrease she grieus now for my paine
ah hapy profferd lyfe w$^{ch}$ this can gaine,
Now shall I goe contented to my graue
though noe more hapines I euer haue; /

      Li:

Now lett mee ask my ioye w$^{ch}$ you must giue
Philisses, you may make mee dy, or liue
your Sister for my wyfe I seeke, alone
I craue butt her, and loue makes her mine owne;
tow bodys wee ar yett haue butt one hart
then rather ioine then lett such deere loue part;

Phi:

My self from bliss I sooner will deuide
then cross your loues; then henceforth thus abide
ioind in firm loue, and hapines attend
your days on earth vntill your liues doe end

Da:

Rustick, what think you is this calld faire play

Ru:

When Venus wills men can nott but obay
yett this I'le sweare I'me plainly cousend heere
butt t'is all one the bargaine may proue deere;

Da:

yett you haue nott lost all this wreath you see
is prou'd your garland, this faire willow tree
you now must reuerence, and brauly weare;

Ru:

I'le sooner dy then such disgrace to bear,
nay sooner marry, and that now I deeme
farr wurse then death though slighter in esteeme

Da

I wowld I might butt name the hapy mayde
showld bee your wyfe; Ru; yoᵣ self name and all's sayd

Da:

will you haue mee then? Ru: rather then my lyfe

Da:

In trothe agreed, I'le proue a louing wyfe

Ru:

T'is all I seek; now god giue you all ioye
and blest ame I who this sweet las inioy

Mu:

A good exchange, and euery one agreed,

Phi:
And as wee loue, and like soe lett vs speed;


Venus;
Now singe a song both priests, and all for ioye
and curst bee they your blessed states anoye


the song; /


[blank space]


Cupid;
Now my warrs in loue hath end
each one heere inioys theyr freind,
and soe all shall henceforth say
who my laws will still obay;
Mother now iudg Arcas fault,
all things els your will hath wrought; /


Venus;
Arcas think nott your villanny's forgott
butt since each now inioys, the better lott
doth fall to you; you heare must still abide
in thes faire plaines wher you shall neuer hide
the shame of faulshood printed in yo$^r$ face
nor hence remoue, butt in the self same place
you did committ that error foule and ill
ther your days left, w$^t$ griefe, and shame shall fill
your gnawing concience; this shalbee your dome


Ar:
O sacred Goddess lett my harts=sute come
beefor your eyes, rather ô lett mee dy
then heere remaine w$^{th}$ shame, and infamy,
this dying lyfe (alas) then death is wurse
nor can you lay on mee a greater curss


Venus;
your dombe is giu'n itt may nott bee recall'd
butt w$^{th}$ your trechery you must bee thrall'd;
And now all dutys ar parform'd to Loue

looke y$^t$ noe more owr powres by scorn you moue
butt bee the treasures of loues lasting glory,
and I your Princeses Crownd w$^t$ Victory; /

       Ar:
Thus still is sinn rewarded w$^{th}$ all shame,
and soe lett all bee that deserue like blame,
I haue offended in the bacest kind
and more ill doe deserue then ill can find
I traitor was to Loue, and to my loue
those who shall thus offend, like mee, shame proue; $ ex:

Finis

# PART II

## JANE CAVENDISH (1621–1669)
## and ELIZABETH BRACKLEY (1626–1663)

# Introduction

## Life and Works

Jane Cavendish (1621–1669) and Elizabeth Brackley (1626–1663) were born into one of the wealthiest families in northern England. Their great-grandmother was Bess of Hardwick, who, over several marriages, amassed enormous wealth and became one of the highest-ranking nobles in the country.[1] The daughters of William Cavendish, the Marquis (later Duke) of Newcastle (1593–1676), and Elizabeth Bassett (1594–1643),[2] Cavendish and Brackley were also the stepdaughters, after their mother's death in 1643, of Margaret Cavendish (*née* Lucas), who married their father in 1645 and whose many plays, scientific treatises, and other literary works continue to be read and studied.[3] Cavendish and Brackley had a sister, Frances (?–1678), and two brothers, Charles, Viscount Mansfield (1626?–1659), and Henry (1630–1691), who became Viscount Mansfield after Charles's death in 1659, the Earl of Ogle in 1665, and second Duke of Newcastle in 1676. In 1641, Elizabeth married John Egerton, Viscount Brackley (later the Earl of Bridgewater).[4] Margaret Cavendish reports that Brackley lived with her family for some time after the marriage on account of her young age.[5] Brackley appears to have still been living with the family at the outbreak of the English Civil War in 1642, and likely remained with her sisters at Welbeck Abbey through 1644–1645, when she and Jane Cavendish are thought to have written *A Pastorall* and *The concealed Fansyes*.[6]

---

1. See Elizabeth Goldring, "Talbot [*née* Hardwick], Elizabeth [Bess; *called* Bess of Hardwick], countess of Shrewsbury (1527?–1608)," *ODNB*.

2. For biographical information on Jane Cavendish, see Jennet Humphreys, rev. Sean Kelsey, "Cheyne, Lady Jane (1620/21–1669)," *ODNB*; on Elizabeth Brackley, see Betty S. Travitsky, "Egerton [*née* Cavendish], Elizabeth, countess of Bridgewater (1626–1663)," *ODNB*; and on William Cavendish, see Lynn Hulse, "Cavendish, William, first duke of Newcastle upon Tyne (*bap.* 1593, *d.* 1676)," *ODNB*.

3. See James Fitzmaurice, "Cavendish [*née* Lucas], Margaret, duchess of Newcastle upon Tyne (1623?–1673)," *ODNB*.

4. See Francis Espinasse, "Egerton, John, second earl of Bridgewater (1623–1686)," *ODNB*. Like Cavendish and Brackley's family, Egerton's family had strong literary interests. Egerton himself acted in John Milton's *Comus* (1634), which was written for performance at Ludlow Castle. The Egerton family also fostered women's involvement in household productions; Lady Alice Egerton, John Egerton's grandmother, devised an entertainment for Queen Elizabeth in 1602 at her house at Harefield. See Sara Mueller, "Domestic Work in Progress Entertainments," in *Working Subjects in Early Modern English Drama*, ed. Michelle M. Dowd and Natasha Korda (Farnham, UK: Ashgate, 2011), 145–59 (155–59).

5. Margaret Cavendish, *The Life of the Thrice Noble, High, and Puissant Prince William Cavendish, Duke, Marquess, and Earl of Newcastle* (London: A. Maxwell, 1667), 95.

6. According to Mary-Louise Coolahan, "the poetry spans a period encompassing events from 1635 up to at least 1648, although the quantity of poems concerned with Newcastle's exile and 'Sister

Cavendish and Brackley's upbringing was privileged not just because of their family's wealth, but also because they were well educated and had a father who encouraged their literary interests.[7] Newcastle himself was a noted theatrical patron and writer, and his positive influence on his daughters' writing is explicitly acknowleged in their dedications of their work to him and, more generally, in the works themselves; both *The concealed Fansyes* and *A Pastorall* are structured around his absence and express longing for his return.[8] The Bodleian manuscript of their writings, entitled *POEMS SONGS a PASTORALL AND a PLAY by the R*[t] *Hon*[ble] *the Lady Jane Cavendish and Lady Elizabeth Brackley*, features numerous tributes to their father, beginning with a poem by Cavendish titled "The Greate Example":

> My Lord.
> You are the Accademy of all trueth,
> And our next worlds greate Example, that's youth,
> Good natures quinticence, you are, all knowes;
> And by your happy sword, conquer'd, your foes.
> For courage, witt, and Judgement, this is true,
> With natures perfect frame, 'tis onely you:
> This Carrecter of trueth, none can but see,
> 'Tis Newcastle's Excellence; none but hee.[9]

Cavendish conceives of her father as her "example," and in her writing seeks to emulate him. While Cavendish and Brackley's works highlight the influence of their father, their mother, who died not long before their plays were written, is

---

Brackley' … locate the volume predominantly within the mid-1640s." "Presentation Volume of Jane Cavendish's Poetry," in Millman and Wright, *Early Modern Women's Manuscript Poetry*, 87–89 (87).

7. Newcastle's efforts to train his children to write witty verse is noted in Jane Milling, "Siege and Cipher: The Closet Drama of the Cavendish Sisters," *Women's History Review* 6, no. 3 (1997): 411–26 (414). Betty S. Travitsky observes that their education lacked the rigor of other famously well-educated women, like Sir Thomas More's children: "No one would—or should—equate the exercises Cavendish designed for his young children with the Latin compositions assigned the young More children or suggest that the worldly Cavendish was creator of a humanist academy on the austere model of More's home in Chelsea, but such manuscript witnesses attest to his pride in and nurturing of his very young children, and particularly to his fostering their interest in letters and their efforts at composition." *Subordination and Authorship in Early Modern England: The Case of Elizabeth Cavendish Egerton and Her "Loose Papers"* (Tempe: Arizona Center for Medieval and Renaissance Studies, 1999), 29.

8. Newcastle was patron to playwrights such as Ben Jonson, James Shirley, William Davenant, and others. He also wrote plays himself, including a masque for his daughters that he called a "Christmas toye." See *Dramatic Works by William Cavendish*, ed. Lynn Hulse (Oxford: Oxford University Press, 1996), 26–27.

9. Rawlinson MS Poet. 16, 3.

commemorated in a short elegy that is included in their poems.[10] Interestingly, Cavendish and Brackley's plays do not mention their mother, nor do any of their central female characters have a mother.

Cavendish and Brackley's plays reflect the benefits of their education and the environment in which they were raised. As Lisa Hopkins puts it, "The sisters were thus part of an extended family circle with copious and intimate knowledge of the dramatic productions and conventions of the thirty or so years preceding the English Civil War."[11] Accordingly, their works show a familiarity with genres popular in the commercial theater and at court. *A Pastorall* is written as a masque, a form of drama that flourished at court throughout the first half of the seventeenth century.[12] As noted above in the general introduction, Newcastle hosted King Charles I on two occasions and for those visits commissioned masques from Ben Jonson, a leading masque writer at court.[13] *The concealed Fansyes* also uses elements of the masque. Moreover, it includes references to the works of Shakespeare and other dramatists, making it likely that Cavendish and Brackley read plays in print as well as seeing plays performed in their own or others' households.[14] The sisters' two plays, along with over eighty short poems, are collected in two extant manuscript books, one now in the Bodleian Library at the University of Oxford, and the other in the Beinecke Rare Book and Manuscript Library at Yale University.[15] Their collaborative writing appears to have taken place when they were living together, though both of them continued to write after their marriages.[16]

10. Rawlinson MS Poet. 16, 31.

11. Lisa Hopkins, "Judith Shakespeare's Reading: Teaching *The Concealed Fancies*," *Shakespeare Quarterly* 47, no. 4 (1996): 396–406 (399).

12. For a detailed definition of masque, see below, Content and Analysis section of *A Pastorall*.

13. The masques were *The King's Entertainment at Welbeck* (1633) and *Love's Welcome at Bolsover* (1634). Newcastle used these lavish entertainments as many courtiers did: to gain advantage at court. His efforts bore fruit, and in 1638, he became a member of the privy council and governor to Charles I's son, the future Charles II. See Hulse, "Cavendish, William," for further details on Newcastle's attempts in the 1630s to win favor at court.

14. Hopkins, "Judith Shakespeare's Reading," 399–405.

15. Based upon evidence from the Beinecke manuscript, Alexandra G. Bennett and Mary-Louise Coolahan argue that Jane Cavendish was the sole author of the poems. See Bennett, "'Now Let My Language Speake': The Authorship, Rewriting, and Audience(s) of Jane Cavendish and Elizabeth Brackley," *Early Modern Literary Studies* 11, no. 2 (2005): 1–13 (6); Coolahan, "Presentation Volume," 87. Ezell says of the Bodleian manuscript that since "few of the pieces are specifically attributed … the volume suggests a collaborative and cooperative effort rather than pieces of individual workmanship." "To Be Your Daughter in Your Pen," 284.

16. Jane Cavendish's elegy on her sister Elizabeth's death is printed in Germaine Greer et al., eds., *Kissing the Rod: An Anthology of 17th Century Women's Verse* (New York: Farrar Straus Giroux, 1988), 108–9. Travitsky, *Subordination and Authorship*, 174–207, gives transcriptions of Elizabeth Brackley's

During the English Civil War (1642–1651), Cavendish and Brackley found themselves without parental supervision in a castle that was, at different times, besieged, occupied, or captured. Paradoxically, it was this circumstance that allowed the sisters the time and the freedom to write plays that reimagined their own lives and to think through issues as varied as the roles of women in marriage, class politics, the tragedies of war, courtship, witch controversies, and familial and sisterly bonds.[17] The Civil War is thus an essential context for understanding Cavendish and Brackley's plays. The war was fought between the Royalists and the Parliamentarians, primarily about the role of parliament in governance. The Parliamentarians advocated for an increased, formalized role of an elected parliament in the governance of the country, whereas the Royalists sought to protect the power of the monarch. The war saw tens of thousands of deaths and, shockingly, led to the execution of Charles I in 1649. Newcastle was captain general of the king's northern forces and, with his two sons, fought actively until 1644. After suffering defeat at the Battle of Marston Moor in July, 1644, Newcastle went into exile, first in Hamburg, then Antwerp, and finally in Paris at the court of Queen Henrietta Maria.[18] Cavendish and Brackley, along with their younger sister Frances, remained at the family home of Welbeck Abbey. A letter from Jane Cavendish establishes that at some point in the mid-1640s, she and possibly her sisters also spent time at Ashridge, a royal residence that belonged to the Egerton family.[19] Welbeck was captured on August 2, 1644, by the Parliamentarians under the Earl of Manchester, who vowed that Newcastle's daughters would remain safe.[20] Welbeck was briefly recaptured by the Royalists in 1645 and then finally

---

"Loose Papers" (Brackley, due to the complicated nature of aristocratic naming conventions, was also known as Elizabeth Cavendish Egerton and, after 1649, the Countess of Bridgewater). The "Loose Papers" were compiled after Brackley's death by her husband and contain short poems and prayers. Three manuscript copies of the "Loose Papers" are extant; Travitsky transcribes one of two versions held by the Huntington Library (Ellesmere MS 8377; the other copy is Ellesmere MS 8376). The third manuscript of the "Loose Papers" is held by the British Library (BL MS Egerton 607). For more on Brackley's "Loose Papers," see below.

17. Findlay, *Playing Spaces*, 53. Sarah C. E. Ross, *Women, Poetry, and Politics in Seventeenth-Century Britain* (Oxford: Oxford University Press, 2015), 102, notes that Cavendish and Brackley's situation at Welbeck was not unique; other gentlewomen of this period, like Lady Fanshawe, Lady Halkett, and Lady Brilliana Harley, took charge of their family's houses during the war. Deanne Williams, *Shakespeare and the Performance of Girlhood* (London: Palgrave Macmillan, 2014), 189, argues that alongside these increased opportunities and responsibilities that came with the Civil War, Cavendish and Brackley also experienced a protracted girlhood because of their circumstances.

18. Hulse, "Cavendish, William," *ODNB*.

19. Huntington Library, Ellesmere MS 11143, quoted in Travitsky, *Subordination and Authorship*, 64–65, and Greer et al., *Kissing the Rod*, 107. Further examples of letters written by Jane Cavendish can be found in the University of Nottingham's Portland Collection MSS Pw 1/86–90.

20. Edward Montagu, Earl of Manchester to Committee of both kingdoms, August 6, 1644, in *Calendar of State Papers Domestic Series of the Reign of Charles I, 1625–1649*, ed. William Douglas Hamilton

surrendered at the end of the year, at which time the family was forced to leave the house.[21]

In addition to the poems and plays preserved in the Bodleian and Beinecke manuscripts, letters written by Jane Cavendish during this period offer insight into what life at Welbeck was like under siege and while Newcastle was in exile. We do know that the family was in communication with one another; indeed, Cavendish wrote a poem about receiving a letter from her father.[22] The sisters were active in the war cause and took pains to do what they could to preserve their family's estate, including "salvaging the family plate."[23] The paintings at Welbeck Abbey, including one by Van Dyck, were reportedly saved by Cavendish.[24] She relayed "military information to the King's commanders at Oxford" on behalf of her father,[25] sold her jewels to raise cash, and sent Newcastle 1,000 pounds while he was in exile.[26]

After the war, Jane Cavendish married Charles Cheyne, who became Viscount of Newhaven in 1654. Madeline Dewhurst's analysis of family letters from this period shows that Cavendish, like her character Luceny in *The concealed Fansyes*, chose her own husband and also had to advocate for the marriage because Newcastle did not think Cheyne was wealthy enough for her.[27] In a letter from 1656, Lady Jane Cheyne, as Cavendish was known after her marriage, gives a glimpse of a happy marriage: "Did I not know my self Maried, I should think by what hee writs, that hee was still a woer, which puts mee in mind of your woords, for you tould mee it would bee allwayes so, beeing the nature of the person."[28] According to the *ODNB*, the couple lived in the former royal palace at Chelsea, which was purchased with her dowry.[29] Cheyne had three children and it is known

---

(London: Eyre & Spottiswoode, 1888), 19:404–5.

21. For a full account of the events that saw the family lose both Welbeck and Bolsover, see Nathan Comfort Starr, "*The Concealed Fansyes*: A Play by Lady Jane Cavendish and Lady Elizabeth Brackley," *PMLA* 46, no. 3 (1931): 802–38 (804).

22. Rawlinson MS Poet. 16, 29. This manuscript is the copy-text for the present edition of Cavendish and Brackley's plays.

23. University of Nottingham, Portland Collection, Pw 1/367, 368, quoted in Travitsky, *Subordination and Authorship*, 64n115.

24. Margaret Cavendish, *Life of William Cavendish*, 91.

25. Travitsky, *Subordination and Authorship*, 64, 115. See Edward Nicholas to the Earl of Forth, Lord General of his Majesty's Army, April 21, 1644, in Hamilton, *Calendar of State Papers*, 19:131.

26. Margaret Cavendish, *Life of William Cavendish*, 90.

27. Madeline Dewhurst, "True Relations: Piecing Together a Family Divided by War," *Lives and Letters* 2, no. 1 (2010): 1–20 (9–10).

28. University of Nottingham Portland MS Pw 1/88, quoted in Greer et al., *Kissing the Rod*, 108.

29. Humphreys, rev. Kelsey, "Cheyne, Lady Jane."

that she paid to have the roof of Chelsea church replaced.[30] Elizabeth Brackley, or Elizabeth Cavendish Egerton as she became known after her marriage, seems to have been happily married as well. On her death, Brackley's husband expressed great grief at her loss and never remarried.[31]

Dewhurst's discussion of the Cavendish family letters after the mid-1640s (when the Bodleian and Beinecke manuscripts are thought to have been transcribed) shows that there were significant tensions between Newcastle and his children, and that the idealized portrait Cavendish and Brackley present of their father in their plays and poems does not continue into the 1650s.[32] The sisters, however, appear to have remained very close. When Brackley died in 1663 (in premature labor in prison, where she had joined her husband, who was being held on a dueling charge), Cavendish wrote a moving elegy, "On the death of my Deare Sister the Countesse of Bridgewater."[33] Jane Cavendish herself died six years later, in 1669.

While there is no evidence to suggest that after their marriages the sisters had the kind of opportunity their circumstances in 1644–1645 offered them to write plays together, there is evidence that both continued to write and were recognized for their literary interests and abilities. Jane Cavendish's tomb at All Saints Church in Chelsea features a sculpture of her by Bernini in which she is depicted, as Bennett says, "as a young woman reclining on one elbow with an open book before her while a scroll below lists her many virtues as 'the most pious and devout Heroine, made famous not so much by the long line of her ancestry, as by her own virtues.'"[34] Moreover, a poem written after her death by Thomas Lawrence claims that poetry was "an Art she knew and Practised so well / Her Modesty alone could it excell."[35] Lawrence's poem was published with a sermon by Adam Littleton, delivered at Cavendish's funeral, which states that "she took,

---

30. Humphreys, rev. Kelsey, "Cheyne, Lady Jane."

31. Francis Espinasse, rev. Louis A. Knafla, "Egerton, John, second earl of Bridgewater (1623–1686)," *ODNB*.

32. Dewhurst, "True Relations," 9–12. In a letter to her brother Charles, preserved in manuscript at the University of Nottingham (Pw 1/89) and transcribed by Dewhurst, Jane Cavendish writes, "the sattisfaction I receave when you are pleased to like any Expression in Mr Cheynes letter wherin your likeing & kind acseptance of them wee both acknowlidge is more then can bee deserved. I could wish you neere nighbours beeing confident you would both take much contentment in one an others companies" (12). Ann Hughes and Julie Sanders, "Disruptions and Evocations of Family amongst Royalist Exiles," in *Literatures of Exile in the English Revolution and its Aftermath, 1640–1690*, ed. Philip Major (Aldershot, UK: Ashgate, 2010), 45–63, give additional details from the postwar letters of the Cavendish family evidencing the tensions between the siblings and their father after his remarriage.

33. Huntington Library, Ellesmere MS 8353, quoted in Greer et al., *Kissing the Rod*, 118.

34. Bennett, "Now Let My Language Speake," 6.

35. "An Elegy on the Death of the Thrice Noble and Vertuous Lady the Lady Jane Cheyne, Eldest Daughter to William Duke of NEWCASTLE," bound with Adam Littleton, *A Sermon at the funeral of the Right Honourable the Lady Jane eldest daughter to His Grace, William, Duke of Newcastle, and*

when Young, special delight in her *Father's* Excellent Composures. And she hath left in Writing a considerable Stock of Excellent ones of Her own, ever spending the time that best pleased Her with her Pen."[36] Emily Smith notes that this passage demonstrates both that Cavendish "continued to write after her marriage" and that "her 'Stock of Excellent' works, which could include the plays written with Brackley, formed a canon of writings that continued to be read."[37]

Elizabeth Brackley also continued to write. Her husband collected her prose meditations and prayers and had them transcribed for her children under the title "True Coppies of certaine Loose Papers left by ye Right ho.ble Elizabeth Countesse of Bridgewater Collected and Transcribed together here since Her Death, Anno Dm. 1663." Three copies of the "Loose Papers" survive: two are at the Huntington Library and one is at the British Library. They have been transcribed by Betty Travitsky and include forty-four compositions, most of which Travitsky says "seem to have been composed at moments of stress."[38] Travitsky further states that "the tone is uniformly sober, and religious concerns permeate almost every section. More than half deal directly with personal, domestic or interpersonal concerns."[39] The "Loose Papers" reveal anxieties about childbirth, motherhood, and expressions of loss at the deaths of her infant children; they do not contain any dramatic works. Brackley also wrote "Devine Meditations upon every particular Chapter in the Bible," including a commentary on Genesis that finds Adam to be as guilty of sin as Eve. Like her "Loose Papers," these "Devine Meditations" survive in multiple manuscripts.[40] While relatively few documents about Cavendish and Brackley are extant or have been discovered from the years after their marriages, what does remain speaks to the importance of writing to their lives and raises the fascinating possibility that they may have written more dramatic literature after the war ended.

## The Beinecke and Bodleian Manuscripts Containing the Dramatic Works of Cavendish and Brackley

The dramatic works of Cavendish and Brackley are preserved in two manuscripts, one held at the Beinecke Library at Yale (Osborn MS b.233) and the other at the

---

*wife to the Honourable Charles Cheyne, Esq, at Chelsey, Novem. I, being All-Saints day* (London: John Maycock, 1669), no pagination.

36. Littleton, *Sermon*, 45.

37. Emily Smith, "The Local Popularity of *The Concealed Fansyes*," *Notes and Queries* 53, no. 2 (2006): 189–93 (190).

38. Travitsky, *Subordination and Authorship*, 158.

39. Travitsky, *Subordination and Authorship*, 158.

40. Travitsky, *Subordination and Authorship*, 136–46, describes the manuscripts in which the "Devine Meditations" are preserved.

Bodleian Library at Oxford (Rawlinson MS Poet. 16). The two volumes contain much of the same material, and among these shared texts there are few substantial variants. Despite these similarities, however, there are significant differences between the manuscripts, which have a bearing on date and on authorship. The Beinecke manuscript includes two poems that are not in the Bodleian manuscript. One is a dedication of the volume by Jane Cavendish to her father; the other, at the end of the manuscript, is an unsigned poem praising Cavendish herself as the author.[41] The Bodleian manuscript, on the other hand, contains significantly more of Cavendish and Brackley's works, including everything contained in the Beinecke manuscript save for the two poems mentioned above, eight additional poems, and the unique text of *The concealed Fansyes*.[42] It also includes a title page that ascribes authorship of the volume to both sisters. To complicate matters, both manuscripts are widely considered to be written not in the hand of the authors, but in the hand of John Rolleston, their father's secretary. The relationship between these two manuscripts, the attribution of their contents to one or both of the sisters, and the agency of the scribe in copying their work have been the subject of much scholarly discussion.

The Bodleian manuscript is part of a collection given to the library in 1755 by Richard Rawlinson. It is bound in black leather and has the initials "W N" (albeit upside down), separated by a fleuron, tooled in gold on the front and back covers (see Figure 5). It consists of 176 folio pages of which 24 are blank and is written in an elegant fashion on a single stock of paper. The manuscript features two tables of contents, neither of which is in the hand of the principal scribe, John Rolleston. One of these is at the beginning of the volume, preceding the title page, and the other is at the end. The table of contents at the beginning is incomplete. Peter Beal ascribes the complete table of contents at the end of the volume to John Egerton, Elizabeth Brackley's husband, who we know took an interest in compiling and editing her writings after her death in 1663.[43] The manuscript is

---

41. Osborn MS b.233, 1, 77. Elizabeth Clarke suggests that John Rolleston, the likely scribe of both manuscript versions of Cavendish and Brackley's works, is the author of the unsigned poem that praises Jane Cavendish. "The Garrisoned Muse: Women's Use of the Religious Lyric in the Civil War Period," in *The English Civil Wars in the Literary Imagination*, ed. Claude J. Summers and Ted-Larry Pebworth (Columbia: University of Missouri Press, 1999), 130–43 (133).

42. The additional poems are "The Angry Curs" (25), a song with the first line "A man and a wife once they marry" (26), "The discoursive Ghost" (26), "The speaking Glass" (42), "Loves Conflict" (45), "On my Worthy freind M^r Richard Pypes" (44), "On my Worthy freind M^r Haslewood" (44), and "Hopes Still" (45). Except for these additional works, the poems are in almost exactly the same order in the two manuscripts, with the poem "Misfortunes Weather Glass" (31) in the Beinecke manuscript renamed "Life's weather Glass" (27) in the Bodleian manuscript. The poems beginning on page 42 of the Bodleian manuscript continue on from where the poems in the Beinecke manuscript stop.

43. Peter Beal, "Jane Cheyne and Elizabeth Egerton," in *Catalogue of English Literary Manuscripts 1450–1700*, http://www.celm-ms.org.uk/introductions/CheyneJaneEgertonElizabeth.html, accessed May 6, 2018. See also Mary-Louise Coolahan, "Literary Memorialization and the Posthumous

neatly and elaborately ruled, is paginated consecutively, and has been described by Margaret Ezell as "handsomely produced," "neatly and formally designed," and showing "great care" in the preservation of the Cavendish sisters' writings.[44] It is commonly thought to be a presentation volume. The present edition prints the plays in the order in which they appear in the Bodleian manuscript, with *A Pastorall* appearing before *The concealed Fansyes.*

The Beinecke manuscript is less formal than the Bodleian manuscript and may be incomplete. It, too, is handsomely bound in black leather and features gilt decoration on its front cover, but has no table of contents and no title page (see Figure 6). Like the Bodleian manuscript, each page is neatly and elaborately ruled and the volume is paginated consecutively, including blank pages. The volume has seventy-four folio pages, including eleven blank pages. Mary-Louise Coolahan has suggested that it appears to have been designed as a presentation copy, but was not completed as planned.[45] It also has more corrections than the Bodleian manuscript, although scholars differ on their extent and nature.[46]

It is possible that the Beinecke manuscript represents an earlier version of Cavendish and Brackley's work. Given that the paper used in the Bodleian and Beinecke manuscripts is not from the same stock, it is likely that the manuscripts were written at different times.[47] As mentioned above, John Rolleston, the Duke of Newcastle's secretary, is widely thought to have copied both the Bodleian and Beinecke manuscripts; these claims are substantiated by Lynn Hulse's paleographic analysis of Rolleston's hand.[48] Betty Travitsky is less confident than Hulse that Rolleston penned both volumes, citing the differences in the neatness of the respective manuscripts and the canceled lines and blank pages of the Beinecke, but Hulse notes that Rolleston's hand shows "considerable variation of style" over his career and that he "constantly developed his skill as a penman."[49] Although Marion Wynne-Davies and Alexandra Bennett have suggested that the manuscripts could

Construction of Female Authorship," in *The Arts of Remembrance in Early Modern England: Memorial Cultures of the Post Reformation,* ed. Andrew Gordon and Thomas Rist (Farnham, UK: Ashgate, 2013), 161–76 (167).

44. Ezell, "To Be Your Daughter in Your Pen," 282, 294.

45. Coolahan, "Presentation Volume," 87–88, gives a full description of the blank pages.

46. Travitsky notes that it has "many cancelled lines and contains many blank pages" (*Subordination and Authorship,* 54), while Coolahan finds "very few emendations or deletions" ("Presentation Volume," 88). Alexandra Bennett, ed., *The Collected Works of Jane Cavendish* (London: Routledge, 2018), 14–15, 134n2, describes both the Beinecke and Bodleian manuscripts. In addition to noting many of the characteristics described in the present edition, Bennett also determines that the Bodleian manuscript originally had "medium blue silk ribbons to tie it closed, of which only nubs remain" (134n2).

47. Bennett, "Now Let My Language Speake," 11.

48. Kelliher, "The Newcastle Manuscript," 153, 171n55; Hulse, "King's Entertainment," 361. Rolleston (1597?–1681) was employed by the Cavendish household for most of his long life.

49. Travitsky, *Subordination and Authorship,* 53n101; Hulse, "King's Entertainment," 361, 364.

Figure 5. Front cover of the Bodleian manuscript, *POEMS SONGS a PASTORALL AND a PLAY by the R$^t$ Hon$^{ble}$ the Lady Jane Cavendish and Lady Elizabeth Brackley*. Rawlinson MS Poet. 16. © By permission of the Bodleian Library, University of Oxford.

be in Jane Cavendish's hand, Hulse's description of the characteristic features of Rolleston's hand matches both the Bodleian and Beinecke manuscripts, making it likelier that Rolleston was the scribe of both.[50]

Despite their physical and textual similarities, the Bodleian and Beinecke manuscripts present the Cavendish sisters' authorship in significantly different ways. Jane Cavendish's dedication of the Beinecke volume to her father implies that she is the sole author of the poems: "As nature ownes my creation from you, & my selfe my / Education; soe deuty invites mee to dedicate my workes / to you."[51] Furthermore, as Bennett points out, "though there are numerous poems in both manuscripts addressed to, and written about, Cavendish family members both living and dead, not a single poem is written to or about Jane herself."[52] By contrast, the numerous poems written to Elizabeth Brackley place her in the position of reader, rather than author. The commendatory poem on Cavendish's authorship at the end of the Beinecke volume reinforces this impression that the manuscript is the work of a single writer. And yet the volume also contains a version of the coauthored masque *A Pastorall*, which ascribes individual scenes of the entertainment to one of the two sisters ("J.C." or "E.B."), thus complicating the claim made in Cavendish's dedication to their father that the volume is a compilation of "my workes."

The Bodleian manuscript presents the authorship of the poems and the plays differently. It lacks Cavendish's dedication to her father, and its title page asserts that the whole volume is collaborative: *POEMS SONGS a PASTORALL*

---

50. Hulse, "King's Entertainment," 359–64; Bennett, "Now Let My Language Speake," 5; and Marion Wynne-Davies, "My Fine Delitive Tomb: Liberating 'Sisterly' Voices During the Civil War," in *Female Communities, 1600–1800*, ed. Rebecca D'Monté and Nicole Pohl (London: Macmillan, 2000), 111–28 (113, 127). It is unclear whether Rolleston was on the continent with Newcastle or at Welbeck with Cavendish and Brackley when *The concealed Fansyes* and *A Pastorall* were written (Jane Cavendish does not list Rolleston among the domestic staff at Welbeck in her poem "The Carecter" [Rawlinson MS Poet. 16, 23]). However, Hulse writes that it is "not impossible that both manuscripts … were copied sometime later," and that "Rolleston's hand cannot be traced in Newcastle's papers dating from his sixteen years in exile." "King's Entertainment," 370. Rolleston may well have been at Welbeck throughout the war. He was, in any event, active as a scribe of dramatic entertainments for Cavendish and his circle before and after the period when *A Pastorall* and *The concealed Fansyes* are thought to have been written. Included among his manuscripts are Jonson's *King's Entertainment at Welbeck* and *Love's Welcome to Bolsover*, a transcription of the Duke of Newcastle's *Witts Triumvirate or the Philosopher* (a play intended to be performed before King Charles), and a play recently ascribed to Margaret Cavendish, the duke's second wife and prolific author and dramatist, titled *The Lotterie*. On these and other Rolleston manuscripts, see Kelliher, "The Newcastle Manuscript," and James Fitzmaurice, "'The Lotterie': A Transcription of a Play Probably by Margaret Cavendish," *Huntington Library Quarterly* 66, no. 1/2 (2003): 155–67. For further discussion of Rolleston's handwriting and career, see Hulse, *Dramatic Works by William Cavendish*.

51. Osborn MS b.233, no pagination.

52. Bennett, "Now Let My Language Speake," 6.

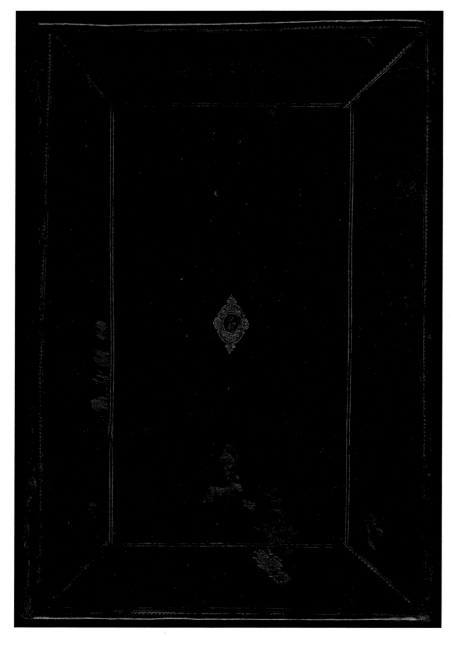

Figure 6. Front cover of the Beinecke manuscript. Osborn MS b.233. © By permission of the Beinecke Rare Book & Manuscript Library, Yale University.

*AND a PLAY by the R^t Hon^{ble} the Lady Jane Cavendish and Lady Elizabeth Brackley.*[53]
Yet there remain some inconsistencies in how authorship is ascribed. The joint
authorship of *A Pastorall*, for example, is signaled here as in the Beinecke manuscript by the initials "J.C." or "E.B." at individual scenes of the masque, but the text
of *The concealed Fansyes* does not follow this practice even though it is addressed
to the Duke of Newcastle in a distinctly collective voice: "My Lord / If that your
judgement doth approve of *wee* [emphasis added]."[54] This difference could suggest that the collaborative process behind *The concealed Fansyes* may not have
been the same as for *A Pastorall*, even though both works are, in Kelliher's terms,
"demonstrably joint enterprises."[55] Adding to the complexity of this primary evidence, some scholars have argued that Cavendish and Brackley's sister Frances
may have had a role in authoring the plays.[56] Given that both plays were conceived
for household performance and feature groups of three women (the witches in
the antemasque of *A Pastorall* and Cicilly, Sh., and Is. in *The concealed Fansyes*), it
certainly is possible that Frances, the youngest of the three Cavendish sisters, was
somehow involved in their creation.

Within the Bodleian manuscript itself there are notable differences between
how the two plays are presented on the page. *A Pastorall*, with its running title and authorial attributions of individual scenes differs, as noted above, from
*The concealed Fansyes*, which has none of these characteristics. Conversely, *The
concealed Fansyes* relies heavily on short forms of words such as "your," while *A
Pastorall* does not. The differences between the two plays are significant enough
to raise the question whether the copy texts used by Rolleston were transcribed by
different people (i.e., that *A Pastorall* was copied out by Cavendish and *The concealed Fansyes* by Brackley, or vice versa). Alternately, the plays could have been
copied at different times, in which case variations between them are evidence of
the scribe's evolving style. This claim is difficult to substantiate, particularly since
the same paper stock is used throughout the book (see Note on the Text, below).

Despite the differences between the Beinecke and Bodleian manuscripts
and the variations in scribal practice within the Bodleian manuscript itself, both
texts were clearly designed to be read. The characteristics of both manuscripts
indicate that attention is being paid to the reader's experience: the hand is mostly
very clear and neat, there are relatively few corrections or deletions, and generous amounts of white space are used to create pages that are elegant in design.

---

53. This is also noted by Ezell, "To Be Your Daughter in Your Pen," 284.

54. Rawlinson MS Poet. 16, 88.

55. Kelliher, "The Newcastle Manuscript," 153.

56. Dorothy Stevens, *The Limits of Eroticism in Post-Petrarchan Narrative: Conditional Pleasure from Spencer to Marvell* (Cambridge: Cambridge University Press, 1998), 146; and Jane Cavendish and Elizabeth Brackley, *A Pastorall, A Drama by Jane Cavendish and Elizabeth Brackley*, ed. Lynn Smith (San Antonio: Independent Scholars Press, 2011), 23.

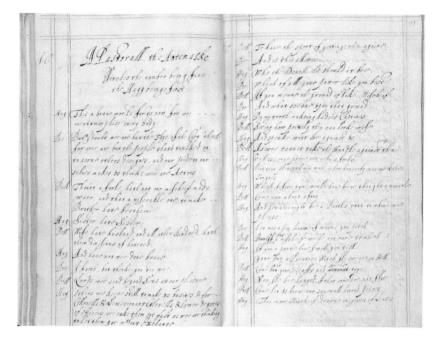

Figure 7. First two pages of *A Pastorall* in the Beinecke manuscript. Osborn MS b.233, pages 46–47. © By permission of the Beinecke Rare Book & Manuscript Library, Yale University.

Rolleston's careful ruling of the page organizes the text into distinct, readable components, delineating one poem from another and clarifying the structure of the dramatic works. Neither manuscript is a working copy or draft; both present finalized versions of the works, as is indicated by the very few variants in wording between the texts they share. Both volumes are durably bound and show care for the preservation and presentation of the poems and plays they contain. It is evident that Cavendish and Brackley wrote with a sense of purpose and audience: they were authors who had something to say and a desire to be heard.[57]

57. Ross, *Women, Poetry, and Politics*, 108, maps out the circulation of some of the sisters' poems, demonstrating that their readership certainly went beyond their family circle. See also Ezell, in "To Be Your Daughter in Your Pen," who discusses the extensive social network within which Cavendish and Brackley's poetry is positioned.

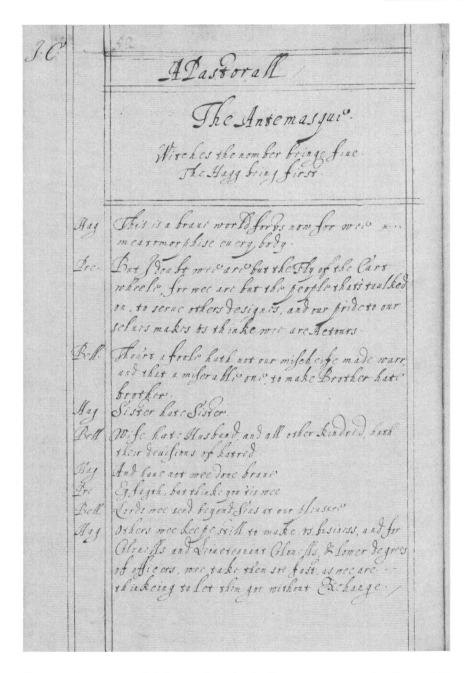

Figure 8. First page of *A Pastorall* in the Bodleian manuscript. Rawlinson MS Poet. 16, page 52. © By permission of the Bodleian Library, University of Oxford.

## *Content and Analysis of* A Pastorall

Jane Cavendish and Elizabeth Brackley explicitly call the text discussed here both a "pastorall" and a "masque," but the work inhabits these genres rather uncomfortably and is perhaps best understood as a hybrid of the two. The masque was a dramatic form popular in the courts of James I and Charles I that used lavish scenery, costumes, music, singing, and dancing to celebrate the king and his power. Pastoral was a mode found in many plays, prose romances, and poems of the English Renaissance that glorified the simple lives of shepherds as opposed to the corruption of the city and court. While invoking these instantly recognizable genres, Cavendish and Brackley complicate them, undermining audience expectations and representing a topsy-turvy world that quite effectively communicates the anxiety, fear, and dislocation of life during the Civil War. No evidence exists to confirm that *A Pastorall* was ever performed, but it was clearly written with household performance in mind, and, as conceived, makes a powerful statement about the distress and hardship caused by war.

As a masque, *A Pastorall* employs a form of elite drama that flourished in the first half of the seventeenth century. The form took its shape most prominently at the court of James I with the masques written by Ben Jonson and designed by Inigo Jones. These masques were lavish spectacles featuring such elaborate stage properties as wave machines (*The Masque of Blackness*, 1605), aerial ballets (*Chloridia*, 1631), elaborate scenery (*The Masque of Queens*, 1609), and spectacular costumes, feasts, and revelry.[58] In addition to its popularity at court, the masque was also popular at aristocratic households, including Cavendish and Brackley's own (see above, general introduction, Household Drama).

A common structure in masque is to begin with a scene of comedy or disorder, also called an "antimasque" (or "antemasque"). Then there is a moment of reversal that functions as a transition from the antimasque to the masque proper. As Graham Parry puts it, "comedy was allowed a brief reign before the sublime movement of the main action began, or spirits of disorder were given license to appear before they were subdued or dispersed by the forces of the principal masque."[59] Where antimasques often depict mischief and can be very humorous, the masque proper celebrates order and the supreme power of the king or

---

58. Dudley Carleton's letter to John Chamberlain famously depicts the wild revelry that followed the performance of *The Masque of Blackness* on January 7, 1605: "A banquet which was prepared for the king in the great chamber was overturned, table and all, before it was scarce touched. It were infinite to tell you what losses there were of chains, jewels, purses, and suchlike loose ware, and one woman amongst the rest lost her honesty, for which she was carried to the porter's lodge, being surprised at her business on the top of the terrace." *Dudley Carleton to John Chamberlain, 1603–1624: Jacobean Letters*, ed. Maurice Lee (New Brunswick, NJ: Rutgers University Press, 1972), 68.

59. Graham Parry, "Entertainments at Court," in *A New History of Early English Drama*, ed. John D. Cox and David Scott Kastan (New York: Columbia University Press, 1997), 195–211 (202).

patriarch. Not surprisingly, court masques were designed and staged in such a way that there was only one "correct" perspective, that of the monarch positioned at the front and center of the audience whose power and authority were celebrated within the fiction of the play.[60] In both their staging and in their fictional representations, masques are thus an inherently conservative form, confirming royal and elite power and reinforcing the divinely sanctioned nature of the established political order. As Stephen Orgel writes in *The Illusion of Power*, "The masque presents the triumph of an aristocratic community; at its center is a belief in the hierarchy and a faith in the power of idealization.... . As a genre, it is the opposite of satire; it educates by praising, by creating heroic roles for the leaders of society to fill."[61]

*A Pastorall* follows the traditional masque structure closely. It begins with two antimasques: the first, written by Cavendish, features a group of witches plotting the mischief they will carry out that evening; the second, written by Brackley, focuses on the impact this witchcraft has on yeoman farmers.[62] The witches, who represent dangerous forms of female power, talk of attacking men, livestock, and families, and freely admit to their love of the devil. The representation of witches as menaces to prosperity and social harmony has much in common with other early modern witch plays, such as Shakespeare's *Macbeth* (1606) and Richard Brome and Thomas Heywood's *The Late Lancashire Witches* (1634). The disorder created by the witches—which we see from the perspective of the witches themselves as well as their victims—is, in typical masque form, temporary and resolved by the turn to the masque proper, which focuses on the pastoral world of shepherds and their struggles in love. This environment is radically different from the world of the antimasque; here, characters are stylized and named for their attributes (Freedome, Persuasion) and engage in a discussion of how they can enter into loving relationships, given the absence of a paternal authority figure.

Despite their use of conventional masque structure, Cavendish and Brackley employ the form in a unique way. The first antimasque of witches foregrounds disorder, yet the world of the antimasque—which is one of war—mirrors very closely the reality of life for the Cavendish household. Cavendish and Brackley turn things around, however, because it is the witches (who conceivably would have been played by Cavendish, Brackley, and their sister Frances) who are waging war. The play, through its metatheatrical language, confronts this reversal head-on in its first sentence:

60. Stephen Orgel, *The Illusion of Power: Political Theater in the English Renaissance* (Berkeley: University of California Press, 1975), 35–36.

61. Orgel, *Illusion of Power*, 40.

62. As discussed in the Note on the Text, in the introduction to this part of the volume, and as is evident in the play text, the initials "J.C." and "E.B." designate the authorship of individual scenes. Cavendish and Brackley also each wrote separate dedications to their father for both *A Pastorall* and *The concealed Fansyes*.

| | |
|---|---|
| Hag | This is a brave world for us now for wee |
| | meatomorphise every body.[63] |

Two of the witches, Hag and Bell, assert power and control in their description of their actions. In a summary rebuttal of Prentice's doubts, they take credit for the war and its chaos:

| | |
|---|---|
| Bell. | Thou'rt a foole hath not our mischeife made warr, |
| | and that a miserable one, to make Brother hate |
| | brother. |
| Hag | Sister hate Sister. |
| Bell | Wife hate Husband, and all other kindred, hath |
| | their devisions of hatred.[64] |

Unlike Cavendish and Brackley, who were garrisoned in their castle at the time of writing and who were very much victimized by the circumstances of war, the witches revel in tearing families apart (as Cavendish and Brackley's was), sending lords overseas (their father was in exile in France by the time this play was written), and holding soldiers captive (as they themselves were captives). The witches claim, in fact, that their favorite activity is to make "Ladyes Captives":[65]

| | |
|---|---|
| Pre. | Which of all your power like you best? |
| Bell | If you meane the grownd of like. Mischeife. |
| Pre | And what Sceane upon that grownd |
| Hag | By my troth, makeinge Ladyes Captives. |
| Bell | Seeinge how prittily they can Looke wise |
| Hag | And speake witt soe against us. |
| Bell | As wee cannot take the handle against them. |
| Hag | Unlesse wee prove our selves Fooles. |
| Bell | But that pleaseth mee most, is, how hansomely |
| | wee tye Ladyes Tongues.[66] |

The joke and the irony here, of course, is that the authors' tongues are not tied and that, in this work, they are taking the opportunity to speak and to think through their experiences of life during the war.[67] While the antimasque dissolves into the

63. "Antemasque," lines 5–6.

64. "Antemasque," lines 11–16.

65. "Antemasque," line 30.

66. "Antemasque," lines 27–36.

67. Cavendish and Brackley's playful and humorous depictions of witchcraft are typical of their family. Both Newcastle and Margaret Cavendish are dismissive of concerns about witchcraft and the

masque as the Jonsonian/Jonesian structure dictates, the peaceful pastoral world of the masque looks more like a fantasy than an assertion of the order, rightness, and propriety of the status quo.

The masque proper complicates things further, since the world of the masque invokes pastoral, but also repeatedly makes clear how far from bucolic it is. Interestingly, though the text clearly labels the first and second sections as "The Antemasque" and "The 2 Antemasque," the masque section itself is not labeled as a masque. Instead, it is introduced by a stage direction and is referred to as the "Pastorall":

> The Sheppards and Sheppardesses
> the first Sceane onely.
> The Sheppardesses, and one of them from the
> rest, comes from amongest them speakes
> this Speech; as the Prologue to the
> Pastorall.[68]

In a sense, although the third section has the appearance of a masque, one wonders if the authors thought it was far enough from being one as to make that label inaccurate. As is noted above in the Content and Analysis section on Wroth's *Loves Victorie*, pastoral is typically employed to question social, cultural, and political authority: the setting away from city and court allows a discussion and critique of the fundamentals of social order. Embedded in the pastoral genre is also a bias toward the country over the city, and an idealization of the purity of country life. While Cavendish and Brackley's masque uses pastoral for critique and comment, in accordance with the norms of the genre, it conspicuously lacks the idealization of country life, further conveying the abnormal nature of their present circumstance.

The language of the masque shifts markedly from the two antimasques, with the constant talk of cows, economic loss, and devil worship giving way to a

---

supernatural. Newcastle's poem "Loves Ghoste," for instance, mocks the supernatural. See Cavendish, "Loves Ghoste," in *The Phanseys of William Cavendish*, 34. Margaret Cavendish exchanged letters with Joseph Glanvill that demonstrate her disbelief in witches (only Glanvill's letters to Cavendish survive, but as Jacqueline Broad has demonstrated, the letters attest to Cavendish's doubts about witches). See Margaret Cavendish and William Cavendish, *A Collection of Letters and Poems: Written by several persons of honour and learning, upon divers important subjects, to the late Duke and Dutchess of Newcastle* (London: Langly Curtin, 1678), 85, 98–100, 102–3, 104–5, 123–27, 135–36, 137–42; and Jacqueline Broad, "Margaret Cavendish and Joseph Glanvill: Science, Religion, and Witchcraft," *Studies in History and Philosophy of Science* 38, no. 3 (2007): 493–505. I thank James Fitzmaurice for drawing my attention to the Cavendish family's attitudes toward witchcraft.

68. *A Pastorall*, lines 1–6.

peaceful and measured description of a melancholy, wintry environment inhabited by shepherds.[69] The first speech of the masque introduces this change:

Cha:    We're now become a fine coule shady walke
        Soe fit to answeare Lovers in their talke
        And if sad Soules, would mallencholly tell
        Let them then come, to visitt, where wee dwell
        For wee're become a fine thick Grove of thought
        Soe frises even our selves with teares full fraught
        When vendeducts of wind, our sighes makes Ayre
        These are the fruites of passion, restles care.
        And this our Groto; soe who lookes may have
        A welcome to a sad Shee Hermetts Cave.[70]

The markedly different tone of this speech invites speculation that it was meant to be staged in a different space than the antimasques. The masque is consistent in describing the environment as cold, whereas pastorals more usually feature fine weather as the backdrop for the conversation of shepherds. Despite its name, Shakespeare's *The Winter's Tale*, for instance, features beautiful, sunny weather in the pastoral scenes, where shepherds and country folk are shown enjoying a sheep-shearing festival. Autolycus signals the shift in setting, mood, and environment with this song:

Autolycus:  When daffadils begin to peer,
            With heigh, the doxy over the dale.
            Why, then comes in the sweet o' the year,
            For the red blood reigns in the winter's pale.

            The white sheet bleaching on the hedge,
            With heigh, the sweet birds—oh, how they sing!—
            Doth set my pugging tooth on edge,
            For a quart of ale is a dish for a king.

            The lark, that tirra-lyra chants,
            With heigh, with heigh, the thrush and the jay,
            Are summer songs for me and my aunts
            While we lie tumbling in the hay.[71]

---

69. One wonders if the play was conceived for performance in the winter since the speakers dwell so often on the cold.

70. *A Pastorall*, lines 10–19.

71. William Shakespeare, *The Winter's Tale*, in Greenblatt et al., *The Norton Shakespeare*, 4.3.1–12.

The "winter's pale" that dominates Cavendish and Brackley's pastoral is the absence of their father; it is his presence and safe return that will end the reign of "red blood" and allow a harmonious life to resume for the masque's female speakers.

It is difficult to read the pastoral section of the masque without attending to biography. So much of the conversation focuses on feelings of boredom, grief, and the pain of being cut off from one's family that it is difficult not to be reminded repeatedly of the authors' own circumstances. Cavendish's epilogue equates her own captivity with the experience of performing a shepherdess in the play: "My Lord it is your absence makes each see / For want of you, what I'm reduc'd to bee / Captive or Sheppardesses life."[72] The masque shows the three sisters mourning the absence of their father, wishing to remain in a kind of suspension until his return, but having to confront the pressures and demands of their suitors. If conceived for performance by Cavendish, Brackley, and their sister Frances, these roles give each sister a voice in which to register her displeasure and melancholy:

| | |
|---|---|
| Cha | When once the presence of a freind is gone |
| | Not knoweing when hee'le come, or stay how longe |
| | Then greife doth fill it selfe w$^{th}$ a reward |
| | That is when passion flowes without regard. |
| Inn | His absence makes a Chaos sure of mee |
| | And when each one doth lookeing looke to see |
| | That speakeing say, That I'm not I. |
| | Alas doe not name mee for I desire to dye |
| Ver | And I your Sister can noe way goe lesse |
| | As by my Face of palenes you may gesse |
| | Then let us singe in Choros Anthome, pray, |
| | To see our loved freinds, doth make our day.[73] |

As in *The concealed Fansyes*, there is a focus in this play on courtship, but there will be no resolution or marriages here because the masque ends without their father's return. In a scene written by Brackley, who was herself married but living apart from her new husband at the time the play was written, Car. and Ch. have this exchange:

| | |
|---|---|
| Car. | Now knowe you are a Shee, & sure a wife. |
| Ch: | Yes, and am resolv'd to live a Country life |
| | Since from my freinds I cannot heare |
| | I'm smother'd in sighes, Torter, feare. |
| Car: | But whats your consolation. |

72. Epilogue, lines 1–3.

73. *A Pastorall*, lines 210–21.

Ch:      To keepe, pritty sheepe.
               And to bring upp grass, my Teares shall weepe.
Car.     You owne your selfe to bee a wife
               And yet you practice not that life.
Ch:      I'm now become a Bracken, branch & stalke
               Soe sadnes dew recrutes mee to a walke.[74]

The reference to "Bracken" directly suggests Brackley's married name; the circumstances described here can be read as a moving expression of her yearning to begin life as a married woman.[75]

Despite its outdoor setting, the masque feels insular and confined. The world Cavendish and Brackley create is unpleasant, where one is constantly interrupted and faced with unwanted and unwelcome questions. The speakers are trapped, contemplating circumstances to which there is no possible resolution. At one point, Inn. discusses her frustration: "As I could wishe my freinds did now mee see / Not that I take a pleasure in this place / But for discourse."[76] The suitors who pursue the shepherdesses seem to irritate them and disrespect their grief, as in this exchange between Con. and Ver.:

Con:    Since that your greife is tourn'd to love
             You will now sure have thought of mee
             For thus to you I ever had
             An admiration love to owne
             And soe I sent my fate to you
             Who I have found sadly alone.
Ver:     Why doe you take the confidence to speake
             After one forme of Lovers rate of weake
             When that you see mee mallencholly sitt
             Thinkeing onely to milke into my kitt.[77]

A conventional masque ending would see the marriages declared and conclude with a celebration and dancing. But this is not the case in *A Pastorall*, where the suitors make no progress and where there is no father figure to swoop in and resolve the conflict as Lord Calsindow does at the end of *The concealed Fansyes*. A

---

74. *A Pastorall*, lines 139–49.

75. Brackley's first child, John, was born on November 9, 1646, so presumably she was living with her husband at Ashridge for the better part of that year. If so, the writing of *A Pastorall* can fairly confidently be dated to 1644–1645, at which time she would have been at Welbeck with her sisters. See Louis A. Knafla, "Egerton, John, third earl of Bridgewater (1646–1701)," *ODNB*.

76. *A Pastorall*, lines 25–27.

77. *A Pastorall*, lines 108–17.

shepherd named Freedome appears and tries to resolve the conflict and end the masque with a dance. But the sisters resist his efforts, which as a result come off more as a parody of the generic norm than a genuine attempt at resolution. The ending is ambiguous about whether they dance or not:

| | |
|---|---|
| Fre: | If you will dance, wee'le have an Ayre |
| | Shall chyme as chast as devine care |
| Ch: | Our vow will admitt noe such Toye |
| | For absent freinds gives us noe joy |
| | … … … … … … … … … |
| Fre: | How like you now my Country Lasces, |
| | That in love lookes, will bee your Glasses. |
| Car: | Now could wee Ladies have but sh such a dance |
| | That would but fetch your freinds, now out of Fraunce |
| | You then would well approve of this our mirth |
| | But since not soe, you doe appeare sad Earth. |
| Fre: | Come Musicke let's have now a Rownd, |
| | To prove my Country Wenches rightly sound.[78] |

The sisters' final words indicate that they did not join in a dance, since the promise of mirth is linked explicitly with the return of absent "freinds" from France. Freedome's final invitation to dance is thus left open-ended, logically conditional upon the return of the sisters' "freinds." Assuming they did not dance, the masque ends on a somber and deeply unconventional note that reinforces Cavendish and Brackley's use of masque and pastoral to represent more nearly tragic than comic circumstances. If they did dance, the tensions present in the masque nevertheless remain.

Within the context of household performance, the use of genre in *A Pastorall* invokes a wished-for reality while drawing attention to what the authors' current reality is not. Cavendish and Brackley's other dramatic work, *The concealed Fansyes*, likely could not have been staged as conceived, since their father, a central character in the play's conclusion, would not have been there to perform in it or witness it. But it seems useful to mention here that *A Pastorall* was eminently performable as written, and that the absence of the father would, in performance, have served to accentuate the difficult and unhappy circumstances not only of the women in the play, but also of Cavendish and Brackley themselves.

---

78. *A Pastorall*, lines 308–21.

## Content and Analysis of The concealed Fansyes

Given the plot of *The concealed Fansyes*—the central characters live in a castle under siege, endure the absence of their father, try to negotiate courtships with suitors who appear to be less than ideal, and take responsibility for running a complex aristocratic household without parental authority–Jane Cavendish and Elizabeth Brackley could easily have written a tragedy instead of a comedy. *The concealed Fansyes* does not shy away from these challenging circumstances, but it also makes clear that it is these very circumstances that allow the young women at the center of the play freedoms and opportunities they might not have had without the war. As Alison Findlay writes,

> The comedy of *The Concealed Fancies* demonstrates how, in the Civil War, households became spaces in which women took centre stage far more permanently than ever before. In the hands of no-blewomen like Cavendish and Brackley, traditional assumptions about authority, autonomy and subjection within the home were questioned in ways that mirrored the wider culture of change in the commonwealth.[79]

The circumstances faced by Luceny and Tattiney, the central figures in the play, mirror those of Cavendish and Brackley in some respects. The play is also full of depictions of daily life. We see conversations between the cook and his boy, the maids, various soldiers, and even captured prisoners, in addition to numerous exchanges between the sisters and their suitors. Despite these representations of day-to-day life in a castle at war, the play does not lend itself to straightforward biographical readings; instead, it blurs the boundaries between imagined and actual identities. Cavendish and Brackley's play engages in complicated and overlapping ways with the circumstances of their everyday lives to explore the boundary between fantasy and reality, to dislocate their audience, and to provoke thought about critical issues such as courtship, parental authority, and the impact of war.

Scholars have agreed that a performance of *The concealed Fansyes* would have been powerfully resonant in the Cavendish household. Alison Findlay and Lisa Hopkins, for instance, demonstrate the play's theatrical potential and how it could have been staged either at Welbeck or Bolsover, the Cavendish family homes.[80] Nevertheless, it appears that at the time the manuscript of *The concealed*

---

79. Findlay, *Playing Spaces*, 53. While Findlay writes persuasively about the subversive aspects of the play, Kamille Stone Stanton, "The Domestication of Royalist Themes in *The Concealed Fancies* by Jane Cavendish and Elizabeth Brackley," *Clio* 36, no. 2 (2007): 177–97 (177), argues that the play is ultimately socially conservative and invested in patriarchy.

80. Findlay, *Playing Spaces*, 44–53; Lisa Hopkins, "Play Houses: Drama at Bolsover and Welbeck," *Early Theatre* 2, no. 1 (1999): 25–44; and Lisa Hopkins, *The Female Hero in Renaissance Tragedy* (New

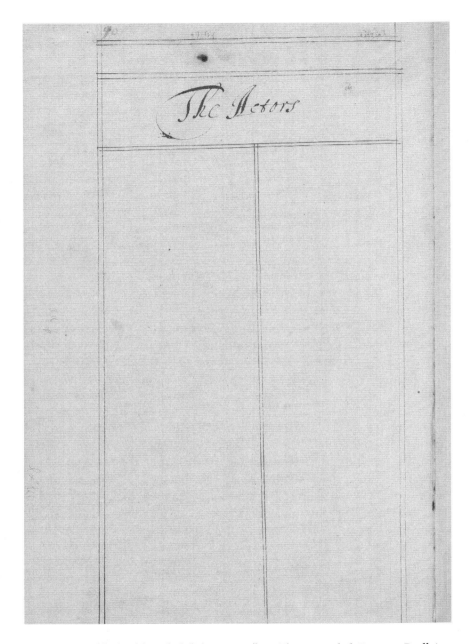

Figure 9. Unfilled table titled "The Actors" in *The concealed Fansyes*, Bodleian manuscript. Rawlinson MS Poet. 16, page 90. © By permission of the Bodleian Library, University of Oxford.

York: Palgrave Macmillan, 2002), 186.

*Fansyes* was produced, the play had not been performed: the page labeled "The Actors" (90), which is apparently designed to serve as the *dramatis personae*, is ruled and takes up a full page but is not filled in (see Figure 9). Interestingly, however, the play includes stage directions in the present tense, resembling stage directions in professional plays written for performance. By contrast, stage directions in other household plays written for occasional performance are in the past tense, as for example in *The Honorable Entertainement given to the Queenes Majestie in Progresse, at Elvetham in Hampshire* (1591): "While the Poet was pronouncing this Oration, six Virgins were behind him, busily remooving blockes out of her Majestie's way."[81] It is interesting to compare this with an example from act 5 of *The concealed Fansyes*, where Courtly and Presumption appear to Luceny and Tattiney as gods to try to persuade them to marriage and sing "A Songe / Sunge by ·2· Gods comeing downe out of / the Skye to the Nunns. Who are. / Courtley & Praesumption."[82] When the women assent to those they assume are "gods" they sing another song as "they are drawne upp."[83] Cavendish and Brackley's circumstances during the war may well have prevented the performance of their play; the war certainly would have prevented their father, who was in exile on the Continent when the play is thought to have been written, from being in the audience or performing the role of Lord Calsindow, as they perhaps originally envisioned. As well, the play would have needed a minimum of nine actors, and the staging as conceived would require some technical skill, particularly the scene cited above in which the actors are descending from and ascending into the sky.[84] Unfortunately we do not know enough about the interior design of Welbeck Abbey to say whether an enactment of this scene would have been possible.

The play's text does, however, reveal that Cavendish and Brackley imagined the play being performed as well as read. It begins with two prologues, which could have been spoken by the authors themselves. The "Prologe to the Stage" asks the women in the audience not to blush when they "see / That I speake a Prologe being a Shee."[85] The same prologue asks for applause, or "hands Playes."[86] The first three of the epilogues that conclude the play, including this one specifically addressed to Newcastle, similarly invoke the image of a performance:

81. *Elvetham: 1591*, 105.

82. 5.69–72. See Figure 10.

83. 5.90.

84. Hopkins, "Judith Shakespeare's Reading," 400. Cadman suggests 14 is a more likely number number of actors for the play's 33 speaking parts. Daniel Cadman, ed., *The Concealed Fancies by Jane Cavendish and Elizabeth Brackley*, in *The Literary Cultures of the Cavendish Family* (blog), 11, https://extra.shu.ac.uk/emls/iemls/renplays/ConcealedFancies.pdf, accessed May 6, 2018.

85. "A Prologe to the Stage," lines 2–3.

86. "A Prologe to the Stage," line 13.

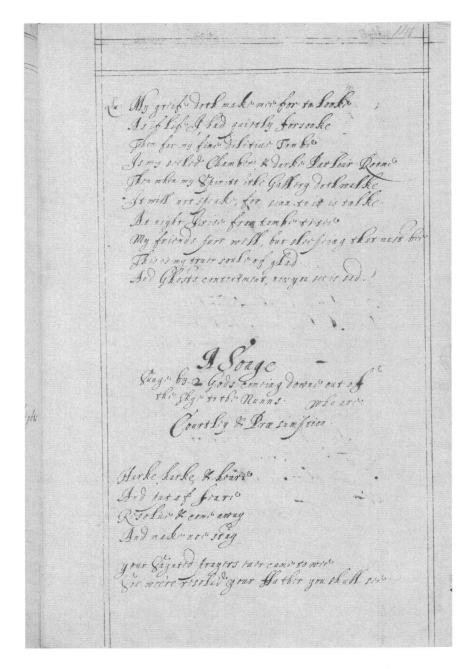

Figure 10. An elaborate stage direction in *The concealed Fansyes*, Bodleian manuscript. Rawlinson MS Poet. 16, page 141. © By permission of the Bodleian Library, University of Oxford.

| Lu: | Now since your Excellence hath thought it fitt |
|---|---|
| Ta: | To stay a three howres Comedy of sitt |
| Lu: | And soe but speake of it as like |
| Ta: | Then are our Sceanes even happy in your sight |
| Lu: | And though wee have, smyles & hats if you dislike |
| Ta: | Wee're totally condemned, for tonight.[87] |

On the next page, however, we find an untitled verse: it is not labeled as an epilogue; nor does it appear in either of the volume's tables of contents as do the other epilogues. Yet this verse clearly refers to their father as a reader of the volume:

Have you now read my Lord, pray doe not speake
For I'm already growne, soe faint & weake
Not knoweing how you will now sensure mee
As rash to thinke, noe witt a present bee
But if you like not, I pray let mee knowe
The Penn & Inke shall have a fatall blowe
If you not pleas'd it will impression make
In my vaine selfe, for indiscretion sake
But if you like you will mee Cordyall give
And soe as witty, I shall ever live.[88]

Notably, there are no blank pages between this verse and *The concealed Fansyes*, though the manuscript is otherwise generous in its use of white space. The verse appears at the end of the volume and explicitly positions Newcastle as a reader of his daughters' works.

In its content, *The concealed Fansyes* engages with the circumstances of Cavendish and Brackley's everyday lives, but complicates and manipulates those circumstances to create an alternate reality. This technique is also found in *A Pastorall*, and both plays work with and against the genres and modes they invoke. While *A Pastorall* does not arrive at the harmonious resolution conventional to masque, *The concealed Fansyes* ends happily, but not, as we will see, without irony or complication. The play evokes Ben Jonson's comedy of humors which was popular earlier in the century. It also anticipates the comedy of manners that came to dominate the late seventeenth-century stage, with its characters that embody types (as indicated by their names—Courtly, Presumption, Corpolant, Action, etc.), its focus on wit and wordplay, and its lack of interest in emotion.[89]

---

87. "An Epilog / In perticuler to your Lo:ᴾᴾ," lines 109–14.

88. "An Epilog / In perticular to your Lo:ᴾᴾ," lines 115–24.

89. Examples of Jonson's comedy of humors include *Every Man in his Humour* (1598) and its sequel, *Every Man out of his Humour* (1599); examples of comedies of manners include William Wycherley's

Cavendish and Brackley were likely influenced by the work of Jonson, and their play very much situates itself in the Cavalier or Royalist drama that was popular in the late Caroline period until the closing of the theaters in 1642. They also refer to the plays of Shakespeare and other dramatists and skillfully deploy various genres, comedy and masque in particular.[90]

Though *The concealed Fansyes* features many allusions to Cavendish and Brackley's lived circumstances, it also deliberately complicates these representations in ways that could be unsettling for its contemporary audience. Luceny and Tattiney, the sisters at the center of the play, refer to themselves as playing their "scenes"; their suitors also refer to them in this way.[91] In a manner often used by Shakespeare, the play begins by giving us other characters' perspectives on Luceny and Tattiney before allowing us to see them ourselves, thus creating distance and complicating our perception of them. We initially hear about Luceny and Tattiney from their suitors, who find them challenging women to woo, and from their servants, who find them to be incompetent household managers. More than this, when we do finally see Luceny and Tattiney, their first words draw attention to the artifice of their appearance:

> Sister pray tell mee in what humour thou wert w[th]
> thy servant yesterday, prethee, tell mee how you acted
> yo[r] Sceane.[92]

In addition to the oblique presentation of Luceny and Tattiney to the audience, the play features another set of sisters whose experiences also mirror those of Cavendish and Brackley. Luceny and Tattiney have three cousins—Cecilly, Sh., and Is.—who live at Ballamo castle, which is under siege.[93] Both sets of sisters live in a castle in a region at war, both are without any evident parental oversight, and both are pursued by suitors. In performance, Cavendish and Brackley could have played both sets of sisters, since they do not speak on stage at the same time (in this scenario, Cavendish and Brackley's sister Frances could have played the third sister living at Ballamo). This would have had an especially interesting effect, since the two sets of sisters spend a significant amount of time talking about one another. Cavendish and Brackley may have expected other actors to

---

*The Country Wife* (1675) and William Congreve's *The Way of the World* (1700). Jane and Elizabeth may or may not have seen Jonson's plays in London, but, given that their father was a major patron of Jonson, it seems very likely that they would at least have known them in print.

90. See Hopkins, "Judith Shakespeare's Reading," 401–5.

91. 1.4.5–6.

92. 1.4.4–6.

93. Some characters—Sh. and Is., for example—are never named except by speech prefixes. Their names may be Charlotte and Isabelle or Isabella.

play the Ballamo cousins: in act 5, when Luceny and Tattiney are on stage just after having been married, we have the stage direction "Enter the ·2· Stellowes w^th their Mistresses." If Cavendish and Brackley were to play both sets of sisters, this stage direction clearly would not work. However Cavendish and Brackley conceived these roles to be performed, the circumstances of both sets of sisters allude humorously and uncannily to different aspects of the authors' lived experience. Alongside this playfulness, the play consistently maintains the various façades and performed identities throughout the play and never allows a moment of revelation where true feelings are expressed. Even when Luceny and Tattiney discuss what it is like to be married after act 5, their role playing continues. Tattiney talks about behaving both as "wife" and "Mistris" to Presumption and claims to write to her husband "In as severall humours as I will dresse / my selfe."[94] The confusion of the boundaries between the two sets of sisters and between the real circumstances of the authors demonstrates the complex representation of identity in the play.

Cavendish and Brackley's unsettling engagement with their lived experience is a powerful use of the self-reflexivity of household theater. As mentioned above, *The concealed Fansyes* ends as one would expect such a play to end: their father miraculously appears, settles the marriages of the central characters, and happiness reigns. The way this ending is represented in the play, however, calls attention to its own fantastical nature. While Courtly and Presumption literally attempt to stage their own masque ending by dressing as gods and descending from above, their conceit is revealed. Lord Calsindow, however, does accomplish the miraculous resolution attempted by Courtly and Presumption. For some scholars, the theatricality of the ending draws attention to the fact that it is forced. Alison Findlay, for instance, finds that the marriages come off as performative and thus contribute to the play's critique of gender politics in the household.[95] It can also be said, however, that the conclusion of the play shows the imperatives of genre: the play ends in marriage because that is what comedies do. In this light, the sudden decision of Lord Calsindow to marry Toy, Lady Tranquility's servant, makes more sense than it does in the context of the play's fictional world, where the pair do not seem to have anything to do with one another (but, in another reversal, the decision of Calsindow to marry Toy is abruptly overturned by the Angel and they do not marry). This sudden turn of events, in the context of a household where things were decidedly not turning for the better in real life, borders on the farcical. The forced resolution at the end of the play may even comment ironically on the reality that the extreme challenges faced by the Cavendish family in the 1640s were not happily resolved. Considered in this context, the comic ending of *The concealed Fansyes* draws attention to a larger tragedy.

94. After act 5, lines 84–85.

95. Findlay, *Playing Spaces*, 52.

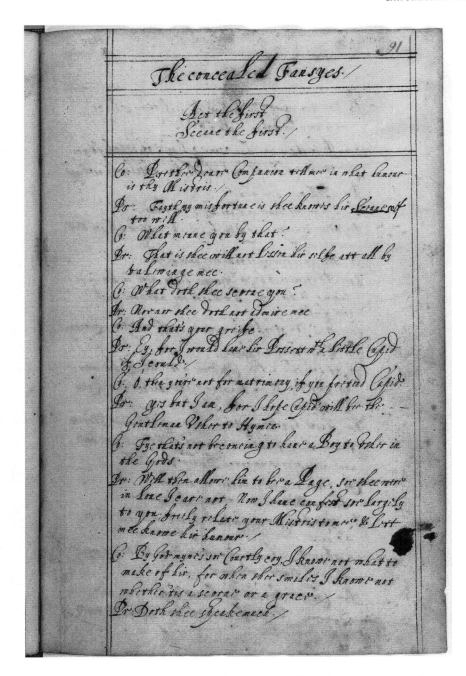

Figure 11. First page of *The concealed Fansyes*, Bodleian manuscript. Rawlinson MS Poet. 16, page 91. © By permission of the Bodleian Library, University of Oxford.

## Afterlives of the Texts

The work of Cavendish and Brackley was largely unknown to scholars until 1931, when Nathan Comfort Starr published a transcription of *The concealed Fansyes* in *PMLA*. He notes that the play was listed by James Halliwell-Phillipps in *A Dictionary of Old English Plays* (1860), but that little notice had been taken of it.[96] Starr dismissed the play quite harshly:

> As a literary production, *The Concealed Fansyes* is practically with-
> out value. Its conformity to the Jonsonian comedy of humors, and
> its specific indebtedness to Jonson are sufficiently obvious without
> detailed comment, nor is it necessary to dwell upon the resemblance
> between the brothers in the play and those of *Comus*. The chief inter-
> est of the work lies in the artless revelation of the activities of seven-
> teenth century ladies of fashion, living in the country.[97]

C. H. Herford and Percy Simpson, the editors of the monumental edition of Ben Jonson's works, identified the scribe of the manuscript as the one who also produced a significant collection of verses, poems, and dramatic entertainments for the Duke of Newcastle (British Library, Harley MS 4955), now known as the "Newcastle manuscript."[98] Although they usefully linked the Cavendish sisters' manuscript to a larger field of scribal practice, Herford and Simpson offered a narrow and belittling description of the works contained in the volume: "Whether the bad grammar and bad metre of these poems is to be attributed to the authors or to the copyist it is impossible to say—probably the former, for the latter in his transcript of *The Gypsies Metamorphosed* faithfully reproduced some senseless blunders of the 1640 Folio."[99]

Not surprisingly, little more was done with the plays until the 1980s and 1990s, when feminist critics were drawn to them on account of their female authorship. S. P. Cerasano and Marion Wynne-Davies's *Renaissance Drama by Women* includes a modern-spelling edition of *The Concealed Fansyes*.[100] More recently, Daniel Cadman has prepared an online modern-spelling edition of the

---

96. Starr, "*Concealed Fansyes*," 802. Halliwell-Phillipps is the James Orchard Halliwell whose wife Henrietta transcribed sections of *Love's Victory* in 1845. James and Henrietta changed their last name to Halliwell-Phillips upon her father's death in 1889. See above, Wroth introduction, note 72, and Salzman, "Henrietta's Version," 159.

97. Starr, "*Concealed Fansyes*," 837.

98. For a detailed study of this manuscript, see Kelliher, "The Newcastle Manuscript."

99. C. H. Herford and Percy Simpson, eds., *Ben Jonson Works* (Oxford: Clarendon Press, 1941), 7:767.

100. Cerasano and Wynne-Davies, *Renaissance Drama by Women*, 127–54.

play.[101] *Kissing the Rod: An Anthology of 17th Century Women's Verse*, edited by Germaine Greer, Susan Hastings, Jeslyn Medoff, and Melinda Sansone (1988) prints selected passages from *A Pastorall*.[102] Lynn Smith's *A Pastorall: A Drama* is a lightly edited original-spelling edition of *A Pastorall* based on the Beinecke manuscript.[103]

Despite the lack of a documented performance history in the seventeenth century, the contemporary interest in Cavendish and Brackley's work has led to numerous recent nonprofessional productions. These include *The concealed Fansyes*, directed by Alison Findlay and Jane Milling and staged on December 14, 1994, in one of the large rooms at Bretton Hall, a country house in West Yorkshire.[104] Findlay also staged scenes from *A Pastorall* in 2000. Videos of this performance, as well as highlights of the performance of *The concealed Fansyes*, are available on Findlay's website.[105]

## Note on the Text

## A Pastorall

This edition is based on the text of *A Pastorall* found in the Bodleian Library (Rawlinson MS Poet. 16, pp. 52–84) in the manuscript titled *POEMS SONGS a PASTORALL AND a PLAY by the R$^t$ Hon$^{ble}$ the Lady Jane Cavendish and Lady Elizabeth Brackley*. The manuscript is a folio volume bound in seventeenth-century black morocco leather with gilt decoration; it measures 31.5 cm x 21 cm. Its 176 pages are numbered consecutively (viii + 168 pages) and include 24 pages on which no text is written. "W N" with a fleuron separating the letters is tooled (upside down) in gilt on the binding, on both the front and back covers. The binding is from the same period as the plays were written, so the upside-down letters may be an error made during the binding process or may indicate a repair done

---

101. Cadman, *The Concealed Fancies*.

102. Greer et al., *Kissing the Rod*, 109–15.

103. Smith, *A Pastorall*. In the final stages of preparing this edition, Alexandra Bennett's edition of Jane Cavendish's complete works became available. Bennett's volume includes the contents of the Bodleian manuscript as well as Cavendish's letters and account books. The inclusion of Cavendish's non-dramatic writings makes Bennett's volume an excellent companion to the present edition.

104. For an account of the performance, see Alison Findlay, Gweno Williams, and Stephanie J. Hodgson-Wright, "'The Play Is Ready to be Acted': Women and Dramatic Production, 1570–1670," *Women's Writing* 6, no. 1 (1999): 129–48 (136–40).

105. http://www.lancaster.ac.uk/english-and-creative-writing/about-us/people/alison-findlay, accessed May 6, 2018. On the performance of early modern women's drama more generally, see Alison Findlay, Stephanie Hodgson-Wright, with Gweno Williams, *Women and Dramatic Production, 1550–1700* (New York: Longman, 2000).

at a later date.[106] The paper used throughout has the same watermark of a double-headed eagle and the letters "LC," similar to Heawood 1287.[107] As indicated in Peter Beal's online *Catalogue of English Literary Manuscripts*, the manuscript is mostly in the hand of John Rolleston (1587?–1681), secretary to Sir William Cavendish, Duke of Newcastle; the list of contents at the end of the volume is in the hand of Elizabeth Brackley's husband, John Egerton, Viscount Brackley and second Earl of Bridgewater.[108] The incomplete contents at the beginning of the volume is in a third, unknown hand. The manuscript contains eighty-nine poems, *A Pastorall*, and *The concealed Fansyes*. The volume is paginated throughout in the hand of the scribe.

Another text of the play is found in the Beinecke Library, Yale University (Osborn MS b.233, pp. 43–76); the variants in wording between the two manuscripts are listed in the Textual Notes.[109] The Beinecke manuscript is somewhat smaller, at 29 cm x 19 cm, and much shorter, at 76 pages, 11 of which have no text written on them. The manuscript is, however, a folio that, like the Bodleian, is bound in black morocco leather with a small fleuron tooled in gilt on its front cover. The image or letter inside the fleuron cannot be deciphered. Two kinds of paper are used: one has a flag watermark, similar to Heawood 137; the second has a letter or initial watermark, similar to Heawood 3100.[110] Both papers are different from the paper used in the Bodleian manuscript. Like the Bodleian manuscript, the Beinecke manuscript is widely considered to be in the hand of John Rolleston,

106. I thank Michael Webb, Curator of Early Modern Archives and Manuscripts at the Bodleian Library, for his assessment of the possible reasons why the book may have been bound in this way.

107. Edward Heawood, *Watermarks, Mainly of the 17th and 18th Centuries* (Hilversum, Holland: Paper Publications, 1950).

108. Beal, *Catalogue of English Literary Manuscripts*, http://www.celm-ms.org.uk/repositories/bodleian-rawlinson-1.html#bodleian-rawlinson-1_id501200, accessed May 6, 2018.

109. The Beinecke manuscript has some deletions that are largely illegible. The corrected text closely resembles the text of the masque in the Bodleian manuscript, perhaps indicating that the Bodleian text was based on the Beinecke. While the text of *A Pastorall* indicates clearly that the play was written collaboratively by Cavendish and Brackley, the Beinecke Rare Book and Manuscript Library online catalogue as of May 6, 2018, ascribes the "poetic dialogue" to Elizabeth and the poems in the manuscript exclusively to Jane: "Manuscript on paper, in a single hand, of 78 poems by Jane Cavendish. Many are addressed to family members, including one titled 'On my sweete brother Charles,' another called 'On my Noble Uncle Sr Charles Cavendish Knight,' and several to her father, as well as others addressed to her sisters, mother, grandparents, and the King and Queen. There are also poems on passion, the 'chamber-mayde,' and 'A noble lady.' The manuscript includes a poetic dialogue by her sister, Lady Elizabeth Brackley Egerton, Countess of Bridgewater, titled 'A Pastorall,' with a cast of witches, country wives, and shepherds, and which is preceded by a verse dedication to their father, William Cavendish, Duke of Newcastle. The manuscript as a whole is prefaced by a dedication by Jane Cavendish to him." http://brbl-dl.library.yale.edu/vufind/Record/3530891, accessed May 6, 2018. The catalogue contains several high-quality images of the manuscript and bindings.

110. Heawood, *Watermarks*.

the Duke of Newcastle's secretary, with the exception of one poem in an unknown hand, copied fifty-six blank pages after the conclusion of *A Pastorall*. The manuscript is paginated in pencil throughout in what appears to be a different hand than Rolleston's.[111] Unlike the Bodleian manuscript, the Beinecke does not have title pages or tables of contents that indicate the authorship of the plays. However, the manuscript does feature the distinctive attribution of each scene of *A Pastorall* to either Jane Cavendish or Elizabeth Brackley, as does the Bodleian manuscript.

This edition preserves the authorial attributions of individual scenes of *A Pastorall*. The Bodleian manuscript frequently features flourishes at the ends of scenes or at transition points in the text; the scribe also routinely ends sentences with both a period and a virgule. Since these features of the text are communicated through the scene breaks and by periods at the ends of sentences, this edition does not reproduce the flourishes or the virgules. Lines in each antimasque and scene are numbered separately.

## The concealed Fansyes

This edition is based on the only known manuscript of the play (Bodleian Library, Rawlinson MS Poet. 16, pp. 87–157). The Bodleian manuscript is described above. As is noted above, the manuscript features flourishes at the ends of many scenes or at a transition point in the text and the scribe routinely ends a sentence with both a period and a virgule. Since these divisions are communicated through the scene breaks and by periods at the ends of sentences, the present edition does not reproduce the flourishes and the virgules. The play is divided into acts and scenes; in the present edition, each act and scene is numbered separately.

---

111. On pages 72–73 of the Beinecke copy of *A Pastorall* the number "3" is written four times. While the manner in which the number is written in the uncorrected text is consistent with Rolleston's hand, both the page number and the corrected "3" at the top of page 72 are in a hand that is not Rolleston's.

# A Pastorall

My Lord                                                                                    [49]

> After the deuty[112] of a Verse,
> Give leave now to rehearse;
> A Pastorall; then if but give
> Your smile, I sweare, I live,                                           5
> In happyness; For if this may
> Your favour have, 'twill ne're decay
> Now let my language speake, & say
> If you bee pleas'd, I have my pay.

That passionately am                                                       10

your Lo:pps[113]

most affectionate, and obedient

Daughter

Jane Cavendysshe.

My Lord                                                                                    [50]

> This Pastorall could not owne weake
> But my intrest which makes mee speake.[114]
> To begg you'l not condem the best
> For thi'll,[115] but chase it, to it rest                               5
> Where I shall owne the word submitt,
> Unto your Judgement of pure witt.[116]

112. Duty.

113. Lordship's. William Cavendish, Duke of Newcastle, father to the authors. See the section Life and Works in the introduction to this part of the volume, for further discussion of the familial context of this masque.

114. The meaning of these first two lines is obscure, though they suggest that the author believes the play to have weaknesses yet presents it to her father to read. Authors of this period commonly invoke the modesty topos when in fact they held their work in high esteem.

115. Thou will.

116. A blank page follows this page.

your Lo:<sup>pps</sup> most affectionate
and obliged

Daughter.                                                                          10

Elizabeth Brackley


J.C.[117]                              A Pastorall[118]                              [52][119]

The Antemasque.[120]

Witches the number beinge five.[121]
The Hagg being first.

| | | |
|---|---|---|
| Hag | This is a brave[122] world for us now for wee[123] | 5 |
| | meatomorphise[124] every body. | |
| Pre.[125] | But I doubt wee are but the Fly of the Cart | |
| | wheele,[126] for wee are but the people that's taulked | |
| | on, to serve others designes, and our pride to our | |
| | selves makes us thinke wee are Actours.[127] | 10 |

117. In the upper left-hand corner of each page of *A Pastorall*, the initials "J. C." or "E. B." identify who authored the text on that page.

118. "A Pastorall" is the running head throughout this portion of the manuscript.

119. There are a number of blank pages and spaces in the Beinecke and Bodleian manuscripts. It is possible the scribe expected to add material at a later time.

120. Antimasques (or antemasques, as they were also known in the period) were commonplace in Jacobean and Caroline court masques. They precede the masque proper and often represent scenes of revelry and disorder that are dispersed by the order established in the masque. See the section Content and Analysis of "*A Pastorall*" in the introduction to this part of the volume.

121. Only three witches speak. Cavendish and Brackley had a sister, Frances, for whom a speaking role may have been intended.

122. Excellent.

123. The scribe wrote an asterisk followed by two mid-line dots next to the end of this line.

124. Metamorphose. Change.

125. Prentice. Colloquial term for an apprentice. See, for example, Thomas Heywood's *The Four Prentices of London* (ca. 1592).

126. Prentice views their actions as being of only passing significance.

127. "A doer, an agent" (*OED*). Prentice suggests that the witches may not be as powerful as they think they are. The use of "Actours" also calls attention to this work as a play. As in *The concealed Fansyes*, Cavendish and Brackley use metatheatrical language (see, for instance, 1.1.6).

| | | | |
|---|---|---|---|
| | Bell.[128] | Thou'rt a foole hath not our mischeife made warr,[129] and that a miserable one, to make Brother hate brother. | |
| | Hag | Sister hate Sister. | |
| | Bell | Wife hate Husband, and all other kindred, hath their devisions of hatred. | 15 |
| | Hag | And have not wee done brave[130] | |
| | Pre | Ey fayth, but thinke you 'tis wee[131] | |
| | Bell | Lords wee send beyond Seas at our pleasure | |
| | Hag | Others wee keepe still to make us business,[132] and for Colonells and Lieutennant Colonells, & lower degrees of officers, wee take them soe fast, as wee are - - thinkeing to let them goe without Exchange.[133] | 20 |
| J.C. | Bell | To have the sport of gettinge them againe. | [53] |
| | Pre | And is this all wee. | 25 |
| | Hag | Who the Devill els[134] should it bee. | |
| | Pre. | Which of all your power like you best? | |
| | Bell | If you meane the grownd[135] of like. Mischeife.[136] | |
| | Pre | And what Sceane[137] upon that grownd | |
| | Hag | By my troth, makeinge Ladyes Captives. | 30 |
| | Bell | Seeinge how prittily they can Looke wise | |
| | Hag | And speake witt soe against us. | |
| | Bell | As wee cannot take the handle against them.[138] | |
| | Hag | Unlesse wee prove our selves Fooles. | |

128. Beldam, possibly, as suggested by Greer et al., *Kissing the Rod*, 110.

129. *A Pastorall* was written during the English Civil War (1642–1651). See the section Life and Works in the introduction to this part of the volume.

130. "Worthy, excellent, good … 'an indeterminate word, used to express the superabundance of any valuable quality in men or things'" (*OED*).

131. But do you think we have done all of this?

132. Hold hostage for our own purposes.

133. This passage indicates that the witches hold so many high- and lower-ranked soldiers captive that they are thinking of releasing them without ransom.

134. Else.

135. Principle.

136. The scribe uses three forms of the letter "m." One is clearly uppercase while another is lowercase. The third form seems to be closer to uppercase than lowercase and has been transcribed here and throughout the manuscript accordingly.

137. Scene. Cavendish and Brackley's plays are characterized by their use of metatheatrical language.

138. Strike them.

| | | | |
|---|---|---|---|
| | Bell | But that pleaseth mee most, is, how hansomely[139] | 35 |
| | | wee tye Ladyes Tongues. | |
| | Hag | Which before tyme would have beene thought a | |
| | | Maracle.[140] | |
| | Bell | Come now, about, about. | |
| | Hag | And let this night bee a Battles rout, to whome | 40 |
| | | wee please. | |
| | Pre. | Let mee then knowe of whome you pitch[141] | |
| | Bell | If but a Mischeife wee'le not care to which | |
| | Hag | If you a partie[142] have I will you tell | |
| | | you're but a Prentice Witch, I'le sweare, in Hell. | 45 |
| | Bell | Come light[143] your distaffes[144] and wee'le try. | |
| | Hag | Now Ile bee hang'd, If that some doe not flye | |
| | Bell | Come let us burne out severall horrid peeces.[145] | |
| J.C. | Hag | Thus is our Mischeife drawne in yeares of Leases | [54] |
| | Pre | If you a Prentice doe call mee | 50 |
| | | Pray' let mee knowe of thee | |
| | | What you intend soe hollyly to burne | |
| | Hag | To sacrafice unto Loves Devills Urne[146] | |
| | Pre. | What's the ingredient of your Perfume | |
| | Bell | All horrid things to burne i'th[147] Roome | 55 |
| | Hag | As Childrens heads | |
| | Bell | Mens leggs | |
| | Hag | Weomens Armes | |
| | Bell | And little Barnes[148] | |
| | Hag | And these wee will you show | 60 |
| | Pre. | Noe thanke you, I will take my leggs to goe. | |
| | Bell | Noe stay wee will not you soe fright | |
| | Hag | That you the better may us like | |

139. Handsomely. Skillfully.

140. Miracle. The authors employ the conventional trope that depicts women's speech as shrewish and improper.

141. Upon whom you have fixed for your mischief.

142. Part. If you participate.

143. Alight on.

144. A tool used in spinning.

145. "An area of land which is enclosed, marked off by boundaries, or otherwise viewed as distinct, esp. in terms of ownership" (*OED*). The witches identify property as the target of their "mischeife."

146. Perhaps a reference to a stage prop.

147. In the.

148. Bairns. Children.

| Bell | For wee're resolv'd that us you shall not slight | |
|---|---|---|
| Hag | For with us you shall oynt[149] and make a flight[150] | 65 |
| Pre. | And must all this bee done to night | |
| Bell | But wee've forgot our Songe | |
| Hag | Let's singe, but let's not bee too longe. | |

### The Songe.

| Hag | Deville thou know'st weer'e thyne | 70 |
|---|---|---|
| Bell | And that in a most stright[151] lyne | |
| Hag | Soe beggs that each may feare | |
| Bell | Us witches every yeare. | |

J.C.  They all ·4· singe in Choros[152] this  [55]

Now oynt and make a flight  75
To see great Lucyfer to night.

all fall[153]

E:B:  The ·2· Antemasque.  [57][154]

### Two Countrye Wives.

| Pr.[155] | Come Naunt Henn[156] I'le tell you a pritty incounter of my selfe now. | |
|---|---|---|
| Hen. | But effeckins[157] I'looke first, whether noe souldier or Witch bee crept under my bed or noe. | 5 |
| Pr. | I care not for them, Naunt stay; | |

149. Anoint.

150. This line is also used in *The concealed Fansyes* (2.1.228).

151. Straight.

152. Chorus.

153. This stage direction is incorporated into a flourish that concludes the scene. It is the only stage direction to conclude a scene in either of Cavendish and Brackley's plays.

154. Page 56 is blank in the manuscript.

155. Pratt or Prat. The associations of the name suggest "a piece of trickery or fraud," "a buttock," and "a cunning person" (*OED*). The name given to this character may help explain the mysterious activities to which she alludes.

156. Aunt Hen. "Hen" was often used to refer to lower-class women.

157. An oath.

|       |     | For I am bigg with talke |   |
|-------|-----|---------------------------|---|
|       | He. | Speake then. |   |
|       | Pr  | Wye, I went to my good Lord, & Maisters howse to | 10 |
|       |     | see his honourable Children, but that was not my |   |
|       |     | occadtions;[158] I darr not tell you what I went[159] |   |
|       |     | about. |   |
|       | He: | Why will you not; I pray you tell mee Gossop[160] |   |
|       | Pr. | Ne fayth your tongue's glibb, & it will twattle | 15 |
|       |     | a little too much. |   |
|       | He: | When did you heare mee speake any thinge against |   |
|       |     | my noble Maister, or against any of his. |   |
|       | Pr. | Well I'le tell you; first I went to the gates, and |   |
|       |     | there I was examined, and my Baskett that | 20 |
|       |     | had the Pigg in it was examined.[161] |   |
|       | He  | Then what sayd they to you Gossopp. |   |
| E.B.  | Pr. | They asked mee what I came for. | [58] |
|       |     | Then I sayd, I came to doe my duety, to present this |   |
|       |     | wreckling[162] Pig, to the Ladies or Gentlewomen, | 25 |
|       |     | I knowe not what you call them, but by'th mack,[163] |   |
|       |     | I knew them well enough fare cheive[164] them. |   |
|       |     | For they have a hard Gamm[165] to play. |   |
|       |     | But when I went upp, I durst not stay, but sent |   |
|       |     | my Baskett upp by one I durst trust. | 30 |
|       |     | 'Twas one of their Maidens, and bid hir, bid hir Lady |   |
|       |     | Looke into my Pigs Tale, & there they would fynd.[166] |   |
|       | He. | What Gossopp. |   |
|       | Pr. | My Pigg fatt,[167] would they not, but I have knowne |   |
|       |     | the day, that, that word would have beene held | 35 |

158. Occasions. Pretexts or excuses.

159. This line ends with a mid-line dot followed by a dash.

160. Gossip. A common term for a friend.

161. Pratt describes the security measures she encountered at the unnamed Lord's house.

162. Reckling. A small, weak animal.

163. Mass. An oath.

164. Possibly "to achieve." To figure out their ruse.

165. Game.

166. The scribe underlined the period at the end of this line.

167. This could refer to the reckling pig becoming fat through some magic related to witchcraft, or "fat" can mean a "vessel" (*OED*). Greer et al., *Kissing the Rod*, 110, follow this reading and suggest that Gossip Pratt alludes here to spying or the passing of secret messages through the pig's "fat." This reading is reinforced by Pratt's name (see note 155), though the topic is never expanded upon or taken

uncivill, for such a word to have beene sent, or
sayd to any one.
Well Naunt Henn, I sayd it, & I repented not,
but wishe I were to say it againe.

<table>
<tr><td>E.B.</td><td colspan="2" align="center">Enter Goodman Rye &<br>Goodman Hay.[168]</td><td>40 [59]</td></tr>
</table>

| | | |
|---|---|---|
| He | You'r welcome Goodman Hay | |
| Pr | And soe are you Goodman Rye | |
| Ha: | I hope you'r well Naunt Henn | |
| Ry | And how doe you Gossopp Pratt | 45 |
| Pr. | Come let's chatt some Newes | |
| Ha: | Wye. Ile tell you a strange thinge. | |
| | I heare there is a strange people to come into | |
| | this Land; They call them Sayters.[169] | |
| He | What are those. | 50 |
| Ry | Wye, they are halfe men, halfe Beasts. | |
| Pr | Barlakeings[170] you may see now Neighbours what learning | |
| | is to knowe these kind of Creatures. | |
| He | But what will they plunder. | |
| Ha: | Noe they understand not that phrase; Plunder. | 55 |
| Ry | But I will tell you, they are very loveing people. | |
| Pr | By my fayth of my body, That's well. | |
| | For then sure wee shall please them | |
| He: | If they bee not rude. | |
| Pr. | But these Witches, out upon them they can cunjer[171] | 60 |
| | our Kine[172] & sheepe from us. | |
| He. | And though wee see them well enough, wee darr not, | |
| | nor cannot speake to them. | |
| Pr | But if these Sayters would come, though they take | |
| | our kine & sheepe from us, as longe as they speake us | 65 |

---

up elsewhere in the masque. Given the occasional nature of the masque, the authors may refer to an incident that would be known to their audience.

168. A goodman is a "yeoman, a farmer" who is "below the rank of gentleman" (*OED*).

169. Part men, part beasts who are often represented in the company of Dionysus, the Greek god of wine and the figurehead of the Dionysian rituals of religious ecstasy. They are often figures of lust and disorder. Goodman Rye later alludes to them as "very loveing people" (56).

170. An oath.

171. Conjure.

172. Cows.

|       |     |                                                                   |      |
|-------|-----|-------------------------------------------------------------------|------|
|       |     | fare, wee should thinke our selves happy.                         |      |
| E.B   | He  | And I speake truely to you all, I had rather bee                  | [60] |
|       |     | amongest the Sayters then the Witches.                            |      |
|       |     | For the Witches they will say truely, & in trueth,                |      |
|       |     | when they plunder, & yet they alwaies thinke of the               | 70   |
|       |     | Devill.                                                           |      |
|       | Pr. | And they say they pray to him.                                    |      |
|       | Ha. | But pray you now let's have a songe before wee                    |      |
|       |     | part.                                                             |      |
|       | He. | Ey pray, for I love songs with all my hart.                       | 75   |
|       | Ry  | Fayth lets singe a songe of all our losses                        |      |
|       | Pr. | Come who shall beginn.                                            |      |
|       | Ha: | Wye my Naunt Henn.                                                |      |
|       | Ry  | Well content and soe wee'le follow.[173]                          |      |
|       | Pr  | For what should wee doe, though wee dye to morrow                 | 80   |
|       | He. | Or be beggers to morrow                                           |      |
|       | Pr. | Come Naunt Henn, hem̃[174] & begin.                               |      |

| E.B. | | The Songe. | [61] |
|------|--|------------|------|

|      |     |                                          |    |
|------|-----|------------------------------------------|----|
|      | He: | I have lost my melch[175] Cow.           |    |
|      | Pr  | And I have lost my Sow                    | 85 |
|      | Ry  | And for my Corne I cannot keepe,          |    |
|      | Ha  | Nether can I my pritty sheepe.            |    |
|      | He. | And I have lost fowre dozen of Eggs       |    |
|      | Pr  | My Pigs are gone, & all their Heads       |    |
|      | Ry  | Come let us wishe for Health              | 90 |
|      | Ha  | For wee can have noe wealth               |    |
|      | He: | Now I will hope for Joy                   |    |
|      | Pr  | And in meane tyme let's bee a Toy[176]    |    |
|      | Ry  | Since that wee have noe plenty[177]       |    |
|      | Ha  | And our Purses, they are empty            | 95 |
|      | He: | Since that wee have noe plenty            |    |
|      | Pr. | And our Purses they are empty.[178]       |    |

173. Rye agrees with Hay's suggestion.

174. Hum.

175. Milk.

176. Be frivolous.

177. Food shortages and other hardships were very common during the Civil War.

178. There are three blank pages following this song, indicating that there may have been plans for more antimasque scenes. The Beinecke manuscript has one blank page following this song.

J.C.                The Sheppards and Sheppardesses                        [65]
                        the first Sceane onely.
                    The Sheppardesses, and one of them from the
                        rest, comes from amongest them speakes
                    this Speech; as the Prologue to the                    5
                    Pastorall.


                The nomber ·4· Weomen &
                the ·4· Men appeares next Sceane.


            The first speech one woman alone speakes from the rest.


Cha:[179]           We're now become a fine coule shady walke[180]        10
                    Soe fit to answeare Lovers in their talke
                    And if sad Soules, would mallencholly tell
                    Let them then come, to visitt, where wee dwell
                    For wee're become a fine thick Grove of thought
                    Soe frises[181] even our selves with teares full fraught   15
                    When vendeducts[182] of wind, our sighes makes Ayre
                    These are the fruites of passion, restles care.
                    And this our Groto; soe who lookes may have
                    A welcome to a sad Shee Hermetts Cave.


J.C.                The ·2· Sceane the Men & Weomen seene,                20  [66]
                        being ·8· in nomber.
                    One woman walkes from all the rest, soe
                        speakes this speeche.


Inn:[183]           My Sheppardes habits, doe become mee soe
                    As I could wishe my freinds did now mee see[184]       25

---

179. This character's name is likely Chastity. The characters in the masque are denoted only by speech prefixes, though their speeches give an indication of their full names.

180. Cha. sets the scene, demonstrating in verse how the world of the masque differs from the baser world of the antimasque. Elaborate changes in scenery were commonplace in masques to show the transition from disorder to order; Cavendish and Brackley do not describe stage properties, using language alone to represent the change in tone.

181. Freezes.

182. Gusts.

183. Innocent. The Beinecke manuscript gives her full name.

184. An allusion to the authors' absent father and brothers. "Friends" in this period was often used for relatives and other close associates (*OED*).

Not that I take a pleasure in this place
But for discourse, of what I them could tell
An Innocence of life, to them relate
That soe my trueth of vertue they may see
My Garments are pure white because that I                    30
Will have noe coullour to hide spots of dye
But in my low Roves[185] I will keepe
And all my fault shalbee my sleepe.
And if I dreame I shall then speake, O.'runn
Or els my prittie Lambe I doubt is gone                      35
And then before I open my Eye lidd
Shall dreame that I was feedeing of my Kidd.

Per.[186]  Your Fathers absence[187] makes you alwaies owne
Your selfe though hansom,[188] still to bee alone.


J.C.                         A Songe.                    40[66][189]


Cha:   His absence makes mee thinke I am
One that should prepare a Lambe
To sacrifice; that is my selfe to bee
A willing Marter for each one to see
The reason why; his absence makes mee sad.               45
And if noe hope, then death to mee makes glad
What am I now sure nothinge but a Butt[190]
And every thought's, greifes Arrowes of my luck
Soe never hit the white,[191] untill I trace
Some happy thought to figure soe his face               50
Then am I happy, but when find him not
I wishe that thought I could have then forgot
Then sit I downe to make my selfe appeare
The Winter of a Summers coulder yeare.


---

185. Robes.

186. He is called "Persw" in the Beinecke manuscript, indicating that his name is likely Persuasion.

187. As in *The concealed Fansyes*, the absence of the father is the chief conceit of the masque. His absence causes the women to be unhappy and unwilling to be wooed by their suitors.

188. Attractive.

189. Two successive pages are numbered "66."

190. "A mark for archery practice; properly a mound … on which the target is set up" (*OED*).

191. A white target placed on the mark in archery practice. She is unlucky.

| | | | |
|---|---|---|---|
| | Per[192] | Come let us walke that wee may sweetely heare | 55 |
| | | The Birds to singe their severall noted tunes | |
| | | As if the yeare was onely made for wee | |
| | | Where nature courts us to each finer shade. | |
| | Inn | O.' noe, the innocence of Sheepe, | |
| | | Shall bee my onely care to keepe. | 60 |
| J:C. | Per | What pleasure is in them to please you soe | [68] |
| | | That you invite your selfe onely to heare | |
| | | The blateings of each Lambe that loves it Pap[193] | |
| | | And afterward, doth lye it downe to sleepe | |
| | Inn | The milke of Kine,[194] I'le huswife,[195] for to make | 65 |
| | | Butter to keepe my thoughts awake. | |
| | Per. | But I should rather thinke to make a prize | |
| | | Of Garlands for to crowne our selves w[th] all | |
| | | And if in love you did become your vow | |
| | | You should my Garland have and mee withall | 70 |
| | Inn: | I owe my selfe to noe ambitious foe | |
| | | For all my thoughts are truely humble low. | |
| | Per | I pray thee bee my Saint and heare my prayer | |
| | | For certainly I have noe other way | |
| | | To hope that you will ever graunt to mee | 75 |
| | | Unlesse I should my forme of man put of | |
| | Inn: | I dedicate my selfe to each sweete feild | |
| | | For to your Sex I'm very loth to yeild. | |
| | Per. | I am resolv'd from you I will not goe | |
| | | Till that your resolution I doe know | 80 |
| | Inn | What in a verse doe you begin to speake | |
| | | And if then witt ther's none can owne you weak | |
| | Per | I sweare as love you nothinge will I say | |
| | | If I may knowe, what's your ambitious way. | |
| | Inn | I darr not that relate for feare some wynn | 85 |
| | | Out my designe, then hate my selfe as sinn.[196] | |
| J:C: | Per | Whispri't in my Eare for further shalt not goe | [69] |
| | | But to my thoughts for then my selfe a foe | |
| | Inn | If that your promise you will keepe | |
| | | I will then singe, but first you'st bee a sleepe | 90 |

192. Persuasion resumes his conversation with Innocent after the song ends.

193. Breast.

194. Cows.

195. Housewife.

196. Innocent will not give in to Persuasion's demands.

Per        Well I will appeare like a dead witherd leafe
                  And soe convert my selfe to sleepe stupid deafe

The Songe.

Inn:        I noe[197] wee're resolved each shall see
                  What's dew,[198] that's duety which word wee'le bee     95
                  For sadnes Earth I hate, should bee my grave
                  But passions teares I'le swim in, to the wave
                  Of happines, then thoughts doe clipp
                  And chalke the way, to bringe mee to a shipp
                  Which will content mee when all Waters see.     100
                  For then shall thinke the Sea is condenst mee
Per.        The sad contynuance of your Teares
                  Allready makes mee Seasick of my feares.

The other Sheppard & Sheppardes walkes     [71][199]
togeather.     105
The Sheppard begins & speakes this
Speeche.

Con:[200]     Since that your greife is tourn'd to love
                  You will now sure have thought of mee
                  For thus to you I ever had     110
                  An admiration love to owne
                  And soe I sent my fate to you
                  Who I have found sadly alone.
Ver:[201]     Why doe you take the confidence to speake
                  After one forme of Lovers rate of weake[202]     115
                  When that you see mee mallencholly sitt

197. Know.

198. Due.

199. There is no authorial attribution for this scene. Page 70 is blank.

200. This character's name may be Confidence or Conceit.

201. This character's name may be Vertue.

202. Presumably Ver. and Con. have just observed Per.'s failed attempt to woo Inn. Ver. wonders why Con. thinks he would be successful with the same approach.

|      |                                                       |          |
|------|-------------------------------------------------------|----------|
|      | Thinkeing onely to milke into my kitt.[203]           |          |
| Con: | When that you take the paps of Kine[204]              |          |
|      | Tell mee what can your fancy make                     |          |
|      | Is it a pleaseing note or tune                        | 120      |
|      | Or are they thus your Preisthood knells.[205]         |          |
|      | Come let us walke that wee may heare                  |          |
|      | The joy of love & then his feare.                     |          |
| Ver: | Noe my remorse shalbee the gentle Spring              |          |
|      | Where sweetely I may heare the Birds to singe         | 125      |
|      | Which makes my fancey, thoughts truely to thinke      |          |
|      | I shall noe more with mallencholly winke.             |          |
|      | For thus I shalbee with my sweeter Sheepe             |          |
|      | And thinke w^ch way to make his Lambe to sleepe.      |          |

E.B.

The third Sheppard & Sheppardes w^ch is  130[73][206]
a Shee Preist whose name is Chast.
The Sheppard begins this Speech

|        |                                                     |     |
|--------|-----------------------------------------------------|-----|
| Car[207] | Your garbe makes mee I knowe you not[208]         |     |
| Ch:    | Have you already mee forgott                        |     |
|        | I'm myne w^ch now full of greife                    | 135 |
|        | And sadnes, doubts, hath noe releife                |     |
|        | But if joyes freinds, once would but come.          |     |
|        | Accounts I'de make up in mirthes sūme               |     |
| Car.   | Now knowe you are a Shee, & sure a wife.             |     |
| Ch:    | Yes, and am resolv'd to live a Country life          | 140 |
|        | Since from my freinds I cannot heare                |     |
|        | I'm smother'd in sighes, Torter,[209] feare.        |     |
| Car.   | But whats your consolation.                          |     |
| Ch:    | To keepe, pritty sheepe.                             |     |
|        | And to bring upp grass, my Teares shall weepe.      | 145 |
| Car.   | You owne your selfe to bee a wife                   |     |
|        | And yet you practice not that life.                 |     |

203. "A deeper vessel with a lid used as a milking-pail" (*OED*).

204. When you milk a cow.

205. Con. mocks Ver's devotion to and interest in her vocation.

206. Page 72 is blank. There is a blank page at the same point in the Beinecke manuscript.

207. Careles, or Careless. He is named at line 247.

208. There are three vertical dots at the end of this line.

209. Torture.

Ch:        I'm now become a Bracken,[210] branch & stalke
                Soe sadnes dew[211] recrutes mee to a walke
                Thus joyed news, did pensell mee with sweete greene   150
                But now not soe greife shalbee all my Queene
                Yet I'le stay to contynew fresh to heare.
                Each Lover thus contemplate of his feare.
                And when their sweeter walke, & wood of thought
                Expres'd I'm not left, but by them I am sought.[212]     155

E.B.       To bee their coullour, sweete & finer seate        [74]
                And then their greife of passion they'l relate
                By each pure Cristall Eye a drop of teare
                And soe their sighes doth buery them just there.
                Thus I'm their Preist, soe they confesse to mee,     160
                Untill, good news my Habits chang'd to bee.

J.C.        The Third Sheppard spake to the Sheppardes     [75]
                    Priest, accompained wᵗʰ the 4ᵗʰ· Sheppardes
                    whose name is ·Jearer·[213]
                    The Sheppard begins this Speech.      165

Car       If you our sacred Preist then bee
                I pray you then give leave to mee
                To tell how I'm condem'd to heare
                The simple ill nature of a jeare
                For never doe I speake, my trueth of witt     170
                But this gives mee a scornefull skitt
                And I doe vow before your holly soule
                I will in love to hir as Snow grow coule
                For if hir witt bee scorne to rayle[214]
                I'le leave hir as a horrid stale.        175
Pr:[215]     You have great reason if shee will not mend
                In Justice then, to let your Love's knott end

---

210. Possibly a reference to Elizabeth Brackley's married name. She married John Egerton, Viscount Brackley, in 1641, but likely remained with her sisters at Welbeck Abbey until 1645. See the section Life and Works in the introduction to this part of the volume.

211. Due.

212. A catchword is used here. Catchwords are not generally used in this manuscript.

213. Jeerer. One who jeers or taunts.

214. Rail. Complain or rant. Careles does not want his wife to be a scold.

215. Despite the different speech prefix, this is presumably Per.

| | | | |
|---|---|---|---|
| Sh:<sup>des216</sup> | | Ha, ha, ha, what a Complaintive²¹⁷ bee | |
| | | Thou makes thy selfe for each to see. | |
| Car. | | Thy empty witt I now will tell | 180 |
| | | Your rayle made Devills whipp you out of Hell. | |
| | | Goe, goe thy way, I'le tell thy fate | |
| | | Each sex, each creature shall thee perfect hate | |

E.B.   Per   My love is pure, serene & cleare,
          Which ownes not courser witt, of Jeare.²¹⁸   185
E.B.      Now I doe begg your Hollynes will say   [76]
          I may bee happy in this my loves day
          And when but happy, as of hir to thinke
          Her witt condemps mee in dispare to sinke
          Sayeing shee 'sad, sad as greifes soule   190
          Which makes mee wishe, for mee the Bell should toll
   Ch:   I can noe Cordiall²¹⁹ give, since say,
          I am hir Sister in greifes pay.
   Con   My Mistris is a Cristall that's select
          None but pure witt to hir can just reflect   195
          And I'm contented if shee give a looke
          To dayly studdy on hir Features book
   Ch:   Come let us goe to our God duety pay
          That is to singe him Anthome²²⁰ every day.
J.C.   Je:   If not my company allow I'le make a Jeare,   200
          And afterwards I'le sit mee downe & fleare.²²¹
   Ch.   Ill nature Jearer is in loves Church a sinn
          Then in their Temple sure cannot come in.

      The three sad Sheppardesses, goe to a little   [77]
      Table, where they singe this Songe in parts.   205
      The Sheppards sadly sitt on the grownd,

216. Jearer.

217. "Given to complaining" (*OED*).

218. Jearer's coarser wit. The authors manipulate her name for the sake of the rhyme scheme.

219. Medicine.

220. Anthem. "A composition, in prose or verse, sung antiphonally, or by two voices or choirs, responsively" (*OED*).

221. Fleer. "To laugh mockingly or scornfully; to smile or grin contemptuously; hence, to gibe, jeer, sneer" (*OED*).

and the Jearer wench apart from them.
The Shee Preist begins.

Songs Anthome.

E.B.  Cha  When once the presence of a freind is gone          210
           Not knoweing when hee'le come, or stay how longe
           Then greife doth fill it selfe w<sup>th</sup> a reward
           That is when passion flowes without regard.

J.C   Inn:  His absence makes a Chaos sure of mee
            And when each one doth lookeing looke to see       215
            They speakeing say, That I'm not I.
            Alas doe not name mee for I desire to dye

      Ver   And I your Sister can noe way goe lesse
            As by my Face of palenes you may gesse²²²
            Then let us singe in Choros Anthome, pray,         220
            To see our loved freinds, doth make our day.

J:C:        The ·3· Sheppardesses Sisters speakes        [78]
            this in severall lines in answeare to one
            another.²²³
            The Shee Preist begins.²²⁴                        225

      Cha:  The univers mee thinks I see
      Inn:  In little moddle²²⁵ is just wee
      Ver   For wee're as constant to our²²⁶ way
      Cha:  As it can bee of night and day
      Inn   Our mallencholly that's the night               230
      Ver   And when Joyes hope then 'tis day light
      Cha:  Our Winter is sad thoughts dispare
      Inn   Soe mallencholly sighes makes Ayre

222. Guess.

223. This part of the masque echoes the antimasque song of Naunt Henn, Gossip Pratt, Goodman Rye, and Goodman Hay beginning at line 84 of The 2 Antemasque.

224. Greer et al., *Kissing the Rod*, 112, point out that lines 226–43 also comprise a poem titled "Loves Universe," found earlier in the manuscript. The poem is on page 20 of the Bodleian manuscript and page 22 of the Beinecke manuscript.

225. Model.

226. "Loves Universe" has "my" instead of "our" here.

| | | |
|---|---|---|
| Ver | Which w^th feares conflicts makes a wind | |
| Cha | And after doth raine showers of kind | 235 |
| Inn | Our couler hopes of what wee wishe | |
| Ver | Can water freize to Ices Dysh, | |
| Cha: | And passion thoughts of what wee feare | |
| Inn | Can thaw Ice Dyshe, though nea're soe deare | |
| Ver | Our Springe is onely Joyes of thinke | 240 |
| Cha: | Yet frosty feare doth make us shrinke | |
| Inn | Our Summer is, if that could bee | |
| Ver | Father, Brothers, for to see. | |
| | | |
| Cha: | God of our love give happines to say, | |
| | Your welcome, when wee owne him as our day. | 245 |

<table>
<tr><td>E.B.</td><td>The ·3^d· Sheppard speakes this to the rest<br>whose name is Careles.</td><td>[79]</td></tr>
</table>

Now what's here a Hee cave, as was a Shee
Or are you a could Groto for to bee.

> The ·3· sad Sheppards sings this in parts.    250
> And the two last lynes in Choros.

| | | |
|---|---|---|
| Per | Since that our Deares wee cannot have, | |
| | Wee're bueryed in loves cruell Grave. | |
| | | |
| Con: | Noe wee're tortred upon the rack of greife, | |
| | As soe to love wee make our selves a Theife. | 255 |
| | | |
| Per | When steale a looke it is a Plunder, | |
| Con | If bar'd sight, our hearts doe breake assunder.[227] | |
| Car | This to mee is a great wonder. | |

> The ·4^th· Sheppard whose name is
> Freedome sings this as hee comes    260
> in, to the sad Lovers.

---

227. These lines in the Beinecke manuscript have a significant number of corrections. The deleted lines are difficult to decipher, but they appear to have been "Soe heat contracted makes us thunder / When bar'd sight it brakes our Harts a sunder." Bennett argues that this change shifts the characterization of the suitors "from the men's loudness and potential violence ('thunder') to heartbreak in the face of their mistresses' intransigence." "Now Let My Language Speake," 10.

Fre:        Fy, fy, what a coyle is here,
To make love chyme to feare.

J.C                      Freedome then speakes this to the three    [80]
                            sad Sisters ·Sheppardesses·    265

Fre:        You three Devinities of sad, pray 'tell
What kind of way you would like well
Could I but any of you please
I'de runn into Loves high disease
But your most cruell, gentle flame    270
Will make mee tell my courtshipp dreame
For otherwaies I darr not speake to you
Doubting you'l judge mee of a looser crue
But now I begg to freely heare
What one you'l harber in your Eare    275
If this noe word of you can sure begett
Tell mee how I, my Mistris should besett.

J.C.  Cha:    Tell hir noe more your fansyes²²⁸ dreame    [81]
Nor in your Cupps hir health in flame
But if you speake let it bee witt    280
Soe by you shee, may darr to sitt.

I would not have you hir prophane
With formall speeches which proves lame
For in love sure it is a sinn
If not by sword your Mistris winn    285

Your courage should soe well be known
As thoughts of you protected hir alone
And if by chaunce, each speake your publique fame
Then should shee blush, at nameing but your name

And when you meete your carrage should be such    290
As you should speake, but yet not speake too much
But gentle lookes, and after then.
Give hir your gentle language of the Penn.

---

228. The "s" was added in later by the scribe; he did not use a caret to indicate the placement of the insertion.

| | | | |
|---|---|---|---|
| Fre: | This is good Counsaile, & I'le follow it, | | |
| | That is, that if I can, I will have witt. | 295 | |

E.B             The ·4ᵗʰ· Sheppard speakes this to the three   [82]
                                  sad Sheppards.

Fre: Now to you my Country wench I'le bringe
Whose very face sweares shee's right the Spring
Thus I'le bring you every one a lass   300
Whose skinne's as smooth as Cristall ball or Glass
Per Noe by Cupid they shall not bee our Loves
Con: For wee will bee as true as Turkle Doves²²⁹
Fre: Come promise mee with them you'l dance
And then your Eye to them must glance.   305

J.C.              Freedome speakes this to the three
                     sad Sheppardesses.

Fre: If you will dance, wee'le have an Ayre
Shall chyme as chast as devine care
Ch: Our vow will admitt noe such Toye²³⁰   310
For absent freinds gives us noe joy
Car. Come Jearer wee will have you in
Though I doe vow, good nature you'l ne're winn

Fre: How like you now my Country Lasces,
That in love lookes, will bee your Glasses.   315

J.C. Car. Now could wee Ladies have but ~~sh~~²³¹ such a dance   [83]
That would but fetch your freinds, now out of Fraunce
You then would well approve of this our mirth
But since not soe, you doe appeare sad Earth.

Fre: Come Musicke let's have now a Rownd,   320
To prove my Country Wenches rightly sound.²³²

229. Turtledoves often represent devoted love. The mournful voice of the turtledove is also apt, given Con.'s circumstance.

230. Trifle.

231. This is the only strikeout in the play and is therefore retained in this edition.

232. Masques traditionally end with dancing, but the grieving sisters' lack of assent makes it unclear whether they dance. See Content and Analysis in the introduction to this part of the volume.

J·C· My Lord it is your absence makes each see[233]        [84]
For want of you, what I'm reduc'd to bee
Captive or Sheppardesses life
Gives envy leave to make noe strife
Soe what becomes mee better then                    5
But to bee your Daughter in your Penn
If you're now pleased I care not what
Becomes of mee, or what's my lott
Now if you like, I then doe knowe
I am a Witt, but then pray' whisper't low.          10

E·B· My Lord your absence makes I cannot owne,
My selfe to thinke I am alone.
Yet Sheppardesses can see to read.
And soe upon your stock of wit I feede
Soe beggs your blesseing to like this               5
Then am I crown'd w^{th} hight of bliss.

---

233. These two verses lack a heading. In the Bodleian manuscript, they are placed between *A Pastorall*, in which the authors imagine themselves as shepherdesses, and *The concealed Fansyes*, in which they imagine themselves as captives. The poems may thus provide a transition from one play to the next. In the Beinecke manuscript, they are positioned between *A Pastorall* and the short poem that concludes the volume, "Upon the right honourable the Lady Jane Cavendish her booke of verses." As discussed in the Note on the Text in the introduction to this part of the volume, the authorship of this poem is unknown.

These Textual Notes record variants in wording between the Bodleian and Beinecke texts of *A Pastorall*. Differences in spelling or upper- or lowercase letters appear only when they are incidental to other variants. Insertions made by the scribe are surrounded by single quotation marks. Deletions made by the scribe are represented using strikethrough. Editorial insertions are surrounded by square brackets.

The Bodleian text precedes the square bracket; the Beinecke text, based on a microfilm copy of the manuscript, follows the square bracket. The Beinecke text has not been edited.

The Antemasque

| | |
|---|---|
| 43 | If but a Mischeife] ~~But If~~ 'but' a mischeife |
| 46 | Come light your distaffes and weeˈe try] Come [illegible deletion] 'light' your distaffes and [illegible deletion] 'weeleˈ trye. |
| 51 | Pray let mee know of thee] Pray let me know of ~~you~~ thee |
| 77 | all fall] |

2 Antemasque

| | |
|---|---|
| 12 | occadtions] occaˈdˈtions |
| 85 | And I have lost my Sow] And I have lost my 'Fat' Sow |

Masque

| | |
|---|---|
| 10 | Cha] Chast |
| 15 | frises] Fresco |
| 24 | Inn.] Innocent |
| 25 | As I could wishe] As I [illegible deletion] Could wish |
| 38 | Per.] Persw |
| 55 | Per.] Pers. |
| 59 | Inn] Inn ~~Cha~~ |
| 68 | Garlands] Garlans |
| 94 | I noe] I [illegible deletion] noe |
| 135 | I'm myne w$^{ch}$ now full of greife] I'm myne which now 'is' full of greife |
| 145 | And to bring upp grass] And to [illegible deletion] 'bring' up gras |
| 153 | Each Lover thus contemplate of his feare] Each lover thus contemplate of their feare |

154     thought] thoughts
159     buery] b'e'ury
166     Car] Shep:ʳᵈ
174     Snow] [illegible deletion] 'Snow'
180     Car.] ~~Shep:ʳᵈ~~ 'Car'
192     Ch:] Cha
209     Songs Anthome] ~~The~~ Songs Anthome
211     when hee'le come] when ~~theyele~~ 'heele' come
217     Alas doe not name mee] Alas doe not name 'mee'
247     Careles] ~~Freedome~~ Careless
248     Now what's here a Hee cave] 'Now' What's here a Hee [illegible deletion] 'cave'
255     When steale a looke it is a Plunder; If bar'd sight, our hearts doe breake assunder.] ~~"Soe heat contracted makes us thunder / When bar'd sight it brakes our Harts a sunder."~~ When steale a looke it is a Plunder; / If bar'd sight, our hearts doe breake assunder.
255     ] ~~The foureth sheppard whos name is Freedom speakes this~~
258     Car] ~~Fre~~ Car
258     This to mee] ~~Now~~ this to mee
264     Freedome then speakes this] ~~The [illegible deletion] 4ᵗʰ Sheppard~~ 'Freedom then' speakes this
303     Turkle Doves] Turkell Doves
306     Freedome speakes this to the three sad Sheppardesses] Free 'To the 3 sad Sheppardesses'
310     Ch] Cha

The concealed Fansyes

Ladyes I beseech you blush not to see
That I speake a Prologe being a Shee[235]
For it becomes as well if votes[236] cry Eye[237]
Why then should I, a Petticote cry fye,                                      5
Gentlemen if soe you allow, is witt
Why then not speake, I pray your patience sitt
And now to tell you trueth of our new Play
It doth become a womans witt the very way[238]
And I did tell the Poett plainely trueth                                     10
It lookes like ·18· or ·22· youth
Or els it could not bee, as 'tis but well
I'le say noe more untill yo[r239] hands Playes tell[240]


The second Prologe spoke by a Woman.

Though a second Prologe spoke to our Play
I will speake trueth, 'tis woman all y[e] way
For you'll not see a Plott in any Act
Nor any ridged, high, ignoble fact                                           5
Feareing you'll sensure[241] mee now full of Tongue
It is not fitt, that I should speake too longe.

234. The two prologues to *The concealed Fansyes* mirror the two dedications of Cavendish and Brackley's *A Pastorall*, where the first dedication is signed by Cavendish and the second by Brackley. The prologues here are unsigned, but they may have been intended for each of the sisters to speak in performance. A running head is not used in this play; the title of the play appears as a heading only on page 91.

235. For the early modern expectation that playwrights and actors would be male rather than female, see the general introduction.

236. The collective opinion of the audience.

237. Aye.

238. The play is becoming to a woman's intellect and ingenuity. The line also suggests that playwriting and performance in the domestic context are appropriate activities for women.

239. In *The concealed Fansyes* the scribe consistently uses a short form for "your." These short forms are not used in *A Pastorall*, although the plays are clearly written in the same hand. This difference could lend credibility to the claim that the plays were copied at different times. See the introduction to this part of the volume for further discussion.

240. Until the approval of the audience is signaled by applause.

241. Censure.

A perticuler Prologe to your Lo:PP242                                    [88]

My Lord

If that your judgement doth approve of wee,
I pray you smile, that all may truely see,
You like, & doe approve, of what wee say,                     5
And then each one will freely give their pay,
If then your quicker witt doth crowne our Play
Your health shalbee our word today:

242. Lordship. Cavendish and Brackley's father, William Cavendish, Duke of Newcastle.

## The Actors²⁴⁴

243. Page 89 is blank.

244. This page is ruled in the manuscript, but was not filled in. See Figure 9.

The concealed Fansyes. [91]

## Act the first
### Sceane the first.

Co[245]: Prethee deare Companion tell mee in what humour[246]
          is thy Mistris.[247]                                              5
Pr[248]: Fayth my misfortune is shee knowes hir <u>Sceane</u> self[249]
          too well.
Co: What meane you by that?
Pr: That is shee will not lessen hir selfe att all by
          valewinge[250] mee.                                              10
Co: What doth shee scorne you?
Pr: Noe nor shee doth not admire mee
Co: And that's your greife.
Pr: Ey, for I would have hir Possett w^th a little Cupid[251]
          if I could.                                                      15
Co: O.' then you're not for matrimony, if you pretend Cupid.[252]
Pr: Yes but I am, for I hope Cupid will bee the - -

245. Courtly. Most characters in the play—aside from the members of the Calsindow family and the
female characters in the subplot—have names that describe their personality or their function. This
was very characteristic of the works of Ben Jonson, whose influence on Cavendish and Brackley's
works is discussed in the Life and Context section of the introduction to this part of the volume.

246. The balance of the four prevailing fluids of the body (blood, phlegm, choler, and black bile or
melancholy) indicates the temperament of an individual (*OED*).

247. "Mistress" could take on different meanings in the seventeenth century. According to the *OED*,
a mistress could be "a woman having control or authority," "a wife," "a woman loved and courted by
a man," and "a woman other than a wife with whom a man has a long-lasting sexual relationship."
Cavendish and Brackley's play explores many of these meanings of the word.

248. Presumption.

249. Scene self. This phrase is somewhat ambiguous, but it suggests that Presumption believes that
Tattiney, the woman he pursues, plays a role rather than being genuine with him. There is some ambi-
guity in the manuscript; "sceane" appears to be underlined and "self" could have been added at a later
time. The hand that wrote "self" appears to be different from that of the scribe.

250. Valuing.

251. Cupid, often represented as a boy, is the Roman god of love.

252. Elite marriages were typically pragmatic unions, designed to unite family properties, hence
Courtly's distinction between marriage and love.

Gentleman Usher[253] to Hymen.[254]

Co:  Fye that's not becomeing to have a Boy to usher in
the Gods.                                                          20

Pr:  Well then allowe him to bee a Page,[255] soe shee were
in love I care not, Now I have confest soe largely
to you: freely relate your Mistris to mee, & lett
mee knowe hir humour.

Co:  By God myne's soe Courtly coy,[256] I knowe not what to          25
make of hir, for when shee smiles I knowe not
whether 'tis a scorne or a grace.

Pr:  Doth shee speake much.

Co:  Noe but shee is soe full of hir neglecting silence,             [92]
as I am almost in dispare.                                         30

Pr:  But I see you have some reliques[257] of hope left you.

Co:  Wer't not for that I should bee absolutely nothinge

Pr:  Tell mee hir name.

Co:  Tell you hir name, will you bee secret then?

Pr:  Or may I never bee happy if I speake of yo$^r$s till you shall    35
reveale myne

Co:  But my curiosity is to knowe yo$^r$s first

Pr:  What must I bee S$^t$ George,[258] first both in hir - -
humour, & hir name, I will not bee made soe much
your foole.                                                        40

Co:  Well I'le speake hir name in a soft whisper. Lucenay.

Pr:  Sister to myne, I fayth

Co:  If soe shee valews Cupid noe more then if hee were
hir footeboy, & hir language is the[259] Torter[260] to a Lovers
Soule.                                                             45

Pr:  Fayth by yo$^r$ discription, I perceive they are Sisters,

253. A gentleman usher was a man of rank who served a person of a higher rank. In general, a gentleman usher was just under the steward in the hierarchy of large elite households (*OED*).

254. The Greek god of marriage and weddings.

255. Either a lowly youth serving in a household or an elite boy who serves in a noble household as
part of his education (*OED*). It seems the latter is indicated here.

256. A "display of shy reserve or unwillingness" (*OED*). That Luceny is described as being "courtly coy"
indicates that she is coy in a fashionable and refined way.

257. Relics. Remains.

258. England's patron saint, renowned for slaying a dragon.

259. "The" appears to be underlined. If so, perhaps "the" is to be emphasized when the line is spoken in
performance. It could also be marked for deletion since the line makes sense without it.

260. Torture.

|       | for my Mistris, valewes courtshipp, & a rich sute,²⁶¹ noe |
|       | more then signes to catch Dotterells²⁶² wᵗʰall; |
| Co: | Certainely they educate one another |
|       | for my Mistris is in the same humour. | 50 |
| Pr· | Come let's goe to them & see how they will act their |
|       | Sceanes.²⁶³ |
| Co: | Agreed, I'll see yoʳ mistris, & you shall see myne, |
|       | In their pousture²⁶⁴ of Coynes.²⁶⁵ |
| Pr: | Content; but let me knowe before you goe. | 55 |
|       | For wife what Mistris yoᵘ would wooe. |
| Co: | My Mistris truely I would have | [93] |
|       | A pritty Munckey,²⁶⁶ yet seeme grave |
|       | Hir face I'de have it plumpe to kisse |
|       | And that is as my heart doth wishe | 60 |
|       | Hir Stature I would have each see |
|       | A wife or Mistris shee may well then bee |
|       | In private knowe noe matrymony lawe |
|       | In publique, all should thinke I did hir awe |
|       | Hir petulance I'de onely have wᵗʰ mee | 65 |
|       | With others stately for to bee |
|       | I would not have hir thinke of wife |
|       | Nor mee as Husband to make strife |
|       | But justly have hir fraught with witt |
|       | Soe by mee, pritty man, may sitt. | 70 |

| Pr: | You have declar'd yoʳ Mistris life of day |
|       | But I'de have myne, mee more, for to obey.²⁶⁷ |

---

261. Suit. Clothing. The lines play on this sense of suit and a lover's suit in courtly love.

262. A type of bird known for its foolishness.

263. The text does not make it explicit when the two men listen in on Luceny and Tattiney (although in 2.1.281–82 Luceny and Tattiney mention their fear of being overheard).

264. The "ous" in "pousture" appears to have been corrected by a hand that was not the scribe's.

265. Coyness.

266. Monkey. The *OED* lists some contemporary meanings of the verb "monkey" as "to ape the manners of, mimic; to mock, ridicule."

267. They exit.

Act the first         [94]
Sceane the Second
The Lady Tranq:[268] & hir woman.[269]

| | |
|---|---|
| La: | Toy, come hither, I will tell yo$^u$ though I am upp |
| | Yet my designe is for all I am well to keepe my    5 |
| | Bedd, therefore resolve Toy, to dresse mee neately |
| To: | I will Madam, soe well as my education will give |
| | mee leave. |
| La: | Toy, tomorrow I intend to goe to my witts.[270] |
| To: | Who are they?              10 |
| La: | Monsieur Calsindos Daughters,[271] therefore my |
| | keepeing of my bedd is to plumpe upp my face Toy. |
| To: | But truely Madam in my opinion those Ladies lookes |
| | as if they would not mind much, the're too younge. |
| La: | O, Toy, but they can give such Carrecters,[272] as to make a  15 |
| | Lady appeare, or not appeare, besides I am in love w$^{th}$ |
| | their Father, soe I would have them like mee. |
| To: | But yo$^r$ La:$^{pp273}$ will not let them knowe soe much. |
| La: | Thou'rt an Asse Toy, for of my fayth, I will, they |
| | shall not bee ignorant of my love, for then I hope - -  20 |
| | Monsieur Calsindow will know, & in respect to him |
| | I will see the two Ladie Cozins,[274] & will carry[275] one of the |
| | Stellos[276] or both, for then I knowe I shalbee welcome, |

268. Lady Tranquility. This character—who is far from tranquil—is believed by many critics to be based on Cavendish and Brackley's soon-to-be stepmother, Margaret Lucas, later Margaret Cavendish, Duchess of Newcastle. However, Margaret Lucas was eighteen years old when she married Newcastle in 1645, so this assumption may be unfounded.

269. Toy, Lady Tranquility's gentlewoman.

270. Wits are often clever, fashionable groups of friends. See, for instance, the wits in Ben Jonson's *Epicoene* (1609).

271. Lord Calsindow is father to Luceny and Tattiney. When Lady Tranquility does make a visit, it is to Cicilly, Sh., and Is. in act 4; we also hear of a visit she made to Luceny and Tattiney's house in 1.3.26–39.

272. Characters. They can play such roles.

273. Ladyship.

274. The Lady Cousins—Cicilly, Sh., and Is.—appear later in the play (despite the number of cousins mentioned by Lady Tranquility, three cousins appear in the play). The latter two are not named except by their speech prefixes. Since they refer to themselves as cousins and Luceny and Tattiney refer to them as cousins as well, it is safe to assume that they are relatives or close family friends, and not necessarily cousins in the modern sense (*OED*).

275. Bring.

276. The sons of Lord Calsindow.

for they are their servants,[277] & 'tis thought will marry
them, but what say'st thou to that Quiff[278] & Pyner[279]                     25
that hath the Gilly flower,[280] & my best Smockband,[281]
will they not agree well togeather.
Speake, what art thou in a studdy of my marryage
to their Father.

To:      I was thinkeing of y^e Lasces,[282] & truely yo^r La:^PP hath          30 [95]
match'd them very well; If yo^r La:^PP please I will
fetch them.

La:      Noe stay what a Clock ist?

To:      'Tis almost ·10· Madam.

La:      That's well, for I have time to talke & dress ·5·                     35
howres w^th out interruption, Now what say you Toy
to y^e best dress[283] for y^e face? Doe you not thinke Pomatum[284]
will doe well, & rubb it over w^th Scarlett[285] after, & then
use m^r Trantams stil'd water,[286] & there are rarer Cordyalls[287]
in that water to plump upp the face Toy.                                 40

To       Truely Madam, but I conjecture w^th my selfe, the
Scarlett will take too much of y^e Pomatum of,[288] & will
not sufferr,[289] that stil'd Cordyall water to give a gloss.

---

277. Their suitors.

278. Cerasano and Wynne-Davies gloss this as a "lock of hair." "The Concealed Fancies," 209. This is possible, but it would be a very early instance of the word because the *OED* does not list this meaning before 1890. Cavendish and Brackley could mean "coif" (of which the *OED* lists "quoif" as an alternative spelling), "a close-fitting cap covering the top, back, and sides of the head."

279. Pinner. "A close-fitting cap worn by women (esp. of high social status) in the 17th and 18th centuries, having a long flap … on either side, sometimes worn fastened on the breast or pinned up on the head" (*OED*).

280. Carnation.

281. A collar.

282. Laces. Another element of Lady Tranquility's elaborate outfit.

283. The best way to dress or apply makeup to your face.

284. A facial ointment, like modern-day foundation.

285. Makeup to color the cheeks.

286. Distilled water. Waters were often branded as being the recipe of a particular doctor or elite woman.

287. Cordials. In this case, a medicine that stimulates circulation (*OED*).

288. Off.

289. Allow. Toy encourages Lady Tranquility to use fewer cosmetics.

La:     What thou woulest[290] have[291] mee use an oyl'd Maske.[292]
        A pox on't. I saw a Lady the other day that leaned                         45
        hir face to the Glasse of a window, & hir face tooke
        dust, Soe I knewe, 'twas that left soe much grease,
        soe 'tis nastie.
To:     Madam you have left out yo[r]. white Satten[293]
        Wastcote                                                                   50
La:     O impertinent dull braine, dost thou thinke I
        would have forgot that, come Toy away I'm resolv'd
        to take my bedd.[294]

Act the first                                        [96]
Sceane the third.
Gravity[295] & the Kitchen Boy.[296]

Gr:     Jack, what a Clock? Is not the bill for dynner[297]
        gone to my Lady? Speake, have yo[u] lost yo[r] tongue?                      5
        Speake I say.
Ja:     Yes S[r][298] the bill was carryed to the Ladies.
Gr:     Knowe how they like dynner, now ther's noe Tart[299]
Ja:     M[ris] Sage[300] told mee they were not upp
Gr:     Fy, Fy, as I am an honest man these witts will ne're                       10
        bee Housewifes, & nothing angers mee but they'le nether[301]
        chide nor comend[302]

290. Wouldest.

291. The scribe wrote "mee" between "woulest" and "have" and then deleted it.

292. Oiled mask. Face masks were commonly worn by gentlewomen to protect their skin from the sun and preserve their pale complexions, the ideal of beauty in the period. According to Farah Karim-Cooper, they were also worn to "protect their painted complexions." *Cosmetics in Shakespearean and Renaissance Drama* (Edinburgh: Edinburgh University Press, 2012), 54.

293. Satin.

294. They exit.

295. Gravity, the cook in the Calsindow household.

296. Jack.

297. The menu. It was the norm for the lady of the house to review it or at least take an interest in it.

298. Sir.

299. This could be a reference to the lack of availability of food, especially luxury goods like sugar, during wartime.

300. Mistress Sage, a waiting woman.

301. Neither.

302. Luceny and Tattiney's lack of interest in caring for and managing the household makes them fail to meet the ideals of domestic womanhood. As Gravity notes later in the scene, they are more

| Ja: | Yes under favour S$^r$, I remember they chid yo$^u$ for | |
| | not makeing a Quinch[303] Tart sweete enough | |
| Gr: | Before God, that's true, come good memory tell | 15 |
| | mee when they praised mee, speake or I'le make yo$^u$ | |
| | remember. | |
| Ja: | My good Sr, my good Sr, when a Lady was here. | |
| Gr: | When a Lady was here, speake or my stick shalbee | |
| | about yor Eares | 20 |
| Ja: | Wye if you could remember the Ladies name I could | |
| | then tell how[304] they prays'd you. | |
| Gr: | The Ladies name | |
| Ja: | Indeede the Ladies name is a hard one | |
| Gr: | I'le have it out, or I'le pluck yo$^u$ for dynner, & | 25 |
| | send yo$^u$ up as a black bird[305] | |
| Ja: | Wye it beginns w$^{th}$ Tray. | |
| Gr: | Trayvand | [97] |
| Ja: | Noe Tran: | |
| Gr: | Tran. speake | 30 |
| Ja. | Tran, Tran, Tranquility. | |
| Gr: | And what by that Lady | |
| Ja: | Wye, yo$^u$ made a great dynner, such an one as my Lady | |
| | liked | |
| Gr: | But what sayd shee? | 35 |
| Ja: | Wye shee sent yo$^u$ a ·20·$^s$ peece,[306] & hir woman - - | |
| | spoke as well as shee could, to let you knowe my | |
| | Lady was pleas'd, & I thought ·20$^s$· was great | |
| | Comendations[307] | |
| Gr: | The next tyme I stand in expectation for yor noe | 40 |
| | peece of flattery, I'le bee sent upp as a Friday | |
| | dynner.[308] For God knowes I can pretend to nothinge | |
| | but a leane Pike, & were that of a Poetts - - | |
| | dressinge the Ladies would like mee.[309] | |

---

interested in poets.

303. Quince.

304. The scribe wrote the word "you" between "tell" and "how" and then deleted it.

305. Black birds were thought to be bad luck.

306. A coin worth twenty shillings. Cerasano and Wynne-Davies note that this was worth one pound and was "a substantial amount of money, more than a token." "The Concealed Fancies," 210.

307. Here, as elsewhere in the play, the authors contrast Lady Tranquility, who behaves as women were expected to, and Luceny and Tattiney, who do not.

308. Meat was not served on Friday in either the Catholic or the Anglican church.

309. They exit.

Act the first                                    [98]
Scaene the foureth
The ·2· Sisters Luceny & Tattiney.

Lu:     Sister pray tell mee in what humour thou wert w^th
        thy servant yesterday, prethee³¹⁰ tell mee how you acted      5
        yo^r Sceane
Ta:      I beg your excuse, a younger Sister, cannot have
        the confidence to teach an elder.
Lu:     Well then I'le beginn first. I drest my selfe in a
        sleight way of carelesnesse,³¹¹ w^ch becomes as well,         10
        if not better than a set dress,³¹² & when hee made his
        approaches of love, by speaking in a formall way,
        I answear'd him I could not love soe dull a braine
        as hee had, always to repeate hee loved mee.
        I had rather have him say hee hated mee,                      15
        For that would bee some variety.
Ta:     But what sayd yo^u, when he express'd himselfe
        by oathes & Execrations.³¹³
Lu:     I told him I wondred hee had the confidence, seeing
        I kept my Chamber to trouble mee w^th his ympertinent        20
        language, w^ch ever produceth my vexation. For I will
        tell you Sister, It is ymposible to answeare him to what
        hee spake, but hee will catch some handle to blowe upp
        his ambitious wishes, therefore I put him of³¹⁴ with
        a sharpe reply, as I have told you before, & then sayd       25
        my face coude bee noe wayes invitable³¹⁵ for his affection
        therefore I did not desire to bee his courting stock to - -   [99]
        practize with against hee comes to his Mistris, &
        therefore told him if hee would not make an honourable
        retreate out of y^e howse, I would proclayme him a           30

310. Prithee. Please.

311. In a slightly disheveled way.

312. A more formal manner of dress.

313. A curse or denunciation.

314. Off.

315. Inevitable.

|      | Malignant,[316] or cause M[r317] Steward to make him make his retreate w[th], more confusion, soe bid him thinke of some visitt, for here I was resolv'd hee should not stay. |     |
|------|-----|-----|
| Ta:  | Pray' Sister, is hee a good fortune? | 35 |
| Lu:  | Yes & a very good title. | |
| Ta:  | Then I perceive yo[r] discretion likes him | |
| Lu:  | Ey, & his discretion may very well like mee, For my Father intends to give mee a great Portion,[318] therefore I shall not knowe whether 'tis his wisdome or affection, that makes choyce of mee | 40 |
| Ta:  | And will you contynew[319] this way of discretion w[th] him when your'e marryed? | |
| Lu:  | Wye doe you thinke I take thee shall alter mee,[320] | 45 |
| Ta:  | I heare their comeing I'le them defeate[321] | |
| Lu:  | Leaveing mee onely to their cunning cheate. | |
| Co:  | Madam your Admirer attends you.[322] | [100] |
| Lu:  | And thinkes to bee accepted for your new sute.[323] | |
| Co:  | Still in your insultinge way. | 50 |
| Lu:  | 'Tis tyrany indeed, to tell you trueth you are soe concious to your selfe, as you thinke you are, the onely object of perfection. | |

316. A rebel or one who is disaffected; used ironically to accuse someone of being sympathetic to the Parliamentarian cause in the Civil War (*OED*). *The concealed Fansyes* (ca. 1645) was written during the English Civil War (1642–1651), which was fought between the Royalists, who supported the monarchy, and the Parliamentarians or Roundheads, who supported Parliament as the primary governing body in England. From about 1644, the authors' father was in exile on the Continent, and Cavendish and Brackley were themselves under house arrest at Welbeck Abbey. See Life and Works in the introduction to this part of the volume,

317. "A title of courtesy prefixed to the surname or first name of a man without a higher, honorific or professional title" (*OED*).

318. Dowry.

319. Continue.

320. "I take thee" quotes the marriage vows from the solemnization of marriage in *The Book of Common Prayer* (1549).

321. A suitor is entering the scene. Tattiney, conceiving of courtship as battle, aims to defeat her suitor.

322. Courtly enters the scene. While the play does have formalized act and scene divisions, there are several very long scenes that have within them a number of natural divisions, such as this one.

323. Pursuit. His latest attempt to win her love.

Co:     Noe Madam I[324] am the object of misfortune, not haveing
        the least hope of your La.[pps] good opinion.                              55
Lu:     I should thinke my selfe, deboyst,[325] should I lend you a
        thought, for as I heare you are the onely libertine,[326] in
        the Towne, & I wonder you can bee soe greate an Imposture[327]
        in your pretended love, as to contract that face of—
        freedome to soe serious a peece of formality.                             60
Co:     Noe Madam, It is yo[r] sweeter face of innocence
        that converts the rudest Pesant[328] even into modesty.
Lu:     Ey but when y[e] Species retornes backe; my face mee thinks
        should bee converted into deboysenes,[329] now will not yo[r] next
        posture bee to stand, w[th] foulded Armes, but that posture       65
        now growes much out of fashion, that's altered to a serious
        looke of admiration, as if yo[r] face was soe terrible, as to
        tourne men to Statues.
Co:     I wish damnation Madam rather then thus to bee[330]
        tormented, by your unkinder love.                                         70
Lu:     Away, away, w[th] your Hippocriticall language, for I
        am not yet soe vaine as to beleive your dissembling
        Romances.[331]
Co      Well I'm gone, & am resolved to bee noe more.
Lu:     What you'll give out yo[r] dead to try what vanity of              75
        love I may bee possest withall, goe take what resolution
        you please.
Co:     Ha. I'le love my selfe better then to dye for one that hates      [101]
        mee, but I could bee a willinge Marter[332] to her that loves
        mee.                                                                      80
Lu:     Ha, Ha, Ha, I thinke soe, you would bee a willinge
        Marter to hir that loves you, & doe you thinke that is a
        high expression of love; this showes how much you hated

324. The scribe wrote "the" between "Madam" and "I" and then deleted it.
325. Debased.
326. "A person of dissolute or promiscuous habits" (OED).
327. To deceive or fraud.
328. Peasant.
329. Debasement.
330. There is an asterisk at the end of this line.
331. Luceny challenges Courtly's posturing by comparing his language to prose romances that glorified courtly love. See, for instance, Sir Philip Sidney's *The Countesse of Pembroke's Arcadia* (ca. 1593) and Lady Mary Wroth's *Urania* (1621).
332. Martyr.

|     |                                                                      |     |
|-----|----------------------------------------------------------------------|-----|
|     | hir, that would quitt hir soe soone, besides leaveing hir            |     |
|     | this Legacie to dye of a Consumption[333] for your sake.[334]        | 85  |
| Co: | Madam, am not I worth that Ribbin you hate worst                     |     |
|     | and that will I contemplate upon with adoration.[335]                |     |
| Lu: | I thought you had learnt better manners then to offerr to            |     |
|     | plunder mee of my favours.                                           |     |
| Co: | Give mee leave then passionately to begg a salute, & I will          | 90  |
|     | never see you more unlesse I may be answered w[th] more              |     |
|     | mildnes, for now every word you speake is a rack unto my             |     |
|     | soule, therefore give mee once more leave to begg the favour         |     |
|     | of yo[r] Lipps.                                                      |     |
| Lu: | When did you heare my Lipps were soe rude, as to come w[th]in        | 95  |
|     | distance of yo[r] sex, & to confirme you there is noethinge I        |     |
|     | hate more then a Country Gentleman,[336] who must ever salute        |     |
|     | comeing & goeinge, or else hee will whisper to his next - -          |     |
|     | Neighbour. I am proud, & I sweare, I would rather cut my             |     |
|     | Lipps of then sufferr you a salute.[337]                             | 100 |
| Co: | What a misfortune's this to mee,                                     |     |
|     | To court a wench that doth soe truely see.[338]                      |     |

Act the Second [102]
Sceane the first

|        |                                                                   |   |
|--------|-------------------------------------------------------------------|---|
| Fr:[339] | Presumption, I knowe thou dost presume of thy owne              |   |
|        | witt, & fansye, therefore prethee tell mee thy loved - -          |   |
|        | humour of Mistris.                                                | 5 |
| Pr:[340] | you thinke to catichise[341] mee at your pleasure, if you       |   |
|        | take mee to bee your boy, where's your reward of Plum?[342]       |   |

333. We now refer to consumption as tuberculosis. All that will be left to the woman in this scenario is to die. Luceny understandably finds this less than ideal.

334. Luceny challenges hyperbolic and clichéd statements of love as being empty and meaningless.

335. It was common in the ritual of courtly love for the woman to give favors—such as ribbons—to the man who pursues her.

336. The scribe wrote "Gl" between "Country" and "Gentleman" and then deleted it.

337. Luceny possibly exits the stage at this point, making Courtly's couplet an aside to the audience.

338. Courtly exits.

339. Colonel Free. A cousin to Luceny and Tattiney and a Royalist officer.

340. Presumption.

341. To preach.

342. The fruit. Used here to describe a reward, as in using the word "plum" to describe something good. Cerasano and Wynne-Davies note that Presumption refers, "ironically, to the nursery rhyme in

Fr:      Come prethee bee good natur'd, & let thy voyce relate
         Thy Mistris of thy sweete lov'd fansyes fate.

Pr:                          The Songe.                              10

         My mistris I would have Loves Booke
         Yet innocent should bee hir looke
         In company shee should thus bee
         A stately pritty thinge to see
         Then should shee bee, that when I kiss                       15
         Thoughts makes mee sweare, I still doe miss
         And then to mee a Toy, & witty
         Makeing mee madd for hir selfe pritty.

Fr:      I see sweete Tattyny in your Songe
Pr:      O' that lov'd name's, a Cordyall to my Tongue               20

                 Enter Corpolant[343] and Courtley                   [103]
Cor:     O Courtly my pouch of Gold, w$^{th}$ my way of craft, shall
         gane your Mistris from you
Co:      Doe you thinke your bancke of sordednes,[344] can make hir
         misunderstand hir selfe.                                    25
Cor:     Why S$^r$ what can shee wishe, but shee shall have,
         If title please hir I'le lay out ·20000$^l$:[345] for what honour
         or name shee likes best, & I knowe hir discretion is not
         taken with a rich sute[346] or a faire face, that appeares
         like one of your pollished Pictures                         30
Co:      Noe S$^r$, nor shee is not taken, with yo$^r$ peece of
         deformity of Fatt, whose face appeares as your
         worst Rustick,[347] Have you ever spoke to hir in the
         way of marriage?
Cor:     Noe but I intend first to speake to hir Cozen[348]          35
         to make the way & then to hir Father.

---

which Jack Horner 'pulls out a plum' from his pie." "The Concealed Fancies," 210.

343. A fat, wealthy, boorish, and unintelligent suitor to Luceny.

344. Sordidness. Dirty or filthy; also base, rough, and lacking in refinement (*OED*).

345. Twenty thousand pounds.

346. Clothes.

347. Rustic. A poor, country person. Corpolant, while rich, does not hold as high a rank as Courtly, although he does have the resources to buy himself a title.

348. Cousin. Colonel Free.

Co:     Your'e mistaken because shee carved you once a legg
        of a Capon, & gave you sawce to boote, your puft upp
        bladder thinkes to marry hir, by reason shee gave you
        the civility of the House, as being hir father friend,                    40
        w$^{ch}$ modest curtesye blowes your braine upp as Gunn powder
        into folly, but pray you S$^r$ doe mee the favour, after you
        have spoke to hir in the way of a Sutor, lett mee knowe
        yo$^r$ opinion

Cor:    I will S$^r$, & doubt not of success                                      45

Co:     Of beinge counted an impertinent Ass

Pr:     Come Corpolant if you bee in love, I'le put you into
        a Consumption,[349] what doe you take my friend to bee.

Cor:    A fine peece of vanity in a rich sute                                  [104]

Pr:     Ho: Corpolant, Corpolant, you're deceived hee                            50
        hath a good Estate besides a rich sute, & that
        Mistris Luceny knowes.

Cor:    I believe you not youth, I believe you not.

Pr:     In concernes you to have noe fayth in that

Cor:    Here's hir Cozen come now wee have good Company. Let's                    55
        drinke M$^{ris}$ Lucenys health
        If shee would but love shee should have all my wealth

Fr:     I have other busines then to drinke.

Cor:    What have you to doe.

Fr:     To give order for the Army                                               60

Cor:    Nay then I will comāund your stay
        Orders belongs to mee, soe mee you shall obey
        Bringe Sack[350] & Clarret[351] that wee may
        Make this my M$^{ris}$ Hollyday.

Co:     And I to see my mistris health belched out in severall                   65
        Tunns.[352] I'le stay to give hir an account, & soe revenge my
        selfe of him, for I hate hee should thinke of hir.[353]

Fr:     What thinke you of the takeinge of Ballamo[354]

Cor:    'Tis a very stronge place.

Fr:     The best is to watch them tame[355]                                      70

349. See note 333.

350. Sherry.

351. Red wine.

352. "A large wine-vessel, a cask" (*OED*).

353. An aside to Presumption.

354. The house where Cicilly, Sh., and Is. reside.

355. Be tame. The best action is to not fight.

| | |
|---|---|
| Cor: | Ey, but I would correspond first |
| Pr: | And recognos[356] till you bee soe drunke as you cannot give orders |
| Co | Now hee's drinkeing I'le put myselfe in the habitt[357] of one of my M[ris] servants, & see if I can cozen[358] him 75 of his pouch of Gold[359] |
| Pr: | It wilbee worth your change of habitt |
| Fr: | Come now let's have a tunne |
| Pr: | Our senses sweetly to perfume |
| Cor: | I love a canny brave Scotch Jigg. 80 [105] And afterwards a wench by mee to ligg.[360] |

Enter Courtly in the Habbit of one of<br>his M[ris] Servants.

| | |
|---|---|
| Cor: | O call that fellow back, where are you going? How doth your Mistris? 85 |
| Co: | Very well |
| Cor: | Set him a Chaire, you're very welcome, set him a seat or I'le comitt[361] some of you.[362] |
| Co: | I hope I shall not drinke soe much, but I may stand. |
| Cor: | In troth first I tooke you for a Sage[363] 90 Pray' what's your busines here |
| Co: | Fayth S[r]. my m:[ris] hath sent mee to borrow money for a Jewell shee hath a mind to buy. |
| Cor: | How much wants shee? |
| Co: | Shee sent mee to borrow ·1000[l].[364] 95 |
| Cor: | Here take this Bagg. |
| Co: | By God, I have cozened him Well S[r] I'le let my M[ris] knowe yo[r] kindnes |

356. The sense of this word is obscure; Cerasano and Wynne-Davies gloss it as "reconnoitre." "The Concealed Fancies," 210.

357. Clothing.

358. Cheat.

359. Courtly says this to Presumption out of Corpolant's hearing.

360. To have sex with.

361. Deal with some of you, i.e., fight some of you.

362. Corpolant commands Presumption and Colonel Free to do his bidding.

363. A wise person.

364. One thousand pounds.

| Pr: | What an old dotting foole is this to part w^th his money[365] | |
|-----|-----|-----|
| Co: | But hee's drunke, for were hee in his right sense | 100 |
| | hee would knowe my M:^ris would rather starve then - - | |
| | receive the monye hee had looked upon. | |
| | When hee's sober I'le let him see his drunken act | |
| Cor: | Come let's goe. | |
| Fr: | You meane carryed.[366] | 105 |
| Co: | Now will I to my Mistris & let hir see, | [106] |
| Pr: | What you have made Corpolent to bee. | |

Enter Presumption & Tattyney

| Pr: | Are you in better humour today will you give mee | |
|-----|-----|-----|
| | leave to speake | 110 |
| Ta: | Your Tongues at liberty[367] | |
| Pr: | Fayth soe 'tis but did not knowe whether you would | |
| | sufferr your Lover of admiration to express himselfe | |
| | your perpetuall servant. | |
| Ta: | O, S^r now I understand you, you spoke this yesterday to | 115 |
| | your Mistris, & thinkes to conferr the same upon mee, | |
| | & I to beleive soe foolish a Romancy.[368] | |
| Pr: | Are you still pleased to neglect your Honourer. | |
| Ta: | How you mistake your selfe, did I ever keepe you | |
| | soe much Company, as you to take the freedome, as to title | 120 |
| | my selfe your servant, or my Honourer I beseeche yo^r. - - | |
| | sweetenes to account of mee, as of your sad Creature & | |
| | Vassall.[369] How now your still[370] is nothing, but full | |
| | of ympudence.[371] | |
| Pr: | What will you bee alwayes my Tyrant, Now doe you | 125 |
| | thinke the pulling downe your Hatt & lookeinge | |
| | sadd, shall make mee beleeve yo^r speech for trueth, | |
| | but you are deceived, therefore bee gone to your Mistris | |

365. Presumption to Courtly.

366. Colonel Free carries a very drunk Corpolant off stage.

367. Your tongue is at liberty. You are free to speak.

368. Romance.

369. Vassal, servant, or slave. Cerasano and Wynne-Davies, "The Concealed Fancies," 210, ascribe the part of the speech from "I beseeche you … Vassall" to Presumption. The dialogue does make more sense if we assume that the scribe made errors when copying the text, though we cannot know that this is the case. Starr makes no changes to the text.

370. A vessel for distillation.

371. Cerasano and Wynne-Davies, "The Concealed Fancies," 210, ascribe lines 123–24 to Tattiney.

|     | & let hir knowe to make mirth that you have beene | |
| --- | --- | --- |
|     | w^th mee, & how rarely you have acted your parte, | 130 |
|     | and what a fine foole you will make hir if you can, to | |
|     | bee confident of your affection.[372] | |
| Pr: | By the Gods you would make mee madd, And when I | [107] |
|     | was you would not pitty mee. | |
| Ta: | There's noe danger of your distraction, since you can | 135 |
|     | have that Hiyjaculation[373] | |
| Pr: | I desire you wilbee pleas'd to give mee the happynes | |
|     | to sallute your hand,[374] & then I will bee gone | |
| Ta: | How I vow I hate you begone rude Creature[375] | |
| Pr: | I sweare this coy Wench makes mee not the same | 140 |
|     | But shee takes the right way to make mee tame[376] | |

Enter Luceny & Courtly.

|     | | |
| --- | --- | --- |
| Co: | Looke you here's Corpolants Pouch of gold, for when | |
|     | hee was in his drunken fitt, I named but your name | |
|     | & hee gave it mee. | 145 |
| Lu: | Ha now peece of confidence, Ile make you knowe you shall | |
|     | not make mirth with mee, & soe to find out my humour, & I | |
|     | am soe farr from beinge merrie, as I am very angry, as to | |
|     | thinke you should understand my witt, noe higher then | |
|     | to laugh at your cheate, besides hee was not himselfe | 150 |
|     | soe you have noe reason to bragg. | |
| Co: | Never of your favours, but I thought you had | |
|     | hated M^r Corpolant | |
| Lu: | You meane contemne[377] him, for I never thought | |
|     | him soe valewable[378] as to hate. | 155 |
| Co: | It seemes mee you doe | |
| Lu: | Sure your vanity thought my extreame hate to him | |
|     | would have made mee exprest[379] love to you.[380] | |

372. Cerasano and Wynne-Davies, "The Concealed Fancies," 210, ascribe lines 125–32 to Tattiney.

373. Ejaculation. "The hasty utterance of words expressing emotion" (*OED*).

374. He kisses her hand or tries to do so.

375. Tattiney apparently exits the scene with this insult.

376. Presumption apparently exits.

377. Condemn.

378. Valuable.

379. Express.

380. Luceny apparently exits.

| | | |
|---|---|---|
| Co: | Was there ever such a Tyrant Shee | [108] |
| | As to make noethinge of brave gallant mee.[381] | 160 |

Enter Tatyny.

| | | |
|---|---|---|
| Ta: | Sister have you heard of Corpolants folly | |
| Lu: | Ey, and his indiscretion, besides his over | |
| | great bounty to Courtly. | |
| Ta: | Noe more then Courtly | 165 |
| Lu: | What hath hee made you for him, or that - - | |
| | twatlinge[382] Lady, that thinkes you governe mee | |
| Ta: | Ey & Presumption too thinkes you doe governe mee, | |
| | doe you not mind how his Sister courts you,[383] | |
| | Ey, but I knowe who governes us both. | 170 |
| Lu: | Who prethee lett mee heare. | |
| Ta: | Monsieur Calsindow. | |
| Lu: | Ho, my Father indeede. And that Gentleman shall | |
| | bee my Alpha & Omega[384] of Governem.t: | |
| Ta: | What shall not M.r Courtly bee your Governo.r when | 175 |
| | you're marryed. | |
| Lu: | How often Sister have you read the Bible over | |
| | & have forgotten man & wife should drawe - - | |
| | equally in a yoke.[385] | |
| Ta: | I warrant you Sister I knowe[386] that Text | 180 |
| | as well, as you. | |
| Lu: | How impertinently then dost thou speake? | |
| Ta: | I wishe w.th all my heart Corpolant would come. | |
| Lu: | When ever hee comes, I will not speake to him. | [109] |
| Ta: | What will you lay[387] of that? | 185 |
| Lu: | My distruction or my Happines. | |
| Ta: | What's that? | |

381. Courtly apparently exits after delivering this aside to the audience.

382. Twattling. Chattering.

383. Lady Tranquility.

384. The beginning and the end.

385. Perhaps allusions to 2 Cor. 6:14, "Be ye not unequally yoked together with unbelievers," admonishing people to marry a person of faith, and Phil. 4:3, "And I intreat thee also, true yokefellow, help those women which laboured with me in the gospel, with Clement also, and *with* other my fellow labourers, whose names *are* in the book of life."

386. The scribe wrote a word beginning with "h" between "I" and "knowe" and then deleted it.

387. Bet.

Lu:     My distruction, is that when I marry Courtley I shall
           bee condemn'd to looke upon my Nose, when ever I walke
           & when I sitt at meate[388] confin'd by his grave winke to      190
           looke upon the Salt, & if it bee but the paireing
           of his Nales[389] to admire him.[390]

Ta:     Your Happynes then

Lu:     My happines when I am in the condition of his
           Wife, is still to ymagin him Courtley & I M$^{ris}$      195
           Luceny. and now you shall have noe more of
           mee

Ta:     O my wish Corpolant is here[391]

Cor:    Ladies you looke faire today

Ta:     Speake to your Ambition S$^r$.      200

Lu:     Alas he understands not; you must name my name,
           or els his dull braine understands not.

Ta:     Speake to my Sister S$^r$.

Cor:    How doe you faire Lady, not a word pray
           you, make your servant happy, for if you say—      205
           nothinge, I shall then understand you thinke Ey,
           & soe you will make mee very happy by yo$^r$
           neglectinge silence.

The Songe.      [110]

Lu:     I prethee Foole not speake noe more      210
                For I cannot thee like
           Thy folly hath beene great enough
                For mee to laughing sleight
           Thy face a blacke brus'd hony Combe[392]
                Thy selfe an Uggly Sott[393]      215
           Besides you are a Clogg of dum̃
                Soe I'le not bee your Lott.[394]

           There's none without it bee a Hagg
                Will ever bee your wife

388. A meal.

389. Cutting his fingernails.

390. Luceny dreads the subordination that will come with being Courtly's wife.

391. Corpolant enters.

392. Bruised honeycomb.

393. Fool, also a drunkard.

394. Lot. I'll not marry you.

And for Companions you are such                                          220
    As they will not bee rife
Then all your recreation is
    A full good Cup of Sack
And that your drunkenes doth sipp
    Which makes you beastly fatt                              225

You're onely fit for witches like
    For lookes of horrour you
Then shee to oynt,[395] & make a flight[396]
    In this to sweare shee's true
For sordid acts is your owne life                                        230
    And this each one doth see,
This Devill[397] you doe make a strife
    The Witch take you for mee.[398]

| | | |
|---|---|---|
| Ta: | Sister I sweare I infinitely com̃end your witt. I confesse | [111] |
| | you have wone yo<sup>r</sup> wager, but who must pay it to you? | 235 |
| Lu: | My selfe. | |
| Ta: | I sweare I longe to see't. | |
| Lu: | Nay prethee doe not speake w<sup>th</sup>out a pritty oath. | |
| Ta: | Wye as I hope to contynew Tattyny I longe to see thee marryed, | |
| | but I'm soe feard you will prove a foole. | 240 |
| Lu: | Doe you not doubt Luceny, but minde Tattyny for my observācon | |
| | is, that Præsumption doth through[399] his Cloke[400] as if hee - - | |
| | intended to governe you | |
| Ta: | Ey but as I hope to contynew my owne, I will make him | |
| | lay his Cloke of, if his carrage bee to sleight mee. | 245 |
| | For doe you thinke Sister, the words sayeing in the Church | |
| | shall make mee minde him more, then I doe now hee is my servant | |
| | for I intend to bee his Mistris. | |
| Lu: | You're right, for I intend to bee the same w<sup>th</sup> Courtly | |
| Ta: | But sure you doe not resolve to lett him knowe soe much | 250 |

395. Anoint. Representations of witchcraft frequently pervert domestic or religious practices to demonstrate the demonic nature of the alleged witches' actions.

396. The same line is used by the witches in 1 Antemasque, in line 65 of *A Pastorall*.

397. Devil. Luceny wishes that the witch, who she says is the only person who will marry him, will cause him much strife.

398. Corpolant exits.

399. Throw.

400. Cloak.

Lu:   O' I understand you, that is to say, the wife, but the
      Mistris to make his love contynew the longer
      Ey but Tatteny shall showe obedient when my Lady Knoweall[401]
      visitts hir.

Ta:   And soe I believe will you bee, when Mistris Courtley            255
      your mother in Lawe see yo[u].

Lu:   Yes fayth will I, but though I looke obedient & civill           [112]
      to hir, I will let her discretion understand in silence,
      that I knowe my selfe, & that I deserve thankes for
      comeing into hir familie, therefore I will not lessen my        260
      conversation for hir peece of sobriety.

Ta:   Ey Sister, but I doe not like that word, some Ladyes
      here in towne are much acquainted w[th], the language of
      friendshipp & conversation, as they will thinke.

Lu:   What, for as I hope for happynes I will contynew                265
      my innocent freedome with Courtely, & hee shall have
      a true peece of vertue of Luceny, & you neede not bee
      more jealous Sister of Lucenyes language, then you are
      of your selfe, of makeing who I please beleive I am
      an obedient foole.                                              270

Ta:   Doe you not wonder that Courtly & Præsumption, are
      heald[402] witts, for mee thinks there is noe such marracles[403]
      in their language.

Lu:   Wye that's because wee have beene brought upp in
      the creation of good languages which will make us ever          275
      our selves.[404]

Ta:   And I protest, Præsumption shall never see mee out of
      order when I am marryed, but in a morneinge, & at night
      in my severall Satten Petticotes & Wastcotes, & alwayes
      in my careles Garbe.[405]                                       280

Lu:           Come let us goe for I doe feare
              If att the doore they may us heare.[406]

---

401. Presumably Presumption's mother.

402. Held. Thought to be.

403. Miracles.

404. For a discussion of Cavendish and Brackley's unusually good education compared to many elite women of the Renaissance, see the section Life and Works in the introduction to this part of the volume.

405. Attire.

406. This could be an indication that Courtly and Presumption are seen overhearing Luceny and Tattiney's discussion. See note 437.

Act the Third[407]                                    [113]
Enter Mᵣ Friendly, Mᵣ Proper, & Mᵣ Devinity.[408]

Pr:    Come, what a Seige?
Fr:    By God I thinke soe, but where's the releife
       I'm sure our partie is now as flatt as a flunder.[409]        5
Pr:    And this Garrison flatter then any
Fr:    Pox ont,[410] I knowe that, where's our Officers
Pr:    Wye the old man[411] is att yᵉworkes[412]
Fr:    Have wee noe more?
Pr:    Yes, his Clerke, who you knowe's an Ancient[413]            10
Fr:    What wilt thou doe?
Pr:    Fight as well as a Gentleman Usher shall?
       And what wilt thou doe wᵗʰ thy Bulke?
Fr:    Stand in the halfe moone, & sweare you all into heart,
       & now, & then fight. By god, I thinke the Ladyes have       15
       a mind to see how I shall looke wᵗʰout an Eye.
Pr:    If I should want a legg I were casshier'd[414] from
       Gentleman Usher.
Fr:    Then you must have a Pention,[415] & if it bee a good one
       It will buy Sack & Clarrett enough in tyme to make          20
       you as bigg as I
Pr:    But our Ladyes doe not use to keepe[416] their - -
       Gentlemen Ushers, soe my desire must bee to begg
       as a lame Souldier of yᵉ Kings & the Kings lame
       Souldier.                                                    25
Fr:    Come Devinity, what sayest thou?                            [114]
De:    Fayth I've beene measureing, & the workes are

407. The scene shifts to Ballamo.
408. Three gentlemen ushers to Cicilly, Sh., and Is.
409. Flounder.
410. On it.
411. The man in charge of heading off the siege.
412. The works. Apparently these are barricades being erected to prevent the Parliamentarians from gaining the Royalist Ballamo.
413. An old person. The only surviving manuscript of this play is thought by most scholars to have been copied by the Duke of Newcastle's secretary, John Rolleston (1587?–1681), who would have been in his sixties when this manuscript is thought to have been written.
414. Cashiered. Dismissed from service.
415. Pension.
416. Support.

|     |     |     |
|-----|-----|----:|
|     | not made high enough for y^e Enemyes if shott will |     |
|     | enter into every Chamber of y^e Howse. |     |
| Pr: | Why will you not tell our Enginer[417] Governour soe | 30 |
| De: | I have, but hee is soe confounded. |     |
| Fr: | Why? doth hee doubt his workes? |     |
| De: | Noe hee cannot understand well Englishe |     |
|     | Nor I his language, but I thinke M^r Discretion |     |
|     | will have noe Seige, haveinge noe possibility of | 35 |
|     | releife. |     |
| Pr: | Come M^r Propper let us goe drinke |     |
|     | And afterwards to bed & Winke.[418] |     |

Enter Luceny & Tattyny Mallencholly[419]

|     |     |     |
|-----|-----|----:|
| Lu: | Sadnes I chide you, thou art slowe & dull | 40 |
|     | 'Tis greife w^th passion, makes a heart as full |     |
|     | Of gallant actions, & love gives the Challenge |     |
|     | Soe lif's not weigh'd, in this worlds harder Ballance |     |
|     | Then goe on wisely on a resolute grownd |     |
|     | And make noe question, but goe on y^e Round | 45 |
|     | And doe not make delayes, nor goe about |     |
|     | But shortly put unquiet life quite out |     |
| Ta: | Greife I wonder you should angry bee w^th mee | [115] |
|     | Thou did'st not see mee till after I was thee |     |
|     | But patience I have consider'd w^th my selfe, & can | 50 |
|     | Tell you Sadnes is the best, w^ch I'le bee & am |     |
|     | Your's is a[420] maddnes, for quiett will you see |     |
|     | But I'le greive to the bone, Anothemy[421] will bee. |     |

Enter an Angell

|     |     |
|-----|----:|
| Stay bee not angry sufferr w^th your friends | 55 |
| In like fortune yo^r selfe to them lend |     |
| For I doe hope the happy gaine wilbee |     |
| And that ere longe you joyfully shall see |     |

417. Engineer.

418. Sleep. They exit the stage.

419. Melancholy. The scene now shifts back to the Calsindow household.

420. The scribe inserted this word and indicated its placement in the line with a caret.

421. Cerasano and Wynne-Davies gloss this as "anathema." "The Concealed Fancies," 141.

Soe I'm assur'd you shall not make these ends
For happie shall you bee in your blest friends.[422]                    60

Enter Courtley and Præsumption

Co:       What are you upon marriage?[423]

Pre:     Ey, & I am dayly contemplateinge, how to make M:[ris] Luceny[424]
           fitt to entertayne my mother, & friends in the Country

Co:       That wilbee a hard designe                    65

Pre:     Fayth but I'le tell you the way I thinke of, as soone
           as I am marryed I will let hir knowe I am hir Husband

Co:       How doe you meane? Shee knowes that.

Pre:     Ey, but I meane to fooleyfie[425] hir all I can, & lett          [116]
           hir knowe that Garbe, that doth best become hir, is          70
           most ill favour'd, Soe shee shall nether looke, walke, or
           speake, but I wilbee hir perpetuall vexation, then
           send hir into the Country, where I will stay with hir a
           moneth, then tell hir my occations[426] drawes mee to Towne
           & soe leave hir to comtemplate mee in [    ][427] my absence, &          75
           to obey my Familye.

Co:       O Præsumption, thoul't bee a Devellyshe Husband, prethee
           more of this, that I may learne by thee, to knowe the word
           Husband

Pre:     Wye then who ever my wife fansyes I will not esteeme          80
           of though a femall, for men Servants shee shall nether
           darr to speake to them, nor soe much as to ymploy them
           were it but to knowe who it was that came last into y[e] howse

Co:       You'll bee over Jealous;

Pre:     'Tis but carefull, besides shee shall not stay w[th] hir          85
           owne friends or famyly after shee is marryed not three
           dayes. then once a yeare I'le bringe hir downe a Gowne
           in fashion, w[ch] w[th] contynewinge longe in the Country shee
           shall not knowe how to put on, then all my discourse shalbee
           to prayse the Ladies in London; & if shee doe but behave          90

422. They exit.

423. Are you soon to be married?

424. Presumably this is an error and Presumption should say "Tattiney."

425. Foolify. To make a fool of. Presumption's method for schooling his wife is similar to Petruccio's efforts in Shakespeare's *The Taming of the Shrew* (ca. 1590).

426. Occasions.

427. There is an illegible deletion in the text.

        hir selfe ugglie, then I'le tell hir that was like a good
        wife & an honourable stock to beare Children on
        w^th all I would have hir take the weeke Bookes^428
        w^ch is the onely way to make hir Uncapable of
        discourse or entertaynement, & if shee doe not give      95
        respects to my mother, & Sisters I will tell hir shee
        hath not deserved to enter into my hon:^ble old howse, & I    [117]
        knowe, contynually seeinge old longe Beards make
        leggs to mee,^429 will teach hir the fashion to obey.^430

Co:    Well Companion thou deserv'st the title of a Husband    100
        but if you'll have my opinion, Mistris Tattyny lookes as
        if shee were præpar'd for y^e ridgednes of a Husband.

Pre:   Why doe you thinke soe

Co:    By reason shee lookes, as if shee did not care for y^e
        word, part, & rather then contynue hir owne unquietnes   105
        shee would live w^th hir friends, you knowe hir Father
        is an understanding Gentleman, his dicurse^431 uses not to bee
        dull, catachyseinge, & they very much w^th him.

Pre:   A Poxe on you for your opinion, it hath done mee
        much hurt, prythee how pretend you?          110

Co:    Fayth I pretend to possess my sweete Luceny of my
        seincere affection, & if I can to make hir passionately love
        mee, & soe to gaine hir Fathers friendship, & then
        by love to gaine hir observancye,^432 w^ch I will retorne
        w^th greate respect, & all hir friends shall comāund    115
        mee.

Pre:   And shee too?

Co:    Noe she shall love mee soe well, as shee shall
        thinke mee worthy of my freedome, & soe wee will
        contynue the conversation & friendshipp of Lovers    120
        w^thout knoweing the words, of man & wife.

Pre:   This I understand to bee one of your Courtships    [118]
        to hir.

Co:    Noe fayth, shalbe my contynuall practice

---

428. Account books that were kept by the week.

429. Old men bow to me.

430. Presumption echoes early modern conduct books such as Juan Luis Vives's *A very frutefull and pleasant boke called the instruction of a Christen woman*, trans. Richard Hyrde (1529?) and William Gouge's *Of Domesticall Duties* (1622), which advocate for the control of women by men.

431. Discourse.

432. Observancy. Obedience.

| Pre: | Sure then you have great designes upon hir Father | 125 |
| Co: | Noe fayth I understand Gallentry better then to | |
| | have any designe, but to serve him your way w<sup>th</sup> your | |
| | wife is to educate hir just soe, as to hate hir w<sup>th</sup>in | |
| | 2· or ·3· yeares, or els you are soe proud as you would | |
| | have your selfe the onely valewable peece of perfection, | 130 |
| | beleive it, beleive it your Mistris & myne though they | |
| | have great portions, are not to be tuterd like a rich | |
| | Cittizens Daughter,⁴³³ or a great heire, they are of other | |
| | breedings. | |
| Pre: | Well I'le see in what Garbe, I can bringe hir too | 135 |
| | & tell you a certainty for your opinion | |
| | | |
| Co: | And when you find I say true what will you say | |
| Pre: | Wye I'le say I am wiser then you for I have endeavour'd | |
| | the best I can to make my wife a foole, & you never had soe | |
| | high a designe. | 140 |
| Co | Fayth I hold that noe designe to make my wife a foole | |
| Pre: | Wee shortly shalbee marryed then each shall see | |
| | Which of us a true kind Husband: Co: That's mee⁴³⁴ | |

Enter a Boy, as a Page to Courtely                [119]

| Co: | O' my Boy of hope art thou come? what news? is all well? | 145 |
| | What sad I prethee relate, I care not for a frowne | |
| | Soe, shee bee well, or if shee threw my Lr̃e⁴³⁵ downe | |
| Bo: | S<sup>r</sup> your prophecy is true, I have brought yo<sup>r</sup> Lr̃e back | |
| Pre: | Come give it mee & tell mee pry'thee Boy | |
| | Thy progress, Hast thou not mett a Bug beare,⁴³⁶ thou still | 150 |
| | lookes soe sad. | |
| Bo: | I have another Lr̃e w:<sup>ch</sup> I'de have you read, not my Maister | |
| Pre: | Companion shall I read thy loved fansye of Lr̃e? | |
| Co: | Ey, but I saw the Boy give you another from yo<sup>r</sup> mistris | |
| Pre: | I doubt I never shall enjoye my Deare | 155 |

---

433. Daughter of a London tradesman, perhaps a woman from a newly rich family whose wealth comes from trade.

434. Courtly finishes the line.

435. Letter.

436. Bugbear. To be frightened by a bugbear is to have imaginary fears (*OED*).

For shee my ridgid thoughts certaine did heare[437]
Could shee bee myne I'de dedicated bee
To hir & give hir leave for to bee free
Can any wench enter into my Head
If ever have hir once into my bedd                                        160
When marryed my soule shall not thinke of wife
For shee shalbee my Mistris, Joy of Life.

Co:     A suddaine[438] change
Pre:    A suddaine change indeede.
Co:     Pray' speake, Are they marryed? read that Lr̄e              165
        Are they dead?
Pre:    Read that Letter.
              And I am now in deepe dispaire
              Never againe to see my Faire[439]

                    Enter the three Cozens[440]                        170 [120]

Sh:     O' Cozens our neighbouringe Pesants.
Ci:     Or our pedanticall Servants, have given us upp for
        a pray to the Enemy.[441]
Sh:     Pray' how did I looke in the posture of a Delinquent
Ci:     You meane how did you behave your selfe in the - -           175
        posture of a Delinquent, Fayth as though you thought
        the Sceane would change againe, & you would bee
        happy though you sufferred misery for a tyme, & how
        did I looke?[442]
Sh:     As your selfe, that's great though in misfortune             180
Ci:     Soe did you.
Sh:     How should I doe otherwayes,[443] for I practized
        Cleopatria, when she was in hir captivity, and could
        they have thought mee worthy to have adorned their

437. This indicates that earlier in the play Luceny and Tattiney need to have been shown on stage listening to Courtly and Presumption talking about how they will behave as husbands.

438. Sudden.

439. They exit.

440. Cousins. The cousins are Cicilly, Sh., and Is.; the scene has shifted to Ballamo.

441. They have been abandoned.

442. In the new role of captive. The context is not entirely clear; perhaps Cicilly refers to a meeting with the Parliamentarians who captured the castle in the siege.

443. Otherwise.

|     |                                                                                  |       |
|-----|----------------------------------------------------------------------------------|-------|
|     | Tryumphs, I would have perform'd his gallant                                     | 185   |
|     | Tragidye,[444] & soe have made my selfe glorious for tyme                        |       |
|     | to come.                                                                         |       |
|     | Come[445] Prethee, let's talke noe more of our Captivity, I wish I               |       |
|     | could not thinke, that I might not remember I had beene                          |       |
|     | once happy.                                                                      | 190   |
| Ci: | I am not in your opinion, for then I should remember                             |       |
|     | nothinge but misery, therefore let's recreate[446] our selves                    |       |
|     | with other discourse.                                                            |       |
| Sh: | And make our selves happy by promising hopes                                     |       |
|     | of our absent friends.[447]                                                      | 195   |
| Ci: | But Cozen what shall wee doe today, I'm loath to                                 |       |
|     | learne French, I am soe dull'd with greife.                                      |       |
| Sh: | And I am stupyfyed w[th] a contynuacōn of misery, but                            | [121] |
|     | I'le tell you wee'le looke for our friends Cordyalls[448]                        |       |
| Ci: | But where are the Keyes?                                                          | 200   |
| Sh: | I have them, pry'thee sweete Cozen bid Joane[449]                                |       |
|     | bringe them quickly, for wee hate delayes,                                       |       |
| Ci: | Now wee shall see what rare Cordyalls hee hath                                    |       |
|     | for restoration of health, & makeing one younge.[450]                           |       |
| Sh: | Come let's goe open the Boxe, what's this?                                        | 205   |
| Ci: | 'Tis quinticence[451] of mint & Magisteriam of Pearle[452]                       |       |
| Sh: | Take one of these Cakes, & you Cozen thei're very                                |       |
|     | good ones.                                                                        |       |

444. Cavendish and Brackley possibly refer to Shakespeare's *Antony and Cleopatra* (1607). The play depicts Cleopatra's suicide, which was in part motivated by her determination not to be put on display in a triumphal procession through Rome (5.2).

445. "Come" is written partially in the margin.

446. Amuse.

447. Their suitors, Luceny and Tattiney's brothers, the Stellows.

448. Cordials. Possibly those of Lord Calsindow, although the ownership of Ballamo is never made clear. The *OED* notes that medicines or remedies referred to as cordials are "stimulating, 'comforting,' or invigorating to the heart" and "restorative, reviving, cheering."

449. A waiting woman.

450. Recipe books of the period are full of advice on how to produce fanciful potions and cosmetics using real and sometimes not-so-real ingredients like unicorn hair.

451. Quintessence. Quintessence can mean either "a highly refined essence or extract" or "the most typical example of a category or class; the most perfect embodiment of a certain type of … thing" (*OED*).

452. In alchemy, magisterium or magistery of a substance is a substance "capable of transmuting or changing the nature of other substances." It can also mean the "concentrated essence of a substance" (*OED*).

| Ci: | Wee never saw these before, come weele put them upp | |
|---|---|---|
| Sh: | Noe take another hee'le never want them. | 210 |
| Es: | Truely if hee knewe, hee would wonder how wee durst | |
|  | offerr to looke of them. | |
| Sh: | I wishe hee sawe us in a Prospective.⁴⁵³ | |
| Es: | But 'tis a great way for him to looke in a Prospective | |
| Ci: | 'Tis noe matter, 'tis a wishe, soe Cozen, what Receats⁴⁵⁴ | 215 |
|  | this I sweare 'tis a Lͬe & one of his Mistris Seales⁴⁵⁵ | |
| Sh: | You're mistaken, you judge wronge, 'tis a Cordyall | |
|  | Seale | |
| Ci: | Here are potts of [    ] & Accodeshdry⁴⁵⁶ | |
| Sh: | And potts of preserv'd Nutmeggs & morabollans⁴⁵⁷ | 220 |
|  | & a whole Boxe of my Lady Kents Cordyalls⁴⁵⁸ | |
| Ci: | And rather Essens⁴⁵⁹ of all sorts, Cabynetts of all manner | |
|  | of Spiritts, Gilberts water,⁴⁶⁰ & curious Balmesomes,⁴⁶¹ | |
|  | I am weary with repeateing, wee'le put them upp. | |
| Sh: | Come Cozen this place is very cole,⁴⁶² & wee have seene all | 225[122] |
|  | his Cordyalls, I'le take this halfe pott of Morabollans | |
|  | & soe quit them. | |
| Ci: | Noe take a whole one. | |
| Sh: | Noe I'le have noe more then this halfe pott, for you | |
|  | have more neede of Cordyalls then I, soe this day shalbee | 230 |
|  | youres, & tomorrow myne | |
| Ci: | How yours? | |
| Sh: | Wye I'le invite you, | |
| Ci: | To what? | |

453. A device that "allows one to see objects or events not immediately present" (*OED*).

454. Recipes.

455. Letters were sealed with wax in this period.

456. An herb used in medical recipes. Cerasano and Wynne-Davies gloss this as "couch grass (Agrostidaea)." "The Concealed Fancies," 212.

457. Cerasano and Wynne-Davies gloss this as "Myrobalans, a variety of plum." "The Concealed Fancies," 212.

458. Recipes were often attributed to elite women. Cavendish and Brackley's aunt, Elizabeth Grey, the Countess of Kent, had many recipes attributed to her; they appear in volumes such as *A choice manual of rare and select secrets in physick and chirurgery collected and practised by the Right Honorable, the Countesse of Kent* (1653).

459. Essences.

460. Another distilled water attributed to a personage. See also 1.2.39.

461. Balsams, salves.

462. Cold.

| Sh: | To what? wye I'le picke his Cabinett Locks, & | 235 |
| | there you shall see his Magazine[463] of love. I darr | |
| | sweare you shall see locks of all manner of Colloured | |
| | haires, & favoureing Ribbins, in as many Colours as | |
| | the Rainebow.[464] | |
| Ci: | How know you that? | 240 |
| Sh: | 'Tis my stronge ymagination, & if this fansye of | |
| | myne should prove true, wee shall have rarer - - | |
| | recreation to looke on them. | |
| Ci: | Well on w^th your designe tomorrow | |
| Sh: | Fayth soe I will if noe impertinent Lady[465] - - | 245 |
| | hinder mee | |
| Ci: | Ey, but I doubt a designe of soe much pleaseing | |
| | consequence wilbee defeated.[466] | |

Enter Colonell Free[467] & M^r Corpolant.[468]                [123]

| Fr: | I'le tell you newes m^r Corpolant. Monsieur Calsindowes | 250 |
| | Daughters my Cozens, are become Nunns upon the greife of | |
| | our departure | |
| Cor: | Upon the griefe of my departure. | |
| Fr: | What a selfe lov'd peece of fatt you are, doe you | |
| | not knowe, nor remember how angrye you were, when shee | 255 |
| | scorn'd you,[469] and doe you thinke shee is in love with you? | |
| | Now you are too partiall. | |
| Cor: | By your leave Colonell Free absence increaseth like, | |
| | sometymes | |
| Fr: | I wonder what fansye my wife will bee possest w^thall | 260 |
| | for shee can nether bee Nunn, nor Vestow,[470] shee hath soe | |
| | many Children. | |

463. "A place where goods are kept in store" (*OED*).

464. Love favors.

465. Lady Tranquility.

466. They exit.

467. Cadman suggests that Colonel Free is modeled after Colonel Fretchville, who was a governor of Welbeck Abbey and "led an attempt to recapture the estate in July 1645 before it was retaken by Parliamentarian forces in November of the same year." Cadman, *The Concealed Fancies*, 28.

468. The action shifts back to Lord Calsindow's household.

469. This tells us something of what Corpolant's reaction was to the song Luceny sang rejecting him in 2.1.210–33.

470. Vestal. A virgin, as in ancient Rome's Vestal Virgins.

Cor:    But the sweete Lady wilbee in a Consumption for
        your sake.

Fr:     Did you see our sweete younge Stellowes today?        265

Cor:    Yes and in my knowledge of conceite they are very
        mallencholly, & they would not let mee knowe the
        reason, soe I doubt they are in love. Are not you
        in the same opinion.

Fr:     They have reason to bee sayd;[471] their Mistreses are—    270
        Captives, & their Sisters are Nunns in mallenchollie
        & they say, gives blessing to each poore body, that comes
        to bee healed of mallencholly of y[e] minde.

Cor:    I wonder people can be soe semple to come to
        bee cured of them, that cannot cure themselves.[472]       275

Enter two Prisoners.                      [124]<br/>Action & Moderate.[473]

Ac:     S[r] brought as a Prisoner?

Mo:     Yes S[r].

Ac:     Pray what newes?                                        280

Mo:     Alas S[r] I wish there were noe newes, but that
        my Cowe had newly calv'd, or how much creame makes
        a pound of Butter, I'm onely brought in by reason they
        have a thought I am rich.

Ac:     They would have money of mee too, a pox take them     285
        all, & the Devill goe w[th] them for they are a Company
        of Knaves.

Mo:     Ey, S[r]; but pray' take heede, for since yo[u] are of our
        partie, I must give you counsell, & desire you not to bee
        soe liberall of your tongue, it may doe you hurt, & our    290
        partie noe good.

Ac:     'Tis true for I was put into such a roome for talkeing
        as I had noe bigger a window, to take breath att
        then the biggnes of my little finger; & noe more to
        piss att.[474]                                             295

Mo:     Sure your ymprisonment hath made you madd

471. Sad.

472. They exit.

473. Action and Moderate are Royalist soldiers who have been captured at the siege of Ballamo.

474. Action's language—like other instances of coarse or frank language in the play—is unusual in
women's writing of the period.

| Ac: | Fayth soe it hath to them in hatered, come let's goe | |
|---|---|---|
| | drinke a health to the good success of our party | |
| | & to the Rogues condemnation. | |
| Mo: | This would bee a very good health, but not in | 300 |
| | this Garrison, & thus much knowne may hange yoᵘ. | |
| Ac: | Tut I'le venter⁴⁷⁵ my neck but I'le bee revenged, | |
| | you're all upon the savation⁴⁷⁶ of yoʳ money, & I have | |
| | none to losse. | |
| Mo: | If you have not, you should get upon the grownd of | 305 [125] |
| | keepeing your health | |
| Ac: | Wye soe I doe, for I walke dayly in the Garden, & | |
| | when I see the Rogues goe by mee in scorne, I will | |
| | not put of my Hatt, let's now hansomely⁴⁷⁷ send to our | |
| | party, to come to take their Horses, & if possible to | 310 |
| | take this Howse. | |
| Mo: | By my fayth of my body, I will not bee of this highe | |
| | flowne, noe designe, goe Sʳ & sleepe for this can | |
| | prove nothinge.⁴⁷⁸ | |

Act the Foureth
Enter the 2· Nunns Luceny & Tattiny

| Lu: | Where are the Innocent Soules?⁴⁷⁹ | |
|---|---|---|
| Ta: | Their'e comeinge. | |

Enter ·2· Poore men & 2· poore weomen kneeleinge      5

| Lu: | What's your griefe? | |
|---|---|---|
| Po:M: | Love | |
| Lu: | In what kind? | |
| Po:M: | One that I lov'd as my Soule rejected mee | |
| Lu: | Take this⁴⁸⁰ &, bee assured, you shall growe wiser or | 10 |
| | have your Mistris love you | |
| Lu: | What's yours? | |

475. Venture.

476. Salvation.

477. Carefully.

478. They exit.

479. Having become nuns out of grief, Luceny and Tattiney have assumed the role of alms givers.

480. Luceny gives him something, perhaps a cordial like the ones discussed earlier in the play.

| Po:W: | Love | |
|---|---|---|
| Lu: | In what kind? | [126] |

Po:W:   My friends who I hold more deare then my life are in          15
        a farr Country

Lu:     I have noe remedy for that, but take this, it is such as I
        weare it is a Bowe of hope.[481]

The other[482] Po:M:          And my greife is I lov'd a woman & shee
        would not marrye mee.                                          20

Lu:     Take this as a scurge[483] to whip your folly away.

The other[484] Po:W:          And I have almost lost my witts by Plunder

Lu:     Take this Lawrell[485] as a promiseing hope of Conquest

Ta:     Now I will grind upon this holy stone
        Your doubts mixt altogeather not alone[486]                    25
        Yo$^r$ Griefs
        Yo$^r$ Feares
        Your Seighs; & your sad teares.

Lu:     May you all happy bee, but you I blesse, & wishe
        That you your friends againe may see                          30
        And pray you pray that prayer for mee.


                         The Songe                            [127]


              Courtlyes discovery[487] & Præsumption[488]


Co:     I sweare as you arr faire
        And chast as is the Ayre                                       35
        Since that I sawe you first
        My selfe could never bee
        But still I'm offeringe att your Shrine
        And you will not allowe to see.


481. A favor. Bows and ribbons were often given in this way.

482. "The other" is written in the margin.

483. A whip.

484. "The other" is written in the margin.

485. Laurel, traditionally given to victors.

486. Tattiney's actions are not entirely clear. Cerasano and Wynne-Davies suggest that the "holy stone" is "possibly an altar." "The Concealed Fancies," 212. The language of grinding also suggests an alchemical process.

487. Courtly is seen.

488. Possibly he enters the stage but stays back as Courtly addresses Luceny.

Which makes my Augers[489] not to tell                                    40
What is my fortune well
But I will never cease
To offerr pay my hopefull vowes
Therefore I'le not dispaire to see a day
Wherein I may                                                             45
Most happy bee
And Mortalls envyeing mee to see.

Luceny the Nunn sings.                            [128]

Lu:    I wonder what's the cause about you goe
    Thus to prophane my sacred Priesthead soe                      50
    As to name mee wantonly faire
    Chast that I am, & it shalbee my care
    Your stealeing language further shall not creepe
    Into my sacred Church, where I will weepe
    Prayeing that all may truely, honest keepe                     55
    For my ambitious store in votes[490] ascends
    For my love'd, deare and absent friends
    That each upon their Temples truely may
    Weare severall Lawrells, of each sweeter Bay
    At their retorne then happy shall I bee                        60
    In that blest day, I once them more doe see.

Enter Præsumption

Pre:   And I have found thy most sacred selfe here
    Whose presence tornes all sex to Joy not feare.
    Soe I'le kneele w^th adoration to thee                          65
    And never thinke the tyme too longe, to see
    Thy purer face of Angell beauty faire
    But looke & ymagin what peece yo^u are
    Soe stands w^th admiration that a shee
    Should thus soe like, a pure just Goddes[491] bee               70

Ta:    Bless mee what spirit possesses you
    To speake to mee as if I were not true

489. A prophecy. In ancient Rome, augurs divined the future from the behavior of birds.
490. Prayers.
491. Goddess.

But I am just & wilbee just to greife
And now without my friends have no releife[492]

Enter the ·2· brother Stellowes      75 [129]<br/>the Eldest passionate.

St:[493]  My Lady & mistris Captive, a Prisoner can Stellowe sufferr
that, I'le her releive:

Yo:[494]  But how can you Brother?

St.  Name how: & thy mistris in the like Condition      80

Yo:  But though I'm in love, I am not out of sense

St:  By God thou art out of sense, if thou canst thinke any
ympossibility,[495] an ympossibility to gane yo<sup>r</sup> Mistris Liberty,
though at the rate of your life.

Yo:  I am resolved to hazard my selfe would that releive hir      85
but to dye, & not to release hir, & then my Corps[496] can have
noe possibility of enjoyeing hir, & what doth that proffitt
mee.

St.  Wye it doth proffitt mee if shee could see mee blowne in
a thousand peeces, to show I dye hir Marter, & in that      90
peece of service I shall account my grave my eternall
happynes.

Yo:  By god Brother, I should rather account hir Bedd of
love eternall happynes

St:  Thour't all for thy selfe.      95

Yo:  But meethinkes, your nether for your selfe nor hir.

St:  Well I am resolved of my designe

Yo:  What's that prethee lett mee knowe

St:  That is I will either ruen my selfe or gaine hir
Wilt thou goe w<sup>th</sup> mee I am not for demurrs[497] speake      100

Yo:  I'm not for merry calls,[498] if a possibility I goe

St:  Hang that word possibility, I love then what is - -
ympossible.

Yo:  Soe doe I & yet meethinkes all things are ympossible      [130]
But tell me whose of your designe      105

492. They all exit.
493. Elder Stellow.
494. Younger Stellow.
495. Impossibility.
496. Corpse.
497. Hesitations.
498. Happy visits. Possibly a pun on "miracles."

St   Love & Courage to that hight as thou appear'st to mee
    like a Bedridden fellow, or att best a frozen Stature[499]
    of Ice, that ere longe will consume by my heate of love
    you had best keepe att distance.

  Yo:  Well I darr love as well as thee     110
     Therefore my mistris I will dye but see.

  St  Then let us goe all danger to ymbrace[500]
     Soe wee may see their sweeter face[501]

Enter the Three Lady Cozens

Sh:  Cozen I longe w$^{th}$ great ympatience till the Smyth[502] come  115
Ci:  It may bee hee that knocks, Come in.
Sh:  I have my wishe, harke you friend, you knowe yo$^r$ maisters
    Cabinetts locks, they are very good ones doe you thinke you
    can open them
Sm:  Yes of my life Madam I can     120
Ci:  There are some Bookes there wee would read to passe
    away this sad & sollitary life wee're in

Enter a wayting Woman.  Sage.[503]

Sh:  Ha now Impertinatt,[504] what have you to doe here
Sa:  M$^r$ Steward Madam is come with the Bookes[505] & sayth  125
    you have not seene them this fortnight
Sh:  Goe formality & tell his Formalityship I have other busines
    then to stupyfie my braine w$^{th}$ how many quarters of Mault[506]
    is bought, & in that how much I am cozened, nether care I
    how many Scores of sheepe have beene Plunderd from  130
    mee.
Sa:  I shall tell him soe Madam.     [131]

499. Statue.

500. Embrace.

501. They exit.

502. Blacksmith.

503. The waiting woman's name is Sage.

504. Impertinent.

505. Household accounts.

506. Malt, used for brewing.

Sh:     Noe stay, It is better to please him & tell him, I doe
        not suspect his honesty, therefore he needes not bringe
        the bookes soe soone, & let him knowe this was his plott          135
        to see whether I suspected him; & to let him see I confide
        in him, I will not take the Bookes this moneth.

                    Enter another Mistris Grave[507]

Ci:     Ha now, another
Sh:     Now foole, what comes your peece of gravity for?                   140
Gr:     The Lady Tranquility is come.
Ci:     A poxe goe with you for your ill newes I'le teach you better
        manners then to bringe mee word of my vexation. Where is shee?
Gr.     The Ladie is in the next Chamber
Ci:     I thought this was too happy a designe to prove prosperous         145
Sh:     Well Cozen content your selfe, the Boxes are here, & the
        Smyth lives not farr of, soe I hope wee are not totally defeated.

                    Enter Lady Tranquility.

Sh:     Sweete Madam how longe hath your La:$^{pp}$ beene here?
        How chance I heard not sooner?                                     150
Tr:     I have not beene here longe your La$^{pp}$ neede not bee angry
Sh:     Lord Madam, how happy am I that yo$^r$ La$^{pp}$ can thinke mee
        worthy of a visett, will your La$^{pp}$ goe into my bed chamber
Tr:     I shall attend yor La:$^{pp508}$

                    Enter Courtly who sings this          155 [132]
                            Songe.[509]

Co:     Bringe in Shopps of sadnes now I cry
        Ladyes what lacke you, pray you of mee buy
        Mallencholly Hudds,[510] or Pendant teares of Pearle
        Which if condenced will washe each fyner Gerle[511]                160
        Or fine sweete water sighes, for to perfume
        Your Closset Chamber, or soe any Roome

507. Another waiting woman.

508. They exit.

509. The scene changes back to the household of Lord Calsindow.

510. Hoods. Women wore hoods over their hair in early modern England.

511. Girl.

If I like a Fucus,[512] take my Crimson Heart
'Twill finely redd your Cheekes before you parte
And when you please, it will you panting tell                165
How it doth pray for you, & wishe you well
And if doubts multyplying Glasse you'll have
I've one that adds, most rarely, brave,
Besides a Prospective, wherein you'll see
My greifs of fuller mone,[513] like Rocks to bee             170
What will you nothinge of mee buy
Truely sweete Ladies, you are very shye
But I doe hope ere longe that fortunes Cupp[514]
Will turne about, & hugg mee in hir Lapp.
Then doe not doubt but have great store                      175
Of Ladyes Customers to haunt my doore

Enter Praesumption w<sup>th</sup> his M:<sup>ris</sup> Picture.    [133]

Præ:   Looke on this Picture where you'll see
      A face of pure Devinity
      Adore it with a jealous veiw                         180
      Since it appeares an Angell true.
      The Face is absolute true faire
      As if't was made of select Ayre.
      'Tis sinn if looke, & not adore
      For such a one, was ne're before.                    185

Courtly falls into the like passion w<sup>th</sup><br>fansyeing his M:<sup>ris</sup> Face.

Co:   My Mistris Picture it doth make
      A studdy to expresse each features take
      And when but view, hir sweeter smyle I say            190
      I've seene Cælestyall happynes today
      Then when but see hir quicker Eye 'tis such
      That all sex sweares they cannot looke too much
      Thus shee appeares my innocent delight
      Soe I will call hir my true vertues light[515]         195

512. "Paint or cosmetic for beautifying the skin" (OED).

513. Moon.

514. Things will improve for him.

515. They exit.

Enter Toy with one of hir Ladies Chamber maides[516]　　　　[134]
whose name is Pert.

To:　　Come Pert I'le tell you newes, who doe you thinke makes
　　　　love to mee? Come thinke & tell mee.

Pe:　　Fayth Mistris I cannot say your Lord, for you have　　　　200
　　　　none, for your Ladies a widow, but the Lord of Lords may.

To:　　God bless my Courtshipp I'm not soe devine yet, to have the
　　　　Lord of Lords make love to mee

Pe:　　You mistake mee Mistris I can explaine my selfe

To:　　Wye, prethee doe then, or I vow to God I'le make my　　　205
　　　　Lady angry w^th you for not starchinge hir Band[517] well,
　　　　therefore you had best please mee.

Pe:　　By my troth Mistris I'le please you, for I'le bee as
　　　　secret to your Counsells as you can wishe

To:　　Good wench speake then who thou thinkes　　　　210

Pe:　　Fayth I'm loath to speake, for feare you'le thinke I'le
　　　　tell my Lady.

To:　　Fayth I'le thinke nothinge but what you'll have mee,
　　　　& this is enough for my Ladies Gentlewoman to speake to
　　　　hir Chambermaide, therefore with a Pox to you speake.　　　215

Pe:　　Wye then, I thinke my Lord Calsindow loves my Lady
　　　　a little, to love you more; & now I have spoke

To:　　Thou'st spoke w^th a vengance, but by God if you tell
　　　　my Lady in hope of a Gentlewomanship my carefull
　　　　way of not dressinge my selfe fine, when his Lo:^pp comes　　　220
　　　　Efayth may pull you downe to a washemaide.

Pe:　　Howe's that? pray that againe, I did not heare you

To:　　Wye I'le tell thee, I have noe other way soe good to
　　　　disguise our loves, then to dresse my Lady fine & my selfe
　　　　Uggly.　　　　225

Pe:　　Ha: Ha; Ha: If I did not thinke soe I'm a very Rogue　　　[135]
　　　　but harke you Mistris, what would you doe w^th a Lady that
　　　　understands the world, & if shee were marryed would say
　　　　to hir husband, prethee take my woman, fayth I'm weary
　　　　of your husbandly loved conversation, what would you doe　　　230
　　　　then? now doe you speake.

To:　　Fayth such a careless thinge of knowledge, I thinke I - -
　　　　should serve best

516. A lower-status servant than Toy. A chamber maid is a lady's maid; the term also refers to servants
who were responsible for cleaning bed chambers (*OED*).

517. Collar.

Pe:    I beleive you, but you would have a hard taske, whether
to please my Lord or my Lady.     235

To:    Noe fayth but I should not, for w^ch pleased best
my humour of please, I would please.

Pe:    Fayth but I knowe some Ladyes that wilbee soe much
of y^e wench with their Husband, that thou would prove
at best but a could Mouldy Pye, & this in playne - -     240
Englishe is true.

To:    But I'le tell thee then, I would bee the wife w^th that
Ladies Husband, & make him fond that way.

Pe:    A pox of thy noe witt, this Lady that I meane will have
hir severall sceanes, now wife, then Mistris, then my     245
sweete Platanicke soule,^518 & then write in the like
severall changes of Mistris not onely to confirme love,
but provoke love, then dress themselves always as a
pritty sweete wife or mistris. What say is Mistris
Toy to serve one of these?^519     250

To:    Poxe on you. I knowe where a bouts you are, but I'm not     [136]
like to serve either of these you meane; but I'le tell
you, fayth, they used mee very kindly the last tyme they
sawe mee, but God knowes their not in condition–
now to see any body, God comfort them.     255

Pe:    For sake, sake, thou givest pittie but what say you to
a Gentlewomanship to one of those witts.

To:    I thanke you for nothinge I'le serve none of yo^r Shee
witts, they will not court mee, I'm for your Hee witts
or a Lady that doth not knowe mee, let mee alone to chuse     260
a Lady to serve if I part w^th my good Lady Tranquility,
I'le have a lady of the tymes, if I can gett hir, or one that
thinkes it an honour for mee to serve hir.^520

Enter M^r Caution & M^r Discretion^521

Di:    Did our Ladyes chide you today? come let's walke.     265

Ca:    Noe fayth I valew noe chideing by them, but to say trueth
they gave mee sharpe apprehension & stately,^522 gave mee

518. Platonic love, the ideal union of two souls.

519. Pert outlines different ways of being a wife.

520. A very frank discussion for a play written by two young women. Pert and Toy exit.

521. Caution and Discretion are stewards at Ballamo.

522. They understood me well and in a dignified way.

a litle noe respect, & when wee talked, they spoke of
some designes against them, & soe put a dislike upon mee,
& in good fayth, I sayd I know of noe designe, nor had any          270
designe against them, but I would serve Moningnure[523] - -
Callindow[524] the best I could; they sayd I might very well
studdy & pleade that pretence, as being the onely - -
handle I had & soe convert them to a beleefe, since
wee honour him as our Father, wee can say nothinge                  275
to you in that concerne, then they swore my wisdome
should not alter their resolution, & in good fayth, I knowe          [137]
not their resolutions, nether can I ymagin.

Di:     I see you call nothinge chideing, unless they had power to
        put out a servant, or in a Servant into the Estate, but in   280
        good fayth S$^r$ they trouble us unexpressedly to governe
        them to doe themselves good. find you not that?

Ca:     I doe not find they trouble mee att all, but they trouble
        busines, & I love not interruptions.

Di:     Once I had a designe to vex them, since they will not bee     285
        pleased. I made one of the Groomes say, one of their
        Coach-horses was plunderd, & that I know would passionately
        vex them.

Ca:     And were they angry?

Di:     Noe their quick at fansey[525] & knewe it was a Plott of mee.[526]  290


Act the Fifth                                                        [138]
Enter the three Ladyes Cozens w$^{th}$ this
Songe.


Sh:     In stead of mens drinke
Ci:     Let us merrylie thinke                                        5
Is:     Now wee're at liberty
Ci:     What wee shall wish to thee.
Is:     'Gainst wee you marryed see
Ci:     Thinke not of beauty
Is:     Nor of duety                                                 10

---

523. The second "n" is in superscript.

524. Monsieur Calsindow.

525. Fancy, here a reference to games.

526. They exit.

| | | |
|---|---|---|
| Ci: | But resolve to bee. | |
| Is. | A pritty toyeing Shee. | |

Enter the ·2· Stellowes

| | | |
|---|---|---|
| Sh: | O' friend I have beene in Hell | |
| St: | Noe sure your goodnes cannot that place tell | 15 |
| Sh: | O' yes this world doth ymitate the other | |
| | But this a secrett let it goe noe further | |
| St: | Well on with your discourse. Sh: I will | |
| | And tell you how they good Soules kill | |
| | They have their Tarriers[527] Devills to betray | 20 |
| | Each honest soule, that loves the true right way. | |
| St: | I knowe all this but tell what fires they have | |
| | And when they're burn'd, how pittyfull they rave | |
| Sh: | Fyres, that's fansey, by a hotter flame | [139] |
| | And haveinge noe Joyes sweares greife burnes them lame | 25 |
| | As for bleir'd Eyes, 'tis nether fyre; nor Smoke | |
| | But cryeing, & sad greife them smothering choke. | |
| | For darkenes, that their mallencholly selfe | |
| | If happy they not want of waggish Elfe | |
| St: | They say Hells lowe | 30 |
| Sh: | How can it other bee | |
| | For when misfortune, then you Hell doe see | |
| St: | When you were there would you your friends there wish | |
| Sh: | Noe shee Devills I would not have them kiss. | |

Younge Stellowe speakes to the Lady Cicilley    35<br>this

| | | |
|---|---|---|
| y:St: | Madam doe you this Chatachime[528] knowe | |
| | I like it not, I pray you let us goe.[529] | |

Enter the 2 Nunns mallencholly    [140]<br>speakeing to one another.    40

| | | |
|---|---|---|
| Lu: | When I in sadnes am & this doe thinke | |
| | I'm lul'd a sleepe in mallencholly winke | |

527. Obstructing, hindering.

528. Catechism.

529. They exit.

Each Chamber seeleing doth create true sad
Yet temperd soe as I am quiett, glad,
Then when I walke Nunns Gallerye round                45
My thoughts tells mee I'm falling in a swond[530]
And when that flowers fine I have
Then sure I'm decked for my Grave
Soe, if each one will have a fine lov'd death
Enter your selfe in sadnes sweeter Earth                50
Then when my quiett soule desires to walke
The Gardens doe revive my tongue to talke
Soe in white sheete of Innocence I fray[531]
Each one that wishes mee to stay
For Ghosts doe love to have their owne delights        55
When others thinkes they have designes of frights
Soe even as they I wish noe feare to none.
But on my Friends contemplate alone.

Lu:[532]    My greife doth make mee for to looke.            [141]
As if life I, had quietly forsooke                        60
Then for my fine dilitive[533] Tombe
Is my seeled Chamber, & darke Parlour Roome
Then when my Spiritt i'the Gallery doth walke
It will not speake, for sinn to it is talke.
At night I rise from tombe to see                        65
My friends pure well, but sleepeing that must bee.
This is my truer soule of glad.
And Ghosts contentment, now you see is sad.

A Songe
Sunge by ·2· Gods comeing downe out of            70
the Skye to the Nunns.    Who are.
Courtley & Præsumption.[534]

530. To faint or swoon.

531. Cerasano and Wynne-Davies state that the word "pray" is meant here. "The Concealed Fancies,"
213. "Fray" could also make sense, given the reference to the sheet earlier in the line.

532. It seems likelier that Tattiney would have spoken these lines. If it was Luceny, the speech would
not be broken up; also, Tattiney usually speaks after her sister has had her say.

533. Delightful.

534. Cavendish and Brackley borrow from the stage properties popular in court masques. It was the
fashion in masques to include aerial ballets, wave machines, and other such magnificent feats. See
also the Content and Analysis section on *The concealed Fansyes* in the introduction to this part of the
volume.

Harke, harke, & heare
And put of feare
Resolve & come away                                                              75
And make noe stay

Your Saynted prayers ever came to wee
Soe wee're resolv'd your Father you shall see.[535]

Lu:     At your Comāunds wee make noe stay                          [142]
Ta:     But you greate Gods wee will obey                              80
Co:     These Garments wee you bringe
Pr:     To usher you to your joy'd springe

After their Habitts are on & their Nunns
Habbitts of, y.[ey536] both speake this:

Lu:     Can I soe soone forgett an Nunn                                85
Co:     Ey sure, & bringe loves happie sonn[537]
Ta:     How doe I in this Habbitt looke
Pre:    As loves devinity of Booke

This Songe sunge in parts by them ·fowre
as they are drawne upp                                                          90

Co:     Now let us cut each way away
Pre:    And make rude winds us to obey
Lu:     To bringe us to our happy day.
Ta:     Then blessings wilbee our rich pay.

This Songe sunge over soe often, till they                          95
bee drawne upp.

Enter Mr Corpolant & my Lady Tranquility.                      [143]
Cor:    Come madam you shall bee my Antidote against Mistris
        Luceny. Witt how like you my profferr?
Tr:     What doe you meane your Bagg of Gold? very well.      100
Cor:    Fayth & you shall have my Bagg of Gold if you'le
        have mee to boote.

535. Like the Angel that appears in act 3, no speech prefixes are given when Courtly and Presumption
pose as gods to persuade Luceny and Tattiney to cease being nuns.

536. They. The "y" is smudged; the scribe may have deleted it.

537. Sun.

| | | |
|---|---|---|
| Tr: | And what say you M$^r$ Corpolant to bee my Garrison of profession against all the world. | |
| Cor: | Fayth Madam & I love you soe well as I darr marry you & let the world say what they will, you'st bee my onely Fort. | 105 |
| Tr: | Excuse mee S$^r$ you rather appeare myne. | |
| Cor: | Come in a word if you'le mee have You shall have title Coach,$^{538}$ & all things that is brave.$^{539}$ | 110 |
| Tr: | S$^r$ you looke a great plumpe Bagg I sweare Soe if I shake you well I neede not care. | |

Enter Monsignure Calsindow at the other doore          [144]
Courtly & Præsumption w$^{th}$ Luceny &
Tattyny in their change of Habbits          115
& Courtley & Prasumption still
in the Habbit of Gods.

| | | |
|---|---|---|
| Co: | Looke looke and see | |
| Pr: | Your Daughters, here they bee. | |
| Lu: | Wee you a blessinge Aske | 120 |
| Co: | Then wee'le put of our maske.$^{540}$ | |

They appeare
Courtley & Prasumption$^{541}$

| | | |
|---|---|---|
| Ca: | What am I surprized w$^{th}$ Joy of please But pray you Daughters who are these? | 125 |
| Co: | Your Servant Courtley | |
| Pr: | Yours Præsumption | |
| Lu: | Are you God=Cheaters | |
| Ta: | Or are wee not our selves | |
| Co: | Madam, wee can create | 130 |
| Pr: | And if your Father please, wee are yo$^r$ fate. | |
| Ca: | I thanke you both, for now I see. You love my Daughters, then you must love mee.$^{542}$ | |

538. A title, a coach. These are signifiers of wealth and status.

539. Fine, splendid, grand.

540. A pun on masque, perhaps, as he describes their willingness to remove their costumes.

541. They remove their costumes.

542. They exit.

Enter an Old Woman, & younge Wench w^th hir.^543     [145]

Ca:^544      Passion of God this younge Flirts vex my Soule     135
           out of my body, did not I tell thee, thy carelesnes would
           spoyle the lynnings^545 against the marryage of my Lord
           Calsindow daughters. I tell thee againe Brides lynnings
           out^546 to bee had a care of, but thou'rt afraid thy faire
           face should bee burnt, or thy hands too ruffe,^547 marry     140
           gep^548 w^th a vengance, come out.
Pri:^549      I am sure I have burnt my fingers w^th smoothinge^550
Ca:      Burnt yo^r fingers, & if you had burnt them of
           God would have blest you never a whit the worse,
           but Efayth. Efaith you're a Flirt, you stand when     145
           my Lords men courts you, & sayth away fye, you speake
           not as you thinke, & with this dallyeing discourse
           never minds your busines. Efayth the world's turn'd
           upp side downe since I was younge.
Pri:      Wye forsooth, would you have mee beleeve them?     150
Ca:      Well, well, I knowe what I knowe, and Care will
           say noe more, but thy very name Pritty hath undone
           thee.
Pri:      Truely Mistris, but that name could never undone you.
Ca:      Thou dost provoke mee, but I will not chide you     155
           for a reason best knowne to my selfe, but Efayth
           I could tell.
Pri:      Pray you tell my Lord then
Ca:      You had best tell him your selfe for I am not
           soe familyar^551 w^th his Lo:^pp I will doe him - -     160
           faythfull & true service, for by my troth I
           cannot bee a Flirt; Honesty shall ever bee     [146]
           my worst & none shall say worse of mee

543. They are maidservants in Lord Calsindow's household.

544. Care, the old woman.

545. Linens.

546. Ought.

547. Rough.

548. An expression of derision, "get out" or "go along with you" (*OED*). Also used in talking to horses.

549. Pritty.

550. Ironing linens.

551. Familiar.

Pri:    I thinke it was alwayes the worst w^th

        you.[552]                                      165

Ca:    The worst w^th mee, take heede my worst bee

        not better then your best.

                Take heede I say take heede

                If begg I will not aske you at my neede.

                Enter Luceny & hir waiteing woman with        170

                hir Glasse.[553] And as Luceny opens hir

                      Haire[554] shee sings

                        This Songe.

Lu:    What is't they say must I a wife become

Ma:[555]    Yes madam that's the vote as I doe heare it runn      175

Lu:    Wye then a wife in showe appeare

        Though Munckey I should deare[556]

        And soe upon the marriage day

        I'le looke as if obey.

                      Enter Stellow singeinge        180[147]

St:    Now doe I heare the Ladies what wagers they will lay

        Sayeing surely you'll disallowe obey

        Truely I knowe not what you meane cry you & looke away

        What act you meane

        To bee the Sceane.                         185

        Lost Wagers each must pay.

Lu:    Now doe I veiw my selfe by all soe looked upon

        And thus men whisperinge say fayth shee's already gone

        For witt or mirth I plainly see

        That shee a Wife wilbee                    190

        Noe S^r say I a witt above

        Is Hymens Munckey love.

---

552. There is a deletion at the end of this line. The deleted word appears to be "Care."

553. Mirror.

554. Takes down her hair.

555. Maid.

556. Dare.

Enter Younge Stellow.

| | | |
|---|---|---|
| Y.St: | Well sister for all your reply of Songe | |
| | I sawe an ill signe to day. | 195 |
| Lu: | What wast?[557] | |
| Y.St: | Fayth a very careles Garbe in Courtely | |
| Lu: | In what perticuler?[558] | |
| Y.St: | In puting on his Hatt | |
| Lu: | Fayth Brother, but as I hope to contynew | 200 |
| | my innocent freedome of Luceny. Hee shall put his | |
| | hat of before hee make mee observe his actions | |
| | for I was never borne to bee his danceing Maister | [148] |
| | to have fowre pounds a moneth to observe his Garbe, | |
| | But did not I give him the like retorne of my | 205 |
| | Alleigiance? | |
| Y.St: | Yes I was infinetly pleased to see you, but | |
| | I'm affraid hee should contract your Face to severall | |
| | formes of rediculousnes when you're marryed, as I | |
| | darr not name marriage. | 210 |
| Lu: | Pray you feare your selfe, & leave mee to the | |
| | world, that is a Husband. | |

Enter the Lord Calsindow w<sup>th</sup> his daughter<br>
Tatyny M<sup>r</sup> Courtely M<sup>r</sup> Præsumption<br>
M<sup>r</sup> Corpolant, Lady Tranquility    215<br>
& M:<sup>ris</sup> Toy.

| | | |
|---|---|---|
| Ca: | Sr take you Luceny to your wedlock wishe | |
| | And you Tattyny for a marryage kisse | |

Enter the ·2· Stellowes w<sup>th</sup> their Mistreses    [149]

| | | |
|---|---|---|
| St: | My lord I have brought my Mistris though w<sup>th</sup> my life | 220 |
| | And if you please shee shalbee now my wife | |
| Ca: | Sonn since you loves trueth, soe truely knowe | |
| | W<sup>th</sup> all my heart you to the Church may goe | |
| y.St: | Brothers & Sisters marryed now I see | |
| | If have your leave, I now may marryed bee | 225 |
| Ca: | Madam if that my younger sonn you'll have | |

557. Was it.

558. In what way?

you will as Heaven him surely save.

Cor:    Now I will tell you newes of mee
      My Lady Tranquility my wife wilbee[559]

            She sings this                      230

Tr:    Mais de van que Je vous marriey
      Je vous die que Je nemiey.[560]

Ca:    All here I marryed see
      Excepting you[561] & mee
      Now Madam[562] I will take           235
      Your woman for my M[ris] Mate.

         A Songe sunge by an Angell        [150]

        Fye, fye, let marryage life
        Plant vertue in you, take a wife
        That's truely vertuous & faire       240
        Hansome & innocent as the chast Ayre
        Then since the Gods makes you this choyce
        Marry, marry to rejoyce.

        This change I like Efayth 'tis very fine
        Noe sinn comitt, & yet this wench is myne    245
        Angell you're pay'd in that you will relate
        Unto the Gods, that vertue is my fate
        Then Toy you may bee gone for I'le be true
        My conscyence bids me not to looke of you[563]

        The Fifth Act ended the Musick      250
               playes.

Enter Luceny & Tattyny                 [151]

---

559. "Wilbee" is written in heavy ink over another illegible word.

560. "But it is for vanity that I marry you / I tell you I don't love you."

561. Toy.

562. Lady Tranquility.

563. This stanza is clearly sung by Lord Calsindow, but there is no attribution in the text.

Ta:      As you love mee Sister, now you are marryed, tell
           mee how you agree, did you never fall out?

Lu:      As I hope to contynewe my owne thou'rt growne a
           foole, did not wee resolve to fall out w$^{th}$ our Husbands?    5

Ta:      Yes but I thought hee had alter'd you, but pray Sister
           did hee never chide you?

Lu:      Noe but hee hath given mee very good Counsell

Ta:      O, I understand you, but I wonder you will sufferr him
           to bee soe ymperious.[564]    10

Lu:      Will you judge before you heare.

Ta:      Wye tell mee then

Lu:      Accordinge to yo$^r$ Comāunds I'le tell you upon his
           first good Counsell, I looked soberly, as if I would
           strickly observe him, yet drest my selfe contrary    15
           to his instruction, & my behaviour was according to
           my dress, soe much as hee sayd Sweete Heart, doe
           you goe abroade to day? I sayd noe, is your desire I
           should, noe sayd hee, but meethinkes you're very fine,[565]
           & though I knew I was, yet I sayd fye, why will yo$^u$    20
           reproch your owne soe much, but I am glad you
           sayd soe, for now I shall understand yo$^u$ by - -
           contraryes. Soe Sister I knew hee was to seeke
           aboute againe for a new good Counsell

Ta:      Come deare Sister tell mee his next humour.    25

La:      Sweare you will tell your Husbands humour &    [152]
           your owne, other wayes you shall have mee noe more
           your liberet Foole.

Ta:      What oaths you please I'le sweare.

Lu:      Well I'le trust you, Fayth all that day hee    30
           was in a conflict, betwixt Anger and mallencholly
           not knoweinge whether my behaivour proceeded
           from neglect or ignorance, then hee declared himselfe
           by allygory & praysed a Lady, [   ] - -
           [   ],[566] obedyent Foole in towne, & swore hir - -    35
           Husband was the happyest man in the world. I
           replyed shee was a very good Lady, & I accounted

564. Imperious.

565. Finely dressed.

566. There is an illegible deletion in the text.

him happy that was hir Husband, that hee could
content him self w^th such a Meachanick^567 wife. I
wishe sayd hee shee might bee your Example,                40
& you have noe reason to sleight hir, for shee is of a
noble family. I knowe that sayd I, & doe the
more admire why shee will contract hir family,
Noblenes & Birth, to the servitude of hir husband,
as if hee had bought hir his slave, & I'm sure hir       45
Father bought him for hir, for hee gave a good
Portion, & now in sense who should obey?
Then hee came w^th his old Proverbe, & sayd hee
would teach mee another Lesson, & soe w^th a
forced kind of mirth, went out of y^e Roome, & I         50
understood hee had nothinge els to say soe was
never angry.

Ta:    But is hee never higher?                           [153]

Lu:    Yes once, when hee thought to make mee cry, but
Efayth I observ'd him in his owne way, & told him        55
his teareing Oathes^568 should not fright mee, & for
part, I valewed at the same rate hee did, for I
had noe designe upon him, but to love him, & pray
for him. I would yet if in either of these I
was [    ]^569 inconvenient to him, I could lay those    60
Contemplations at his feete, & would not weepe.

Ta:    Ha: ha: ha: How I am pleased to see Courtley
become Præsumption after marryage.

Lu:    And Præsumption Courtley

Ta:    Noe fayth hee gently sleightes as being madd      65
in Love.

Lu:    How prethee let mee heare.

Ta:    Wye thus, when I am in Company w^th him hee
becomes a Compound of hee knowes not what, that is
hee doth not appeare my Husband, nether is his           70
Garbe my Servant

Lu:    Now I wonder Sister how you can call this a
sleight for in this hee appeares himselfe.
but I see you would have him fond in Company.

---

567. A lowly or vulgar person, typically a manual laborer. See Shakespeare's "rude mechanicals" in *A Midsummer Night's Dream* (ca. 1590).

568. Mean words intended to make her cry.

569. The scribe deleted a word that may be "innocent."

| Ta: | By witt, I hate to see a fond foole, let it | 75 [154] |
| | bee, Hee, or Shee; but in a word I knewe | |
| | I had angerd him, therefore tooke this his | |
| | silence as a neglect, yet I sweare by you | |
| | I was my selfe, & held my petulant Garbe, | |
| | once hee spoke in company according to a | 80 |
| | discreete Husband, then I gave him a modest | |
| | returne of wife, & yet appear'd his Mistris. | |
| Lu: | Howe write you to him? | |
| Ta: | In as severall humours as I will dresse | |
| | my selfe, His Mistris, this you may see is an | 85 |
| | equall marryage, & I hate those people | |
| | that will not understand, matrymony is to | |
| | joyne Lovers. | |
| Lu: | But thinkes Husbands are the Rodd | |
| | of authority. | 90 |
| Ta: | Or a Marriage Clogg | |
| Lu: | That puts mee in mind of my Epilog | |

## Epilog. [155]

| Lu: | Truely the conflicts I did see w$^{th}$in | |
| | Which for to tell you, even would bee a sinn | 95 |
| | The severall wayes, & fansyes of their feares | |
| | And yet they darr not speake for their Eares | |
| | Now I am charged, not a word more to say | |
| | But begg your likes, & then 'tis Hollyday. | |

## Epilog. 100

| Ta: | And I was sent in all hast to you here | |
| | For to assure you there is a great feare | |
| | Not knoweing how the Comedy doth please | |
| | Dislik'd there will bee a white Huds[570] decease | |
| | Ladies from you I begg, a smile of like | 105 |
| | If Hats the Poet's happy in the night | |

570. White hoods.

An Epilog                                    [156]

In perticuler to your Lo:ᴾᴾ.

Lu:  Now since your Excellence hath thought it fitt
Ta:  To stay a three howres Comedy of sitt                  110
Lu:  And soe but speake of it as like
Ta:  Then are our Sceanes even happy in your sight
Lu:  And though wee have, smyles & hats if yoᵘ dislike
Ta:  Wee're totally condemned, for tonight.


Have you now read[571] my Lord, pray doe not speake    1  [157]
For I'm already growne, soe faint & weake
Not knoweing how you will now sensure mee
As rash to thinke, noe witt a present bee
But if you like not, I pray let mee knowe               5
The Penn & Inke shall have a fatall blowe
If you not pleas'd, it will impression make
In my vaine selfe, for indiscretion sake
But if you like you will mee Cordyall give
And soe as witty, I shall ever live.[572]                10

571. Alluding to the play as a manuscript.

572. This verse (lines 115–24) appears after the third epilogue of The concealed Fansyes. Not labeled as part of the play, it may serve as a conclusion to the volume itself. Because it is not listed separately in either of the two tables of contents, the poem is included here.

# Bibliography

## Primary Sources

### Manuscripts and Archival Sources

Cavendish, Jane, and Elizabeth Brackley. "The concealed Fansyes." In *Poems, Songs, a Pastorall, and a Play by the R<sup>t</sup> Hon<sup>ble</sup> the Lady Jane Cavendish and Lady Elizabeth Brackley*. Bodleian Library. Rawlinson MS Poet. 16.

———. "A Pastorall." In *Poems, Songs, a Pastorall, and a Play by the R<sup>t</sup> Hon<sup>ble</sup> the Lady Jane Cavendish and Lady Elizabeth Brackley*. Bodleian Library. Rawlinson MS Poet. 16.

———. "A Pastorall." In *Poems, Songs, and a Pastorall, by the R<sup>t</sup> Hon<sup>ble</sup> the Lady Jane Cavendish and Lady Elizabeth Brackley*. Beinecke Rare Book and Manuscript Library. Osborn MS b.233.

Fane, Rachel. *Manuscript of a Masque Performed by the Fane Children*. Centre for Kentish Studies. Maidstone, UK. U269/F38/3.

Lumley, Jane, trans. *The Tragedie of Euripides called Iphigeneia translated out of Greake into Englisshe*. British Library. MS Royal 15.A.ix.

*Perdita Manuscripts, 1500–1700*. http://www.amdigital.co.uk/m-products/product/perdita-manuscripts-1500-1700/detailed-information/. Accessed May 6, 2018.

*The Perdita Project: Early Modern Women's Manuscript Catalogue*. http://web.warwick.ac.uk/english/perdita/html/. Accessed May 6, 2018.

Wroth, Mary. *The [first and] secound booke of the secound part of the Countess of Montgomery's Urania*. Newberry Library. Case MS fY 1565. W95.

———. *Loves Victorie*. Huntington Library, San Marino, California. HM600.

———. *Love's Victory*. De L'Isle Manuscript. Penshurst Place, Penshurst, UK.

———. *Pamphilia to Amphilanthus*. Folger Shakespeare Library. V.a.104.

### Published Sources

Bell, Ilona, and Steven W. May, eds. *"Pamphilia to Amphilanthus" in Manuscript and Print*. Toronto: Iter; Tempe: Arizona Center for Medieval and Renaissance Studies, 2017.

Bennett, Alexandra G., ed. *The Collected Works of Jane Cavendish*. London: Routledge, 2018.

Brennan, Michael G., ed. *Lady Mary Wroth's Love's Victory: The Penshurst Manuscript*. London: Roxburghe Club, 1988.

Cadman, Daniel, ed. *The Concealed Fancies by Jane Cavendish and Elizabeth Brackley*. Online edition. In *The Literary Cultures of the Cavendish Family* (blog). https://extra.shu.ac.uk/emls/iemls/renplays/ConcealedFancies.pdf. May 6, 2018.

*Calendar of State Papers Domestic Series of the Reign of Charles I, 1625–1649*. Edited by William Douglas Hamilton. London: Eyre & Spottiswoode, 1888.

Carleton, Dudley. *Dudley Carleton to John Chamberlain, 1603–1624: Jacobean Letters*. Edited by Maurice Lee. New Brunswick, NJ: Rutgers University Press, 1972.

Cary, Elizabeth. *The tragedie of Mariam, the faire queene of Jewry. Written by that learned, vertuous, and truly noble ladie, E.C.* London: Thomas Creede, 1613.

Cavendish, Jane, and Elizabeth Brackley. *The Concealed Fancies*. In *Renaissance Drama by Women: Texts and Documents*, edited by S. P. Cerasano and Marion Wynne-Davies, 127–54. London: Routledge, 1996.

———. *The Concealed Fancies by Jane Cavendish and Elizabeth Brackley*. Online edition. Edited by Daniel Cadman. In *The Literary Cultures of the Cavendish Family* (blog). https://extra.shu.ac.uk/emls/iemls/renplays/ConcealedFancies.pdf. Accessed May 6, 2018.

———. "*The Concealed Fansyes*: A Play by Lady Jane Cavendish and Lady Elizabeth Brackley." Edited by Nathan Comfort Starr. *PMLA* 46, no. 3 (1931): 802–38.

———. *A Pastorall, A Drama by Jane Cavendish and Elizabeth Brackley*. Edited by Lynn Smith. San Antonio: Independent Scholars Press, 2011.

Cavendish, Margaret. *CCXI Sociable Letters*. London: William Wilson, 1664.

———. *The Life of the Thrice Noble, High, and Puissant Prince William Cavendish, Duke, Marquess, and Earl of Newcastle*. London: A. Maxwell, 1667.

Cavendish, Margaret, and William Cavendish. *A Collection of Letters and Poems: Written by several persons of honour and learning, upon divers important subjects, to the late Duke and Dutchess of Newcastle*. London: Langley Curtin, 1678.

Cavendish, William. *Dramatic Works by William Cavendish*. Edited by Lynn Hulse. Oxford: Oxford University Press, 1996.

———. *The Phanseys of William Cavendish Marquis of Newcastle addressed to Margaret Lucas and her Letters in reply*. Edited by Douglas Grant. London: Nonesuch Press, 1956.

Cerasano, S. P., and Marion Wynne-Davies, eds. *Renaissance Drama by Women: Texts and Documents*. London: Routledge, 1996.

Douglas, Lady Margaret, and Others. *The Devonshire Manuscript: A Women's Book of Courtly Poetry*. Edited by Elizabeth Heale. Toronto: Iter and the Centre for Reformation and Renaissance Studies, 2012.

*Elvetham: 1591*. In *Entertainments for Elizabeth I*, edited by Jean Wilson, 96–118. Woodbridge, NJ: D. S. Brewer, 1980.

Firth, C. H., ed. *The Life of William Cavendish Duke of Newcastle To Which is Added the True Relation of my Birth Breeding and Life, by Margaret Cavendish, Duchess of Newcastle*. London: Routledge, 1906.

Fitzmaurice, James. "'The Lotterie': A Transcription of a Play Probably by Margaret Cavendish." *Huntington Library Quarterly* 66, no. 1/2 (2003): 155–67.

Gouge, William. *Of Domesticall Duties*. London: John Haviland for William Bladen, 1622.

Herbert, Mary Sidney. *The Collected Works of Mary Sidney Herbert, Countess of Pembroke*. Vol. 1, *Poems, Translations, and Correspondence*. Edited by Margaret P. Hannay, Noel J. Kinnamon, and Michael G. Brennan. Oxford: Clarendon Press, 1998.

Hulse, Lynn, ed. *Dramatic Works by William Cavendish*. Oxford: Oxford University Press, 1996.

Jonson, Ben. *The Alchemist*. Edited by Alvin B. Kernan. New Haven, CT: Yale University Press, 1974.

———. *Ben Jonson: The Complete Masques*. Edited by Stephen Orgel. New Haven, CT: Yale University Press, 1969.

———. *Ben Jonson: The Complete Poems*. Edited by George Parfitt. New Haven, CT: Yale University Press, 1982.

Lawrence, Thomas. "An Elegy on the Death of the Thrice Noble and Vertuous Lady the Lady Jane Cheyne, Eldest Daughter to William Duke of NEWCASTLE." In *A Sermon at the funeral of the Right Honourable the Lady Jane eldest daughter to His Grace, William, Duke of Newcastle, and wife to the Honourable Charles Cheyne, Esq, at Chelsey, Novem. I, being All-Saints day*, by Adam Littleton. London: John Macock, 1669.

Littleton, Adam. *A Sermon at the funeral of the Right Honourable the Lady Jane eldest daughter to His Grace, William, Duke of Newcastle, and wife to the Honourable Charles Cheyne, Esq, at Chelsey, Novem. I, being All-Saints day*. London: John Macock, 1669.

Maxwell, C. H. J., ed. *Loues Victorie*. Master's thesis, Stanford University, 1933.

Montagu, Edward. "Edward Montagu, Earl of Manchester, to Committee of both kingdoms, August 6, 1644." In Hamilton, *Calendar of State Papers*, 19: 404–5.

Nicholas, Edward. "Edward Nicholas to the Earl of Forth, Lord General of his Majesty's Army, April 21, 1644." In Hamilton, *Calendar of State Papers*, 19: 131.

Pulter, Lady Hester. *Poems, Emblems*, and *The Unfortunate Florinda*. Edited by Alice Eardley. Toronto: Iter and the Centre for Reformation and Renaissance Studies, 2014.

Roberts, Josephine A., ed. *The First Part of The Countess of Montgomery's Urania*. Binghamton, NY: Medieval and Renaissance Texts and Studies, 1995.

———, ed. *The Poems of Lady Mary Wroth*. Baton Rouge: Louisiana State University Press, 1983.

Russell, Elizabeth Cooke Hoby. *The Writings of an English Sappho*. Edited by Patricia Phillippy with translations from Greek and Latin by Jaime Goodrich. Toronto: Iter and the Centre for Reformation and Renaissance Studies, 2011.

Salzman, Paul, ed. *Early Modern Women's Writing: An Anthology, 1560–1700*. Oxford: Oxford University Press, 2000.

———, ed. *Love's Victory*. By Mary Wroth. Online edition. http://hri.newcastle.edu.au/emwrn/da/index.php?content=lovesvictory. Accessed May 6, 2018.

Shakespeare, William. *The Norton Shakespeare: Third Edition*. Edited by Stephen Greenblatt, Walter Cohen, Suzanne Gossett, Jean E. Howard, Katharine Eisaman Maus, and Gordon McMullan. New York: W. W. Norton, 2016.

Sidney, Mary. *A discourse of life and death. Written in French by Ph. Mornay. Antonius, a tragoedie written also in French by Ro. Garnier. Both done in English by the Countesse of Pembroke*. London: John Windet for William Ponsonby, 1592.

———. *The Tragedie of Antonie. Doone into English by the Countesse of Pembroke*. London: Peter Short for William Ponsonby, 1595.

Sidney, Sir Philip. *The Countesse of Pembroke's Arcadia (The Old Arcadia)*. Edited by Jean Robertson. Oxford: Clarendon Press, 1973.

———. *A Defence of Poetry*. In *Miscellaneous Prose of Sir Philip Sidney*, edited by Katherine Duncan-Jones and Jan van Dorsten, 71–121. Oxford: Clarendon Press, 1973.

Smith, Lynn, ed. *A Pastorall, A Drama by Jane Cavendish and Elizabeth Brackley*. San Antonio: Independent Scholars Press, 2011.

Starr, Nathan Comfort, ed. "*The Concealed Fansyes*: A Play by Lady Jane Cavendish and Lady Elizabeth Brackley." *PMLA* 46, no. 3 (1931): 802–38.

Taylor, John. *A New Discovery by Sea, with a Wherry from London to Salisbury*. London: Edward Allde for the author, 1623.

Vives, Juan Luis. *A very frutefull and pleasant boke called the instruction of a Christen woman*. Trans. Richard Hyrde. London: Thomas Berthelet, [1529?].

Wroth, Mary. *The Countesse of Mountgomeries Urania*. London: John Marriott and John Grismand, 1621.

———. *The First Part of The Countess of Montgomery's Urania*. Edited by Josephine A. Roberts. Binghamton, NY: Medieval and Renaissance Texts and Studies, 1995.

———. *Lady Mary Wroth's Love's Victory: The Penshurst Manuscript*. Edited by Michael G. Brennan. London: Roxburghe Club, 1988.

———. "*Loues Victorie*." Edited by C. H. J. Maxwell. Master's thesis, Stanford University, 1933.

———. "Love's Victorie." Selections transcribed by Henrietta Halliwell. In *A Brief Description of the Ancient & Modern Manuscripts Preserved in the Public Library, Plymouth*, edited by James Orchard Halliwell, 212–36. London: C. and J. Adlard, 1853.

———. "Love's Victory." In *Early Modern Women's Writing: An Anthology, 1560–1700*, edited by Paul Salzman, 82–133. Oxford: Oxford University Press, 2000.

———. *Love's Victory.* Edited by Paul Salzman. Online edition. http://hri.newcastle.edu.au/emwrn/da/index.php?content=marywroth. Accessed May 6, 2018.

———. *Love's Victory.* In *Renaissance Drama by Women: Texts and Documents*, edited by S. P. Cerasano and Marion Wynne-Davies, 91–126. London: Routledge, 1996.

———. *"Pamphilia to Amphilanthus" in Manuscript and Print.* Edited by Ilona Bell and Steven W. May. Toronto: Iter; and Tempe: Arizona Center for Medieval and Renaissance Studies, 2017.

———. *The Poems of Lady Mary Wroth.* Edited by Josephine A. Roberts. Baton Rouge: Louisiana State University, 1983.

———. *The Second Part of The Countess of Montgomery's Urania.* Edited by Josephine A. Roberts; completed by Suzanne Gossett and Janel Mueller. Tempe: Renaissance English Text Society in conjunction with Arizona Center for Medieval and Renaissance Studies, 1999.

## Secondary Sources

Alexander, Gavin. "Constant Works: A Framework for Reading Mary Wroth." *Sidney Newsletter and Journal* 14, no. 2 (Winter 1996–1997): 5–32.

———. "The Musical Sidneys." *John Donne Journal* 25 (2006): 65–105.

———. *Writing after Sidney: The Literary Response to Sir Philip Sidney, 1586–1640.* Oxford: Oxford University Press, 2006.

Archer, Jayne Elisabeth, Elizabeth Goldring, and Sarah Knight, eds. *The Progresses, Pageants, and Entertainments of Queen Elizabeth I.* Oxford: Oxford University Press, 2007.

Austen, Katherine. *Book M: A London Widow's Life Writings.* Edited by Pamela S. Hammons. Toronto: Iter and the Centre for Reformation and Renaissance Studies, 2013.

Beal, Peter. *Catalogue of English Literary Manuscripts, 1450–1700.* http://www.celm-ms.org.uk. Accessed May 6, 2018.

———. *A Dictionary of English Manuscript Terminology, 1450–2000.* Oxford: Oxford University Press, 2008.

Bell, Ilona. "The Autograph Manuscript of Mary Wroth's *Pamphilia to Amphilanthus.*" In Larson and Miller with Strycharski, *Re-Reading Mary Wroth,* 171–81.

———. "The Circulation of Writings by Lady Mary Wroth." In Hannay, Lamb, and Brennan, *The Ashgate Research Companion to The Sidneys,* 77–85.

Bennett, Alexandra G. "'Now Let My Language Speake': The Authorship, Rewriting, and Audience(s) of Jane Cavendish and Elizabeth Brackley." *Early Modern Literary Studies* 11, no. 2 (2005): 1–13.

———. "Playing by and with the Rules: Genre, Politics, and Perception in Mary Wroth's *Love's Victorie.*" In *Women and Culture at the Courts of the Stuart Queens,* edited by Clare McManus, 122–39. Basingstoke, UK: Palgrave Macmillan, 2003.

Bland, Mark. *A Guide to Early Printed Books and Manuscripts.* Chichester, UK: Wiley-Blackwell, 2010.

Brayshay, Mark. "Waits, Musicians, Bearwards and Players: The Inter-Urban Road: Travel and Performances of Itinerant Entertainers in Sixteenth- and Seventeenth-Century England." *Journal of Historical Geography* 31, no. 3 (2005): 430–58.

Brennan, Michael G. "Creating Female Authorship in the Early Seventeenth Century: Ben Jonson and Lady Mary Wroth." In Justice and Tinker, *Women's Writing and the Circulation of Ideas,* 73–93.

Broad, Jacqueline. "Margaret Cavendish and Joseph Glanvill: Science, Religion, and Witchcraft." *Studies in History and Philosophy of Science* 38, no. 3 (2007): 493–505.

Brown, Pamela Allen, and Peter Parolin, eds. *Women Players in England, 1500–1660: Beyond the All-Male Stage.* Aldershot, UK: Ashgate, 2005.

Burke, Victoria E., and Elizabeth Clarke. "Julia Palmer's 'Centuries': The Politics of Editing and Anthologizing Early Modern Women's Manuscript Compilations." In *New Ways of Looking at Old Texts,* vol. 3, edited by W. Speed Hill, 47–64. Tempe: Arizona Center for Medieval and Renaissance Studies in conjunction with Renaissance English Text Society, 2004.

Burke, Victoria E., and Jonathan Gibson, eds. *Early Modern Women's Manuscript Writing: Selected Papers from the Trinity/Trent Colloquium.* Aldershot, UK: Ashgate, 2004.

Campbell, Julie. *Literary Circles and Gender in Early Modern Europe: A Cross-Cultural Approach.* Aldershot, UK: Ashgate, 2006.

Cerasano, S. P., and Marion Wynne-Davies, eds. *Readings in Renaissance Women's Drama: Criticism, History, and Performance, 1594–1998.* London: Routledge, 1998.

Clarke, Elizabeth. "The Garrisoned Muse: Women's Use of the Religious Lyric in the Civil War Period." In *The English Civil Wars in the Literary Imagination,* edited by Claude J. Summers and Ted-Larry Pebworth, 130–43. Columbia: University of Missouri Press, 1999.

Coolahan, Mary-Louise. "Literary Memorialization and the Posthumous Construction of Female Authorship." In *The Arts of Remembrance in Early Modern England: Memorial Cultures of the Post Reformation*, edited by Andrew Gordon and Thomas Rist, 161–76. Farnham, UK: Ashgate, 2013.

———. "Presentation Volume of Jane Cavendish's Poetry." In Millman and Wright, *Early Modern Women's Manuscript Poetry*, 87–89.

Cox, John D., and David Scott Kastan, eds. *A New History of Early English Drama*. New York: Columbia University Press, 1997.

Davidson, Peter, and Jane Stevenson. "Elizabeth I's Reception at Bisham (1592): Elite Women as Writers and Devisers." In Archer, Goldring, and Knight, *Progresses, Pageants, and Entertainments*, 207–26.

Dewhurst, Madeline. "True Relations: Piecing Together a Family Divided by War." *Lives and Letters* 2, no. 1 (2010): 1–20.

Dubrow, Heather. "'And Thus Leave Off': Reevaluating Mary Wroth's Folger Manuscript, V.a.104." *Tulsa Studies in Women's Literature* 22, no. 2 (2003): 273–91.

Espinasse, Francis, revised by Louis A. Knafla. "Egerton, John, second earl of Bridgewater (1623–1686)." In *ODNB*.

Ezell, Margaret J. M. "The Laughing Tortoise: Speculations on Manuscript Sources and Women's Book History." *English Literary Renaissance* 38, no. 2 (2008): 331–55.

———. "To Be Your Daughter in Your Pen: The Social Functions of Literature in the Writings of Lady Elizabeth Brackley and Lady Jane Cavendish." *Huntington Library Quarterly* 51, no. 4 (1988): 281–96.

Findlay, Alison. "Lady Mary Wroth: *Love's Victory*." In Hannay, Lamb, and Brennan, *The Ashgate Research Companion to The Sidneys*, 211–24.

———. "*Love's Victory* in Production at Penshurst." *Sidney Journal* 34, no. 1 (2016): 107–21.

———. *Playing Spaces in Early Women's Drama*. Cambridge: Cambridge University Press, 2006.

Findlay, Alison, Stephanie Hodgson-Wright, with Gweno Williams. *Women and Dramatic Production, 1550–1700*. New York: Longman, 2000.

Findlay, Alison, Gweno Williams, and Stephanie J. Hodgson-Wright. "'The Play Is Ready to Be Acted': Women and Dramatic Production, 1570–1670." *Women's Writing* 6, no. 1 (1999): 129–48.

Fitzmaurice, James. "Cavendish [*née* Lucas], Margaret, duchess of Newcastle upon Tyne (1623?–1673)." In *ODNB*.

Freeman, Arthur. "*Love's Victory*: A Supplementary Note." *The Library* 19, no. 3 (1997): 252–54.

Goldring, Elizabeth. "Talbot [*née* Hardwick], Elizabeth [Bess; *called* Bess of Hardwick], countess of Shrewsbury (1527?–1608)." In *ODNB*.

Greenfield, Peter H. "Touring." In Cox and Kastan, *A New History of Early English Drama*, 251–68.

Greer, Germaine, Susan Hastings, Jeslyn Medoff, and Melinda Sansone, eds. *Kissing the Rod: An Anthology of 17th Century Women's Verse*. New York: Farrar Straus Giroux, 1988.

Greg, Walter W. *Pastoral Poetry and Pastoral Drama*. New York: Russell & Russell, 1959.

Halliwell, James Orchard, ed. *A Brief Description of the Ancient & Modern Manuscripts Preserved in the Public Library, Plymouth*. London: C. and J. Adlard, 1853.

Hannay, Margaret P. "'Bearing the Livery of Your Name': The Countess of Pembroke's Agency in Print and Scribal Culture." In Justice and Tinker, *Women's Writing and the Circulation of Ideas*, 17–49.

———. "The 'Ending End' of Lady Mary Wroth's Manuscript of Poems." *Sidney Journal* 31, no. 1 (2013): 1–22.

———. "Herbert [*née* Sidney], Mary, countess of Pembroke (1561–1621)." In *ODNB*.

———. *Mary Sidney, Lady Wroth*. Farnham, UK: Ashgate, 2010.

———. "Sleuthing in the Archives: The Life of Lady Mary Wroth." In Larson and Miller with Strycharski, *Re-Reading Mary Wroth*, 19–33.

———. "'Your Vertuous and Learned Aunt': The Countess of Pembroke as a Mentor to Mary Wroth." In Miller and Waller, *Reading Mary Wroth*, 16–34.

Hannay, Margaret P., Mary Ellen Lamb, and Michael G. Brennan, eds. *The Ashgate Research Companion to The Sidneys, 1500–1700*, vol. 2: *Literature*. Farnham, UK: Ashgate, 2015.

Haselkorn, Anne M., and Betty S. Travitsky, eds. *The Renaissance Englishwoman in Print: Counterbalancing the Canon*. Amherst: University of Massachusetts Press, 1990.

Heaton, Gabriel. "Elizabethan Entertainments in Manuscript: The Harefield Festivities (1602) and the Dynamics of Exchange." In Archer, Goldring, and Knight, *Progresses, Pageants, and Entertainments*, 227–44.

Heawood, Edward. *Watermarks, Mainly of the 17th and 18th Centuries*. Hilversum, Holland: Paper Publications Society, 1950.

Herford, C. H., and Percy Simpson, eds. *Ben Jonson Works*. Vol. 7. Oxford: Clarendon Press, 1941.

Hopkins, Lisa. *The Female Hero in English Renaissance Tragedy*. New York: Palgrave Macmillan, 2002.

———. "Judith Shakespeare's Reading: Teaching *The Concealed Fancies*." *Shakespeare Quarterly* 47, no. 4 (1996): 396–406.

————. "Play Houses: Drama at Bolsover and Welbeck." *Early Theatre* 2, no. 1 (1999): 25–44.

Hughes, Ann, and Julie Sanders. "Disruptions and Evocations of Family amongst Royalist Exiles." In *Literatures of Exile in the English Revolution and Its Aftermath, 1640–1690*, edited by Philip Major, 45–63. Aldershot, UK: Ashgate, 2010.

Hulse, Lynn. "Cavendish, William, first duke of Newcastle upon Tyne (bap. 1593, d. 1676)." In *ODNB*.

————. "The King's Entertainment by the Duke of Newcastle." *Viator* 26 (1995): 355–405.

Humphreys, Jennett, revised by Sean Kelsey. "Cheyne [*née* Cavendish], Lady Jane (1620/21–1669)." In *ODNB*.

Johnston, Alexandra F. "'The Lady of the farme': The Context of Lady Russell's Entertainment of Elizabeth at Bisham, 1592." *Early Theatre* 5 (2002): 71–85.

Justice, George L., and Nathan Tinker, eds. *Women's Writing and the Circulation of Ideas: Manuscript Publication in England, 1550–1800*. Cambridge: Cambridge University Press, 2002.

Karim-Cooper, Farah. *Cosmetics in Shakespearean and Renaissance Drama.* Edinburgh: Edinburgh University Press, 2012.

Kelliher, Hilton. "Donne, Jonson, Richard Andrews and The Newcastle Manuscript." *English Manuscript Studies, 1100–1700* 4 (1993): 134–73.

Kidnie, M. J. "Near Neighbours: Another Early Seventeenth-Century Manuscript of *The Humorous Magistrate*." *English Manuscript Studies, 1100–1700* 13 (2007): 187–211.

Kolkovich, Elizabeth Zeman. "Lady Russell, Elizabeth I, and Female Political Alliances through Performance." *English Literary Renaissance* 39 (2009): 290–314.

Knafla, Louis A. "Egerton, John, third earl of Bridgewater (1646–1701)." In *ODNB*.

Lamb, Mary Ellen. "'Can You Suspect a Change in Me?': Poems by Mary Wroth and William Herbert, Third Earl of Pembroke." In Larson and Miller with Strycharski, *Re-Reading Mary Wroth*, 53–68.

————. "Selling Mary Wroth's *Urania*: The Frontispiece and the Connoisseurship of Romance." *Sidney Journal* 34, no. 1 (2016): 33–48.

————. "Wroth [*née* Sidney], Lady Mary (1587?–1651/1653)." In *ODNB*.

Larson, Katherine R. *Early Modern Women in Conversation.* New York: Palgrave Macmillan, 2011.

————. "Playing at Penshurst: The Songs and Musical Games of Mary Wroth's *Love's Victory*." *Sidney Journal* 34, no. 1 (2016): 93–106.

————. "Voicing Lyric: The Songs of Mary Wroth." In Larson and Miller with Strycharski, *Re-Reading Mary Wroth*, 119–36.

Larson, Katherine R., and Naomi J. Miller with Andrew Strycharski, eds. *Re-Reading Mary Wroth*. New York: Palgrave Macmillan, 2015.

Lees-Jeffries, Hester. "Pictures, Places, and Spaces: Sidney, Wroth, Wilton House, and the *Songe de Poliphile.*" In *Renaissance Paratexts,* edited by Helen Smith and Louise Wilson, 185–203. Cambridge: Cambridge University Press, 2011.

Lennam, T. N. S. "Sir Edward Dering's Collection of Playbooks, 1619–1624." *Shakespeare Quarterly* 16, no. 2 (1965): 145–53.

Lewalski, Barbara Kiefer. "Mary Wroth's *Love's Victory* and Pastoral Tragicomedy." In Miller and Waller, *Reading Mary Wroth,* 88–108.

Long, William B. "'Precious Few': English Manuscript Playbooks." In *A Companion to Shakespeare,* edited by David Scott Kastan, 413–33. Oxford: Blackwell, 1999.

Love, Harold. *Scribal Publication in Seventeenth-Century England.* Oxford: Clarendon Press, 1993.

Love, Harold, and Arthur F. Marotti. "Manuscript Transmission and Circulation." In *The Cambridge History of Early Modern English Literature,* edited by David Loewenstein and Janel Mueller, 55–80. Cambridge: Cambridge University Press, 2002.

MacDonald, Joyce Green. "Ovid and Women's Pastoral in Lady Mary Wroth's *Love's Victory.*" *SEL: Studies in English Literature* 51, no. 2 (2011): 447–63.

Marotti, Arthur F. *Manuscript, Print, and the English Renaissance Lyric.* Ithaca, NY: Cornell University Press, 1995.

McLaren, Margaret Anne. "An Unknown Continent: Lady Mary Wroth's Forgotten Pastoral Drama, 'Loves Victorie.'" In Haselkorn and Travitsky, *The Renaissance Englishwoman in Print,* 276–94.

McManus, Clare. *Women on the Renaissance Stage: Anna of Denmark and Female Masquing in the Stuart Court (1590–1619).* Manchester: Manchester University Press, 2002.

Miller, Naomi J. "As She Likes It: Same-Sex Friendship and Romantic Love in Wroth and Shakespeare." In Salzman and Wynne-Davies, *Mary Wroth and Shakespeare,* 137–50.

———. "Engendering Discourse: Women's Voices in Wroth's *Urania* and Shakespeare's Plays." In Miller and Waller, *Reading Mary Wroth,* 154–72.

———. "Playing with Margaret Cavendish and Mary Wroth: Staging Early Modern Women's Dramatic Romances for Modern Audiences." *Early Modern Women: An Interdisciplinary Journal* 10, no. 2 (2016): 95–110.

Miller, Naomi J., and Gary Waller, eds. *Reading Mary Wroth: Representing Alternatives in Early Modern England.* Knoxville: University of Tennessee Press, 1991.

Milling, Jane. "Siege and Cipher: The Closet Drama of the Cavendish Sisters." *Women's History Review* 6, no. 3 (1997): 411–26.

Millman, Jill Seal, and Gillian Wright, eds. *Early Modern Women's Manuscript Poetry.* Manchester: Manchester University Press, 2005.

Montrose, Louis Adrian. "Celebration and Insinuation: Sir Philip Sidney and the Motives of Elizabethan Courtship." *Renaissance Drama* 8 (1977): 3–35.

———. "Of Gentlemen and Shepherds: The Politics of Elizabethan Pastoral Form." *English Literary History* 50, no. 3 (1983): 415–59.

Mueller, Sara. "Domestic Work in Progress Entertainments." In *Working Subjects in Early Modern English Drama*, edited by Michelle M. Dowd and Natasha Korda, 145–59. Farnham, UK: Ashgate, 2011.

Nelson, Karen L. "'Change Partners and Dance': Pastoral Virtuosity in Wroth's *Love's Victory*." In Larson and Miller with Strycharski, *Re-Reading Mary Wroth*, 137–56.

Nicolson, Adam. *Arcadia: The Dream of Perfection in Renaissance England.* London: Harper Perennial, 2009.

O'Callaghan, Michelle. "Publication: Print and Manuscript." In *A New Companion to English Renaissance Literature and Culture*, edited by Michael Hattaway, 1: 160–76. Oxford: Wiley-Blackwell, 2010.

O'Connor, Marion. "Rachel Fane's May Masque at Apethorpe, 1627." *English Literary Renaissance* 36, no. 1 (2006): 90–113.

———. "'Silvesta was my instrument ordained'?: Lucy Harington Russell, Third Countess of Bedford, as Family Marriage Broker." *Sidney Journal* 34, no. 1 (2016): 49–65.

Orgel, Stephen. *The Illusion of Power: Political Theater in the English Renaissance.* Berkeley: University of California Press, 1975.

Orgis, Rahel. "'[A] Story Very Well Woorth Readinge': Why Early Modern Readers Valued Lady Mary Wroth's *Urania*." *Sidney Journal* 31, no. 1 (2013): 81–100.

*The Oxford Dictionary of National Biography Online.* Edited by David Cannadine. 2004–17. http://www.oxforddnb.com. Accessed May 6, 2018.

*The Oxford English Dictionary Online.* Second edition, 1989. http://www.oed.com. Accessed May 6, 2018.

Parry, Graham. "Entertainments at Court." In Cox and Kastan, *A New History of Early English Drama*, 195–211.

Pender, Patricia, and Rosalind Smith, eds. *Material Cultures of Early Modern Women's Writing.* Basingstoke, UK: Palgrave Macmillan, 2014.

Phillippy, Patricia. "Chaste Painting: Elizabeth Russell's Theatres of Memory." *Early Modern Women: An Interdisciplinary Journal* 7 (2012): 33–68.

Roberts, Josephine A. "Deciphering Women's Pastoral: Coded Language in Wroth's *Love's Victory*." In *Representing Women in Renaissance England*, edited by Claude J. Summers and Ted-Larry Pebworth, 163–74. Columbia: University of Missouri Press, 1997.

———. "The Huntington Manuscript of Lady Mary Wroth's Play, 'Loves Victorie.'" *Huntington Library Quarterly* 46, no. 2 (1983): 156–74.

———. "An Unpublished Literary Quarrel Concerning the Suppression of Mary Wroth's *Urania* (1621)." *Notes & Queries* 222 (1977): 532–35.

Ross, Sarah C. E. *Women, Poetry, and Politics in Seventeenth-Century Britain*. Oxford: Oxford University Press, 2015.

Salt, S. P. "Dering, Sir Edward, first baronet (1598–1644)." In *ODNB*.

Salzman, Paul. "Contemporary References in Mary Wroth's *Urania*." *Review of English Studies*, new series, 29, no. 114 (1978): 178–81.

———, ed. *Early Modern Women's Writing: An Anthology, 1560–1700*. Oxford: Oxford University Press, 2000.

———. "Henrietta's Version: Mary Wroth's *Love's Victory* in the Nineteenth Century." In Pender and Smith, *Material Cultures of Early Modern Women's Writing*, 159–73.

———. "Mary Wroth and Hermaphroditic Circulation." In *Early Modern Women and the Poem*, edited by Susan Wiseman, 117–30. Manchester: Manchester University Press, 2014.

———. *Reading Early Modern Women's Writing*. Oxford: Oxford University Press, 2006.

Salzman, Paul, and Marion Wynne-Davies, eds. *Mary Wroth and Shakespeare*. New York: Routledge, 2015.

Sanders, Julie. "Geographies of Performance in the Early Modern Midlands." In *Performing Environments: Site-Specificity in Medieval and Early Modern English Drama*, edited by Susan Bennett and Mary Polito, 119–37. Houndmills, UK: Palgrave Macmillan, 2014.

Shephard, Robert. "The Political Commonplace Books of Sir Robert Sidney." *Sidney Journal* 21, no. 1 (2003): 1–30.

Sidney, Philip. "Introduction: Penshurst, Place, and Performance." *Sidney Journal* 34, no. 1 (2016): 1–14.

Smith, Emily. "The Local Popularity of *The Concealed Fansyes*." *Notes and Queries* 53, no. 2 (2006): 189–93.

Smith, Helen. "Women and the Materials of Writing." In Pender and Smith, *Material Cultures of Early Modern Women's Writing*, 14–35.

Stanton, Kamille Stone. "The Domestication of Royalist Themes in The Concealed Fancies by Jane Cavendish and Elizabeth Brackley." *Clio* 36, no. 2 (2007): 177–97.

Stater, Victor. "Herbert, William, third earl of Pembroke (1580–1630)." In *ODNB*.

Stern, Tiffany. *Documents of Performance in Early Modern England*. Cambridge: Cambridge University Press, 2009.

Stevens, Dorothy. *The Limits of Eroticism in Post-Petrarchan Narrative: Conditional Pleasure from Spencer to Marvell*. Cambridge: Cambridge University Press, 1998.

Stewart, Alan. *Philip Sidney: A Double Life*. London: Chatto & Windus, 2000.

Straznicky, Marta. "Lady Mary Wroth's *Love's Victory*." *Early Modern Women: An Interdisciplinary Journal* 9, no. 2 (2015): 166–70.

———. "Lady Mary Wroth's Patchwork Play: The Huntington Manuscript of *Love's Victory*." *Sidney Journal* 34, no. 1 (2016): 81–92.

———. *Privacy, Playreading, and Women's Closet Drama, 1550–1700*. Cambridge: Cambridge University Press, 2004.

———. "Private Drama." In *The Cambridge Companion to Early Modern Women's Writing*, edited by Laura Lunger Knoppers, 247–59. Cambridge: Cambridge University Press, 2009.

———. "Reading through the Body: Women and Printed Drama." In *The Book of the Play: Playwrights, Stationers, and Readers in Early Modern England*, edited by Marta Straznicky, 59–79. Amherst: University of Massachusetts Press, 2006.

———. "Wilton House, Theatre, and Power." In *The Intellectual Culture of the English Country House, 1500–1700*, edited by Matthew Dimmock, Andrew Hadfield, and Margaret Healy, 217–31. Manchester: Manchester University Press, 2015.

Swift, Carolyn Ruth. "Feminine Self-Definition in Lady Mary Wroth's *Love's Victorie* (c. 1621)." *English Literary Renaissance* 19, no. 2 (1989): 171–88.

Travitsky, Betty S. "Egerton [née Cavendish], Elizabeth, countess of Bridgewater (1626–1663)." In *ODNB*.

———. "His Wife's Prayers and Meditations: MS Egerton 1607." In Haselkorn and Travitsky, *The Renaissance Englishwoman in Print*, 241–62.

———. *Subordination and Authorship in Early Modern England: The Case of Elizabeth Cavendish Egerton and Her "Loose Papers."* Tempe: Arizona Center for Medieval and Renaissance Studies, 1999.

Walker, Greg. *The Politics of Performance in Early Renaissance Drama*. Cambridge: Cambridge University Press, 1998.

Waller, Gary. "'Like One in a Gay Masque': The Sidney Cousins in the Theaters of Court and Country." In Cerasano and Wynne-Davies, *Readings in Renaissance Women's Drama*, 234–45.

Warkentin, Germaine. "Robert Sidney's 'Darcke Offrings': The Making of a Late Tudor Manuscript *Canzoniere*." *Spenser Studies* 12 (1998): 37–73.

Werstine, Paul. *Early Modern Playhouse Manuscripts and the Editing of Shakespeare*. Cambridge: Cambridge University Press, 2013.

West, Susie. "Finding Wroth's Loughton Hall." *Sidney Journal* 34, no. 1 (2016): 15–31.

Westfall, Suzanne. "'A Commonty a Christmas Gambold or a Tumbling Trick': Household Theater." In Cox and Kastan, *A New History of Early English Drama*, 39–58.

———. *Patrons and Performances: Early Tudor Household Revels*. Oxford: Clarendon Press, 1990.

Whyte, Rowland. *The Letters (1595–1608) of Rowland Whyte*. Edited by Michael G. Brennan, Noel J. Kinnamon, and Margaret P. Hannay. Philadelphia: American Philosophical Society, 2013.

Williams, Deanne. *Shakespeare and the Performance of Girlhood*. London: Palgrave Macmillan, 2014.

Woudhuysen, H. R. "Sidney, Sir Philip (1554–1586)." In *ODNB*.

———. *Sir Philip Sidney and the Circulation of Manuscripts, 1558–1640*. Oxford: Clarendon Press, 1996.

Wynne-Davies, Marion. "Editing Early Modern Women's Dramatic Writing for Performance." In *Editing Early Modern Women*, edited by Sarah C. E. Ross and Paul Salzman, 156–75. Cambridge: Cambridge University Press, 2016.

———. "'For *Worth*, Not Weakness Makes in Use but One': Literary Dialogues in an English Renaissance Family." In *'This Double Voice': Gendered Writing in Early Modern England*, edited by Danielle Clarke and Elizabeth Clarke, 164–84. Houndmills, UK: Palgrave Macmillan, 2000.

———. "'Here Is a Sport Will Well Befit this Time and Place': Allusion and Delusion in Mary Wroth's *Love's Victory*." *Women's Writing* 6, no. 1 (1999): 47–64.

———. "The Liminal Woman in Mary Wroth's *Love's Victory*." *Sidney Journal* 26, no. 2 (2008): 65–81.

———. "My Fine Delitive Tomb: Liberating 'Sisterly' Voices During the Civil War." In *Female Communities, 1600–1800*, edited by Rebecca D'Monté and Nicole Pohl, 111–28. London: Macmillan, 2000.

———. "'My Seeled Chamber and Dark Parlour Room': The English Country House and Renaissance Women Dramatists." In Cerasano and Wynne-Davies, *Readings in Renaissance Women's Drama*, 60–68.

———. "Performance of Lady Mary Wroth's Love's Victory: A Review." *Sidney Journal* 34, no. 1 (2016): 123–26.

Yakimyshyn, Lindsay Jenelle. "Security and Instability: Mary Wroth, the Cavendish Sisters, and Early Stuart Household Plays." Ph.D. diss., University of Alberta, 2014.

# Index

actors, 5, 7, 11, 29, 40, 44, *165*, 166, 169,
    199n235, 201; traveling, 1, 2n6, 3.
    *See also* women: as performers
Agincourt, 6
alchemy, 228n452, 233n286
Anne of Denmark, Queen consort,
    18–19
Apethorpe, 4
Apollo, 49, 50n102, 67n164
authority, 17, 32, 35, 157, 159, 164,
    202n247, 252; authorial voice,
    9, 35n61. *See also* gender: and
    authorship; manuscript culture:
    and authorship

Ballamo Castle, 169–70, 214, 222n407,
    222n412, 227n440, 228n448,
    231n473, 240n521
Bassett, Elizabeth, 141
Baynards Castle, 18, 44n80
Beal, Peter, 148, 174
Behn, Aphra, 5
Bell, Ilona, 29, 43n75
Bennett, Alexandra G., 41n69, 143n15,
    146, 149, 151, 173n103, 193n227
Bernini, Gian Lorenzo, 146
Bess of Hardwick, 141
Bible, 146, 218
Bisham, 3
Bolsover Castle, 5, 145n21, 164
Brackley, Elizabeth: authorial voice,
    154, 161; children, 146–47;
    *The concealed Fansyes* (see *The
    concealed Fansyes*); education, 143;
    marriage, 141, 146–47; *A Pastorall*
    (see *A Pastorall*); relationship
    with father, 142–145 (*see also*
    Cavendish, William, first Duke of
    Newcastle: in daughters' works);
    youth, 141–42. *See also* Cavendish,
    Jane

Brennan, Michael, 42, 113
Brome, Richard, 157

Cadman, Daniel, 166n84, 172, 230n467
Carleton, Dudley, 156n58
Cary, Elizabeth, 1n2
catchwords, 30, 52n111, 59n133,
    80n206, 91n230, 190n212. *See also*
    manuscript qualities; Wroth, Mary
    Sidney: style
Cavendish, Charles, Viscount
    Mansfield, 141, 174n109
Cavendish, Elizabeth. *See* Bess of
    Hardwick
Cavendish, Frances, 141, 144, 153, 157,
    161, 169, 178n121
Cavendish, Henry, second Duke of
    Newcastle, 141
Cavendish, Jane: authorial voice, 154,
    161; children, 145; *The concealed
    Fansyes* (see *The concealed
    Fansyes*); education, 143; letters,
    145–46; marriage, 145–47; *A
    Pastorall* (see *A Pastorall*); poetry,
    145–46; relationship with father,
    142–45 (*see also* Cavendish,
    William, first Duke of Newcastle:
    in daughters' works); tomb, 146;
    youth, 141–42. *See also* Brackley,
    Elizabeth
Cavendish, Margaret, Duchess of
    Newcastle, 141, 151n50, 158n67,
    205n268
Cavendish, William, first Duke of
    Newcastle, 141–46, 149, 151n50,
    158n67, 174–75, 205n268,
    223n413; in daughters' works,
    142–43, 153, 166, 168, 177, 200;
    as patron of the arts, 5, 141–43;
    wartime exile, 141n6, 144–45. *See
    also* Newcastle manuscript